HOOKED:
DRUG WAR FILMS IN BRITAIN, CANADA, AND THE
UNITED STATES

Drug prohibition laws began to emerge in the United States, Canada, and Britain during the same era that saw the discovery of film. In *Hooked*, Susan C. Boyd explores over a century of American, British, and Canadian films containing fictional representations of drug use, the drug trade, and the war on drugs. She examines not only popular, mainstream films but also counter-culture, alternative, and 'stoner' movies, including *Harold and Kumar Go to White Castle*, and *Trailer Park Boys: The Movie*.

On-screen depictions of drug use and trafficking are powerful indicators of evolving socio-cultural attitudes towards illegal drugs. Using films such as *Broken Blossoms*, *The Trip*, *Superfly*, *Traffic*, and *Trainspotting*, Boyd explores how illegal drugs are linked to discourses of the Other, nation building, and law and order. Her discussion takes into account issues of race, class, and gender, and includes an important analysis of representations of women. A fascinating and groundbreaking study, *Hooked* uncovers the links between cinema and the cultural production of myths and stereotypes related to illegal drugs.

SUSAN C. BOYD is a professor in Studies in Policy and Practice at the University of Victoria.

Hooked

Drug War Films in Britain, Canada, and the United States

Susan C. Boyd

UNIVERSITY OF TORONTO PRESS
Toronto Buffalo London

First published in hardcover in 2008 by Routledge
© 2008 Taylor & Francis
This edition published by University of Toronto Press Incorporated
Toronto Buffalo
www.utppublishing.com

Published by arrangement with Routledge, part of Taylor & Francis Group L.L.C.

Printed in Canada

ISBN 978-1-4426-1017-0

∞

Printed on acid-free, 100% post-consumer recycled paper with
vegetable-based inks.

Library and Archives Canada Cataloguing in Publication

Boyd, Susan C., 1953–
    Hooked : drug war films in Britain, Canada, and the United States /
Susan C. Boyd.

    Includes bibliographical references and index.
    ISBN 978-1-4426-1017-0

    1. Drugs in motion pictures.   2. Motion pictures – Great Britain.
    3. Motion pictures – Canada.   4. Motion pictures – United States.
    I. Title.

    PN1995.9.D78B692 2009   791.43'6556   C2009-904504-4

University of Toronto Press acknowledges the financial assistance to
its publishing program of the Canada Council for the Arts and the
Ontario Arts Council.

University of Toronto Press acknowledges the financial support for its
publishing activities of the Government of Canada through the Book
Publishing Industry Development Program (BPIDP).

For Diana

Contents

List of Film Stills

x   *List of Film Stills*

Acknowledgments

I would like to thank Benjamin Holtzman and Gerhard Boomgaarden of Routledge for their interest and support in the publication of this book and Carey Nershi for her composition of the manuscript and James Barbee for his copyediting. I am indebted to the Social Sciences and Humanities Research Council of Canada; without their support, this project might not have been completed. I am also indebted to my colleagues at Studies in Policy in Practice, University of Victoria.

I am grateful to Craig Reinarman and Dennis Sullivan for agreeing to review my book proposal and the first chapter and providing feedback to me. I would also like to thank Karlene Faith for reading the first draft. Her critical insight and helpful comments contributed to this book. Similarly, Dara Culhane and Sunera Thobani were essential supports in writing this book. They painstakingly read over my draft proposal and introduction and provided support over the three years that I was researching and writing the book. Their friendship, scholarship, and activism have helped to shape my own work, although any errors or mistakes are completely of my own making.

I would also like to thank Nedjo Rogers for his editorial help on my original research proposal for this research and Starla Anderson for her insightful comments on my book proposal. I am grateful to Mark Stoddart, who worked as a research assistant on the project for almost two years. His contributions were invaluable and his enthusiasm for the project helped carry it forward. Research assistants Catherine Van Mossell and Connie Carter also contributed to this book, and their input was significant. I am indebted to Connie for her thoughtful editorial comments and her help with formatting and securing copyright permission for the photos in the book, a task that seemed insurmountable at times. I would also like to thank Barbara Hodgson and Mark Starks for their insights about copyrights and film stills. A special thanks to Gloria Watkins for helping me with the title of the book.

Finally, I would like to thank Val Zwicker, Marjorie van Orden, Cheryl Anderson, Carolyn Crichton, Morgan LeBlond, Don Forsyth, Nuszia Mordasiewicz, Gazella Mordasiewicz, Dawne Graham, Jeannie Kamins,

Marilyn Green, and my family for all of their support. My son Iain suffered through three years of film viewing and offered his technical help more times than I can say. My daughter Jade gratefully read my first draft and lent her support to the project. Her own research and writing on film introduced me to a new field of research and inquiry.

Some of the material in this book was previously published in two journal articles. I am grateful for their permission to reprint the material in this book:

Contemporary Justice Review, no. 10 (3) (September 2007)

International Journal of Drug Policy, no. 13 (2002)

Introduction

THE STORIES WE TELL

Since the advent of film, stories about drugs, drug users, addiction, traffickers, and criminal justice have entertained audiences. Drug prohibition emerged at the same time as the discovery of film, in the late nineteenth century and early twentieth century, and their histories intersect in significant ways. Early silent films, like *Chinese Opium Den,* produced in 1894, were only half a minute long and they were featured at penny arcades. Only stills exist of *Chinese Opium Den*, yet they are telling. Asian men portrayed as foreigners lay semiconscious on wooden bunks smoking opium out of long pipes. From their inception, film narrative and imagery racialize drug use and associate specific drugs with foreigners and racialized people. The nation, whether it be Britain, Canada, or the United States, is represented in illegal-drug films as under constant threat by street drugs and those associated with them.

Contemporary films also produce similar discourses about foreigners and racialized people. The popular U.S. film *Traffic* (2000) was heralded as an accurate portrayal of the "war on drugs" by politicians and reporters; in fact, a few politicians actually participated in the movie. It is loosely based on the earlier British made-for-television miniseries *Traffik* (1989). In the U.S. film, Mexico, which is represented as the illegal-drug-source country, is depicted as barbaric and uncivilized, where life is cheap and the military and police are violent, corrupt, and involved in drug trafficking. The military authorities are depicted as ruthless and sadistic (evidenced by a torture scene). Scenes shot in the United States situate Black men, and street dealers, in the inner city. The film follows the plight and degradation of Caroline, a young innocent White upper-class teenager who uses crack cocaine. Following Caroline's quick descent into crack addiction, a heated confrontation with her father, and a few days in drug treatment, she is shown fleeing to the inner city and then lying in bed with a Black man. They are having sex and the camera focuses in on Caroline's body underneath him. They are interrupted by a knock on the door and the Black man gets up and walks away to conduct a drug transaction. When he returns to the bedroom, he finds Caroline going through his satchel of drugs and hypodermic needles near the bed. He asks her, "Want to do that?" In the next scene he is shown injecting drugs into a vein in her foot. She has never injected drugs before. Afterwards, she lies back in the bed, oblivious to her surroundings, and he resumes having sex with her. Caroline has hit rock bottom and the message in *Traffic* is very clear. Poor Black men who deal drugs are represented as violent sexual predators who lure innocent White women into addiction. Similar discourse about Asian men informed early illegal-drug films. The opium den was depicted as a site of addiction and degradation. Fears about the "mixing of the races" and White women's morality informed film narratives. Asian men were depicted as a threat to Western Anglo-Saxon nations and moral women, just as racialized men are today.

Of course, fictional illegal-drug films are produced for entertainment and, above all, profit, and audiences learn about illegal drugs and justice from a myriad of sources. Yet friends and students at the university where I teach continually point to films as a frame of reference and as a source of information and disinformation about drugs and criminal justice. I care about films, especially drug films, because they tell a story not only about drugs but about nation building and criminal justice, pleasure and threat, and occasionally they challenge war-on-drugs narratives. Film, our contemporary mode of storytelling, provides both a narrative and visual experience. Thomas King, the author of *The Truth About Stories: A Native Narrative*, writes that "Stories are wondrous things. And they are dangerous."[1] He reminds us that the stories we tell and the stories we listen to are important. In his book, he tells the story of Charm, a native creation story, and Genesis, a Christian creation story.

The stories King presents are quite different. The story of Genesis provides a hierarchic worldview of a Christian universe of law and order, punishment, and governance. The story of Charm presents a native universe characterized by cooperation, harmony, and equality. King writes that if we accept the world through the eyes of Adam in the story of Genesis, we may blind ourselves to the story of Charm. We may see one story as sacred and the other story as secular, thus falling into the Western "pairing as dichotomy."[2] He asks if "the stories we tell reflect the world as it truly is, or did we simply start off with the wrong story?"[3] What if we start off with a flawed story, or what if the story were different? Would the world we have created look different too? In relation to the story about Charm, King asks if "you would live your life differently if only you had heard this story."[4]

Fellow writer Gerald Vizenor agrees, claiming that "You can't understand the world without telling a story."[5] Watching the British and U.S productions *Traffik* (1989) and *Traffic* (2000), respectively, and noting how very different they are (see chapters 4 and 7 for a fuller discussion), led me to think about the different ways we imagine and portray the world we live in. It led me to write about the two films and to conduct a three-year study of illegal-drug films produced in Britain, Canada, and the United States.[6]

I was interested in the stories presented in illegal-drug movies—and the stories that film producers ignored. Whereas I examined drug myths in my earlier analysis of *Traffic*,[7] in this study I wanted to look more closely at drug discourse, film narrative, and visual representations. I was interested in exploring the ideological assumptions embedded in the narrative and imagery of illegal-drug films. I wanted to look more closely at illegal-drug films because they involve the "production of meaning and truth-claims"[8] about drug use, pleasure, addiction, and responses to it by criminal justice (and social-service and medical professionals). Contemporary illegal-drug films, just like the story of Genesis, provide a hierarchical worldview of a Christian universe of evil, repentance, retribution, law and order, punishment, and governance. Yet occasionally, similar to the story of Charm, illegal-drug films challenge and disrupt, providing equally powerful and diverse stories that rupture conventional narratives about illegal drugs. We might ask ourselves if our drug laws and policies would be different if we saw and heard stories different from those that celebrate punishment.

Since the emergence of film in the late 1800s, knowledge is often transmitted through pictures rather than the written word or through oral history. In the early 1920s and 1930s, Britain instigated a number of trade conferences attended by Canadian and U.S. representatives where film was an "important topic" of discussion. Film historian Zoe Druick notes that film and its "powers of propaganda and persuasion, in the words of the time, were feared to be enormous . . . it was widely agreed that its powers need to be used for the benefit of the empire."[9] These concerns shaped film productions. Although the emergence of TV in the late 1940s succeeded in capturing a larger viewing audience, films continue to be popular and accessible in theaters, at home on TV, and through video and DVD releases. U.S. viewers watch over four hours of TV, video, or DVDs each day.[10] U.S., and Canadian and U.K, viewers are more likely to watch movies at home than in cinemas. We are inundated with illegal-drug representations.

The criteria for my sample was simply any Canadian, British, or U.S. film with a focus *primarily* on illegal drugs, trafficking, and their consequences. Although their history differs, British, Canadian, and U.S. drug policies and regulations draw on similar ideologies about morality, gender, race, family, and nation-state. They also share a colonial history. I watched comedies, action films, and dramas; I did not include documentaries in my sample. My sample consists of 120 films produced in Britain, Canada, and the United States from 1912 to 2006 (see the Appendix for the full list of films). Because the British and Canadian film industries are smaller than the United States', U.S. films dominate in the sample.

Illegal-drug films present ideas about pleasure, justice, the nature of addiction, morality, criminality, the drug user and trafficker, and the effectiveness of treatment, social services, law enforcement, criminal justice, and punishment. They also transmit ideas about the nation, colonization, militarization, and the intersection of the war on drugs and the war on terrorism. However, illegal-drug films are not homogeneous, and we should not lose sight of ruptures and alternative scenes that serve to shake us up, revealing alternative representations of drugs, drug users, and sellers. Both conventional and alternative themes embedded in illegal-drug films are investigated in this book.

THEORETICAL LENS

Theory is useful in helping us understand our world and imagining other ways of being. By looking at films produced between 1912 and 2006 in Britain, Canada, and the United States, drawing from critical criminology, feminist studies, and cultural criminology, I am able to provide a critical analysis of representations in drug films prior to criminalization to the present. However, this book is not a survey of drug films. Rather than discuss in depth all of the films in the sample or all of the drug films produced since 1912, specific films are highlighted in the book to examine more fully representations, themes, discourses, and tensions embedded in them.

Cultural criminology is "a mode of analysis that embodies sensitivities to image, meaning, and representation in the study of deviance, crime, and control"[11] in popular culture. It provides ways to understand the continuous interplay of "moral entrepreneurship, moral innovation and transgression" and the proliferation of media representations of crime and deviance.[12] At the core of cultural criminology is the questioning of the expansion of criminal justice and militarism in Western nations. The criminalization and militarization of civil society has been augmented by the war on drugs and terrorism.[13] As we will see, addiction, criminalized drugs, and "addicts" are most often portrayed as isolated from the social, political, and economic factors that shape them. And where drug dealing is depicted as the only job in town for disenfranchised men, the ghetto is represented as spreading, violent, contagious, and threatening.

The drugs examined in this study are criminalized: marijuana, ecstasy, LSD, heroin, cocaine, and methamphetamine. But they were not always categorized as illegal drugs. Less than a century ago, cocaine and heroin were legal substances. Drug movies depict the demonization of drugs, and, more often than not, criminalization and prohibition are celebrated. The illegal status of specific drugs, and prohibition, shapes drug use and selling just as it shapes the films that we watch. I am interested in what Ward Churchill refers to as "unraveling the codes of oppression"[14] and in revealing oppositional discourse about pleasure, play, transcendence, and social and political shifts.

Western cultural discourses (criminal justice, medical, literary, film, etc.) about illegal drugs, users, and sellers does not exist in a vacuum; rather, it speaks volumes about national identity and our attempts to govern, regulate, punish, and subjugate people seen and categorized as alien to ourselves, the Other. The construction of the Other is tied to narratives about national identity. Feminist scholar Sunera Thobani illuminates how in the West the "exalted" citizen is White and law-abiding. She reveals how racialization was integral to nation formation and is "constitutive of the modern state formation."[15] Writing about nationhood and the Other provides a lens to understand the war on drugs, addiction-as-disease discourse, and subsequent drug-treatment practices that legitimate repressive drug policy.[16] It reveals how acquiescent we are and how hegemonic assumptions shape our understanding of illegal drugs.

Film is one medium that serves to intensify cultural stereotyping of illegal-drug users and sellers. Drug discourse is played out through the war on drugs via the state and its representatives (criminal justice), by the professions (social workers, the medical and psychiatric), institutions, drug-treatment workers, and through self-regulation. Edward Said notes that it is one thing to study to gain knowledge, compassion, and understanding of a people or activity; it is another thing to gain "knowledge" to "reaffirm or self-affirm" domination.[17] Illegal-drug films are one medium that people gain knowledge from, and it can be easily argued that they reaffirm domination through war-on-drugs narratives. Said states that the identity of "self" or of "other" "is a "much worked-over historical, social, intellectual, and political process that takes place as a contest involving individuals and institutions in all societies."[18] Illegal-drug users and sellers have long been constructed as the Other. However, Said warns that human nature and human reality are not natural or stable; rather, they are constantly being made and unmade, and anything that resembles essentialism is constantly shifting. Michel Foucault also provides insight into how the self is governed and how the Other came to be identified by the newly emerging professions in the 1900s. New techniques of surveillance to identify, categorize, regulate, and discipline the population and delineate criminal and noncriminal, addicted and nonaddicted bodies emerged. The panopticon design by Jeremy Bentham provided a visual model for the regulated society and for the building of the penitentiaries of the late nineteenth century. The subject is observed at all times and soon participates in the governance of the self.[19]

Rather than understand drug movies as individualized stories, one might look at some films as an "accomplice to empire" building and domination;[20] thus, films that "rupture" empire and domination are noteworthy. Although discourse about illegal drugs speaks volumes about the "powerful and the powerless in each society,"[21] the powerful (and the powerless) are not homogeneous and drug discourse remains a contested place—where criminal-justice, medical, and social-service professionals contest and collude with one another and grassroots groups and moral reformers clamour for attention. To a lesser degree, illegal-drug users' voices have been heard. The unrepentant marijuana users seen in the Cheech and Chong movies such as *Up in Smoke* (1978) provides one example.

MEDIA AND CRIME STUDIES

Critical criminologists and other scholars brought our attention to the "manufacturing" of news and its relation to crime and justice. Stanley Cohen and Jock Young's 1973 edited book, *The Manufacture of News: Social Problems, Deviance and the Mass Media*, sensitized a growing number of critical criminologists and students to how the news is produced and how the media construct deviance and social problems. It set the stage for future investigations of the media.[22] News came to be seen as a cultural product and law and order as a news category.[23] Print, television, and radio news provide both narrative and visuals. Thus, photos in news media are viewed as "facts" that "speak for themselves."[24] Stuart Hall states that photos have ideological significance because they "can *enhance*, *locate*, or *specify* the ideological theme, once it has been produced, by a sort of reciprocal mirror-effect."[25] Applying Hall's exploration of news photos to images in film, we can see how representations of illegal-drug users, drugs, and drug paraphernalia are fetishized in both news photos and film "refracting the ideological theme at another level," one that we come to recognize. Who does not recognize the visual image of the illegal-drug user shooting up? Over and over again this image is depicted in the news and film as "natural" and it takes on a life of its own, falsely encapsulating the boundaries and practices of illegal-drug users' interests. Just as significant, we attach specific understanding and meaning to the visual image of "shooting up."

Jock Young states that not all drug use is condemned or represented in a negative fashion in the news, rather only those drugs that are constructed as pleasurable and "taken for hedonistic reasons . . . unrelated to productivity."[26] Young draws from Richard Blum, who claims that people are "fascinated with drugs—because they are attracted by the states and conditions drugs are said to produce . . . it is the desire for release, for escape, for magic, and ecstatic joys. That is the derivation of the menace in drugs—their representation as keys to forbidden kingdoms inside ourselves. The dreadful in the drug is the dreadful in ourselves."[27] Our fascination is also related to how specific drugs are associated with racialized groups, dangerous classes, and criminalized groups (which are often conflated); deviance and violence; and with the abandonment of "rational consciousness." Colonization was and continues to be accompanied by the suppression of drugs used for ritual and spiritual purposes. The fact that some drugs were conduits to spiritual and social cohesion was not lost on colonizers.[28] Thus, the suppression of pleasure is not the only motivating force behind drug prohibition. Drugs are cultural products that have multiple meanings. The stories we tell about drugs are important, for they lay out the parameters around the issue.

Feminist, critical criminology, and cultural studies scholars have drawn our attention to how women in conflict with the law are depicted in film and contribute to our understanding of race, class, and gender representations.[29] Feminist criminologist Karlene Faith discusses how women in conflict with the law are often characterized as masculinized monsters situated outside of normative heterosexuality.[30] Rebecca Johnson also brings our attention to representations of sexuality and normal and deviant families in film.[31] She examines, with Ruth Buchanan, film narratives about nation building and the origins of law and how narratives serve "to hold colonial relations in place." White frontier justice (a world of violent masculinity) is envisioned as separating the "savage" from the West. They suggest that frontier justice "is embedded" deeply in international discourse.[32] Frontier justice in the form of civil and police vigilantism and protection of borders is a dominant narrative in illegal-drug films.

Theorists such as bell hooks[33] and Richard Dyer[34] also sensitized us to representations of "whiteness" and the "black body" in film.[35] Dyer examines how Whiteness is associated with "order, rationality, rigidity, qualities brought out by the contrast with black disorder, irrationality and looseness."[36] hooks explores how black female bodies and sexuality are negatively represented in film. She also examines imperialist "nostalgia at its best—potent expression of longing for the 'primitive'? One desires 'a bit of the Other' to enhance the blank landscape of whiteness."[37] A number of other researchers examine film representations of racialized people, crime, and place in Western films, including depictions of Mexican-Americans;[38] black males;[39] resentment and suburban security;[40] ghetto aesthetic;[41] and women of colour.[42] Historically, criminalized drugs and the people who use them are racialized, and this phenomenon is represented in drug films.

Complimenting the research outlined above, a number of critical writers have begun to look more closely at print media and representations of illegal drugs.[43] Drug researchers Craig Reinarman and Harry Levine explain that, while the news media in the United States offer narrow misrepresentations of drugs, drug use, selling, and criminal-justice responses, they also attempt to shape public opinion about crime, especially drug crime.[44] For example, media reporting during the Ronald Reagan era that proclaimed that drugs were killing our children, Nancy Reagan's "Just Say No" campaign, and later George Bush Senior's infamous speech while holding up a bag of crack cocaine (said to be bought only minutes from the White House) contributed to public perceptions about drugs, and especially crack, as the number one evil to be battled in the United States. Drug scares have been a popular media creation throughout the twentieth century. Dramatic and sensationalized stories about killer weed, LSD, angel dust, crack, and methamphetamine spread misinformation about drugs and drug users. Today's "war on drugs" is characterized by the *"routinisation of caricature,"* which promotes worst-case scenarios as the norm and sensationalizes and distorts drug issues in the media.[45]

THE DRUG-FILM GENRE

Although there are a number of research articles about drug films,[46] only three books on the subject have been published (authored by Michael Stark, Jack Stevenson, and Harry Shapiro),[47] and none of these texts focus on criminal justice. Michael Starks's 1982 groundbreaking book *Cocaine Fiends and Reefer Madness* is an illustrated history of drugs in the movies. Starks includes numerous stills from movies around the world, including a still from the first studio film about drugs, produced by Thomas Edison in 1894, titled *Black Maria*, and a later 1905 film titled *A Pipe Dream*. Starks does not confine himself to "drug movies" per se because he is interested in any movie that depicts illegal drugs. He defines a drug film "as a film having any reference to psychoactive drugs." Thus, films that include a comment such as "What's he been smoking?" are included in his exhaustive sample.[48]

Drug-film researchers owe a tremendous debt to Michael Starks. Many of the films he includes in his excellent book are difficult to access and view. He includes films produced in Germany, France, Italy, the United States, and Britain. The stills and the narrative of the book provide an extensive illustrated history of representations of drugs in movies up until the 1970s.

Although Starks,[49] Stevenson,[50] and Shapiro[51] contribute significantly to the drug-film genre,[52] they do not consider illegal-drug films against the backdrop of criminal justice and the war on drugs. In contrast to other work, my sample consists of 120 Canadian, British, and U.S. productions. I also provide a sociohistorical lens through which to understand illegal-drug film discourse in Britain, Canada, and the United States from 1912 to 2006. This book focuses on fictional representations of users and traffickers, drug services and treatment, and the intersection of criminal justice and treatment.[53] I also discuss counterculture, alternative, and stoner flicks. This book provides an analysis of race, class, and gender, and, importantly, maternal drug use and film representations of women are examined. What also distinguishes this book from others is the focus on how cinematic representations of illegal-drug use and trafficking (regardless of drug type) are associated and linked to discourses about the Other, nation building, law and order, and punishment. In other words, it is not the drug per se that is significant; rather, it is our associations with them. This book explores these themes and more in relation to the war on drugs and global politics.

Chapter 1, "Moral Regulation, Film Censorship, and Law," introduces the reader to film censorship in Britain, Canada, and the United States. In the twentieth century, moral-reform movements saw films and drugs as sites for regulation; thus, the regulation of illegal drugs and film narrative and imagery will be discussed. In addition, I explore the convergence of government, censorship, film, and drug law. Chapter 2, "Illegal-Drug Users and Addiction Narratives: The Early Film Years," examines illegal-drug films until the late 1950s with an emphasis on depictions of drug users, illegal drugs, and addiction and treatment models. Chapter 3, "The 60s On: Counterculture, Addiction-as-Disease, and Mandatory-Treatment Narratives," discusses illegal-drug films produced from 1960 to the 1990s. Representations of the drug user, addiction, and treatment models are explored, including positive portrayals of marijuana and LSD, criminal addicts, and twelve-step treatment models. Chapter 4, "Ruptures in Addiction Narratives: Pleasure, Harm Reduction, Consumer Culture, and Regulation," examines alternative films about illegal-drug use and addiction, drug treatment, and therapeutic use of drugs. The drug-treatment industry and its intersection with law enforcement are also explored. Chapter 5, "Drug Dealers: A Nation Under Siege," explores U.S. films and ideologies about punishment, criminal justice, law and order, prison, nationhood, and colonization, as well as representations of the intersection of the war on drugs and the war on terrorism. Chapter 6, "Vilified Women and Maternal Myths," examines representations of women who use and sell illegal drugs and maternal-state conflicts (the intersection of the regulation of reproduction and the war on drugs) in illegal-drug films. A number of films that depict maternal drug use and "fetal harm" are discussed. In chapter 7, "Challenges to the Drug War: 1980 to 2006," I discuss "stoner flicks" and other alternative films that challenge conventional drug-war narratives. In these films, illegal-drug use is portrayed as pleasurable and positive and the drug war is seen as negative and destructive. In addition, I discuss the British series *Traffik* in order to look more fully at global politics, alternative representations of drug-source nations, poppy growers, the war on drugs, and the war on terrorism.

1 Moral Regulation, Film Censorship, and Law

DRUG HISTORY

From time immemorial, wild and cultivated plants have been valued for medicinal, spiritual, and ritual use.[1] Plants provide food sources and substances that affect both body and mind. Contemporary ethnobiologists continue to be amazed at the pharmacological genius of early people who were able to discern and identify plants for nutrition, healing, and spiritual uses. In the seventeenth and eighteenth centuries, British subjects used alcohol and indigenous plants for healing. White colonizers from Britain and Europe brought their own remedies to North America, alcohol being one of them. Beer and wine were available on ships in lieu of scarce and often contaminated water. European physicians had long warned about the dangers of drinking water, so beer was the national beverage. By the mid-1700s all types of alcohol (beer, wine, distilled) were cheap and used as a "food, medicine, tonic, and stimulant." For example, in French Canada in 1795, breakfast might consist of bread and a glass of rum. A small glass of whisky was drunk in the morning to ward off colds and to enable hard work.[2] Although there was concern about the public consumption of distilled alcohol, more specifically "gin" in Britain in the early to mid-1700s, there was no public condemnation of beer.[3]

In contrast, apart from one or two small groups at the southern tip of what is now North America, aboriginal peoples did not use alcohol prior to colonization. When it was used, it was for ritual purposes, and there are no accounts of problematic alcohol use prior to colonization. In fact, a number of early missionaries wrote about aboriginal abhorrence to the drug when they were first introduced to it.[4] Aboriginal peoples had an array of plants they used for medicinal and ritual purposes. Over time, many of these plants were introduced to and used by the colonizers. Others, such as peyote, were later condemned, as were other aboriginal social, political, economic, and spiritual practices. Both Canada and the United States enacted legislation in the 1800s prohibiting aboriginal people from consuming alcohol (these laws were in effect for over 100 years).

Prior to the mid-1800s, drug use of all kinds was considered to be a personal matter if one was not a colonized subject. If it was discussed at all, it was seen as a bad habit. Drug use, sales, and production were not criminalized in Britain, Canada, and the United States until the late 1800s and early 1900s, although sales and production were taxed and sometimes regulated for trade purposes. Therefore, people who used drugs such as opium, or later morphine, cocaine, and marijuana were not cut off from the rest of society. Rather, drugs were obtained legally and most often consumed in the form of home remedies, patent medicine, tonics, and/or elixirs. The occasional and regular use of these drugs was not perceived as dangerous or negative. In fact, right up until the mid-1800s, the term *addict* referred to pleasurable pursuits such as reading. It did not refer to negative or destructive drug use.[5]

British and European settlers to North American also brought with them opiates, derivatives from the opium poppy (*Papaver somniferum*). It had long been an important medicine in India, China, the Middle East, and Europe, traced to the third millennium BC.[6] Opium was considered an important trade item right up until contemporary times, as evidenced by the Opium War of 1840–42, in which China was forced to open its ports to opium exports by the British (the East India Company was making huge profits). Opium is a narcotic (as are morphine, heroin, and codeine) that can be consumed by mouth or smoked. Opium is used to relieve pain. It is also used to induce sleep, to ease intestinal problems and stabilize mental disorders, to relax users, to reduce spasms and fever, and to suppress coughs. It was especially useful in easing stomach ailments for infants and adults alike. Opiates were also used for a number of women's ailments related to painful menstruation and childbirth.

Historians Virginia Berridge and Griffith Edwards explain that oral preparations of opium were widely used by all classes of people in Britain and elsewhere during the 1700s and 1800s. At that time, there was no distinction between "medical" and "nonmedical" use.[7] Poppy plants were cultivated in Britain and the United States (as well as in India and other nations). A wide array of liquid elixirs, home remedies, and patent medicines was available in Britain, Canada, and the United States, including laudanum, an opium tincture (which might contain opium, saffron, castor, ambergris, musk, and nutmeg) that was widely used until the early twentieth century.[8] Recipe books provided details on how to make home remedies, and a wide selection of patent medicines was sold. Advertisements for Mrs. Winslow's Soothing Syrup, A Pennyworth of Peace, and Godfrey's Codial were directed to mothers in their care of infants. A number of these remedies also contained alcohol. These soothing syrups for infants contained opiates to settle upset stomachs, a common ailment in Britain and other nations at the time. Poverty, poor housing, and lack of sanitation contributed to gastrointestinal complaints and infant mortality was high. The syrups were cheap, popular, and available. They offered palliative care for treating infants and adults for pain, stomach ailments, coughs, and diarrhoea right up until the early 1900s, especially for the poor who could not afford a doctor or rural families who lived hundreds of miles away from the nearest doctor.[9]

Opium eating, popularized by Thomas De Quincey's 1821 book *Confessions of an English Opium-Eater*, brought attention to this aristocratic vice and recreational use of the drug. However, most people used opium and its derivatives more modestly; more typical famous opium users were Elizabeth Barrett Browning, a well-balanced habitual user, and Florence Nightingale, who used opium for medical reasons following the Crimean war.[10] Eaton's and Sears, Roebuck and Co.'s mail-order catalogues advertised patent medicines right up until the 1930s, and these ads targeted rural women who lived far away from doctors and whose services were too expensive. It was assumed that women would turn to these remedies to care for their family's health.[11]

The isolation and extraction of the alkaloid morphine from the poppy plant in 1806 (named after the god of dreams, Morpheus) and the invention of the hypodermic needle in 1843 were heralded as advances in medical treatment. The discovery of the hypodermic needle brought about changes in pain management and treatment for illness. Now, medicine could be delivered more rapidly, bypassing the stomach. Originally, injections were hypodermic, injecting right under the skin. Physicians recommended morphine for medicinal purposes and it was widely used during the U.S. Civil War and the Crimean and Franco-Prussian wars. Morphine injection to reduce pain became common. Besides its use for pain management, it was also recommended for "hysterical women" and to cure morning sickness in pregnancy.

In the 1800s, a number of British novels and autobiographies refer to the use of laudanum and other opiates. Although all classes of people used opiates, the typical user was a middle- to upper-class White woman. Prior to the criminalization of opiates in the United States, 80 percent of people addicted to opiates had "jobs, home, families, and [good] reputations."[12] Drug researcher Stephan Kendall suggests that the women's temperance movement to prohibit alcohol inadvertently raised women's opium use, because alcohol was not seen as a viable option. Other drug researchers note that in the 1800s and early 1900s "husbands drank alcohol in the saloon; wives took opium at home."[13] However, by the end of the 1800s physicians began to write about the habit-forming propensity of morphine, coupled with injecting as the route of administration. The first recorded morphine addict was the wife of Alexander Wood, who is credited with the discovery of the hypodermic needle.[14] Physicians came to label addiction to morphine *morphinomania*. Habitual use of morphine and laudanum usually derived from medical treatment rather than recreational use.[15]

A derivative of morphine—heroin—was discovered in 1874, although it was not marketed until the late 1880s.[16] A semisynthetic drug, heroin was produced by Bayer (of Bayer aspirins), which marketed products containing the drug. Physicians saw it as a very effective pain medication, similar to morphine and most often consumed by mouth in cough syrups or in tablet form. Opium and heroin have zero toxicity (as does marijuana).[17] The Stevenson Report discusses the effects of narcotics in 1956: "To our surprise, we have not been able to locate even one scientific study on the proved harmful effects of addiction. Earlier investigators had apparently assumed that the ill effects were so obvious as not to need scientific verification, or they, too, had accepted without question the traditional beliefs on the harmful effects of narcotics."[18] Of course, opium and heroin are powerful depressants: thus, drug overdose is a risk, especially when mixing the drug with other depressants such as alcohol or taking doses of unknown quality and quantity, a risk factor related to the illegal market.

Marijuana was also a favoured ingredient in elixirs and patent medicines in the mid-1800s and early 1900s.[19] Marijuana is one of our oldest drugs, a product of the hemp plant, *Cannabis sativa*. The hemp plant provides fiber, paper, oil, seeds, and it is used as a medicine. Ancient Chinese herbal books record medical use of marijuana, and the plant was also used in Africa, India, and medieval Europe. It was recommended for a host of ailments, including the treatment of malaria, rheumatic pain, and "women's problems." However, it did not become popular in the West until the mid-nineteenth century, when Western doctors began to praise the drug and recommend its medicinal use, and a number of patent medicines containing the drug became available.[20] Although marijuana was used in liquid form in patent medicines, it was not until the early 1900s that Mexican labourers looking for work in the United States introduced it to residents in a smokable form.[21]

Similarly, the coca plant had long been cultivated in Peru and Bolivia and recognized for its medicinal qualities. However, it was not until the late 1800s, especially after cocaine was isolated and extracted from the coca leaf in 1860, that it became popular in the West (there is 0.5% cocaine in the coca leaf; refined cocaine can contain up to 100% pure cocaine). Cocaine was a central ingredient in a number of patent medicines and was used as a local anaesthetic. Recreational use of drinks that contained cocaine were also popular. Cocaine was an ingredient in a number of wines (i.e., Vin Mariana) and in the popular drink Coca-Cola. These wines, tonics, and coca extracts were popular and also recommended by physicians; and the 1901 text *History of Coca*, written by a U.S. doctor, W. Golden Mortimer, outlined its diverse uses.[22] Fictional characters like Sherlock Holmes brought powder cocaine to the attention of English readers.

SHIFTING PRACTICES

By the mid-1800s, the newly emerging medical profession began to stake out its fields of expertise and regulation. Doctors started to take an interest in opium eating, a pastime of middle-and upper-class White people, and in what they termed *morphinomania,* people addicted to morphine. Where these people were mostly introduced to morphine for medical treatment, the smoking of opium was perceived as a recreational vice associated with foreigners. There was already some opposition to smoking opium, specifically against Chinese men who were thought to use or supply the drug, and San Francisco criminalized the smoking of opium in dens in 1875.[23] Class, race, and gender tensions began to surface and became more explicit following the completion of the national railways in Canada and the United States. Early on, Chinese workers were welcomed and seen as good workers by their White counterparts. When the railway was complete, followed by an economic slump, Chinese workers were vilified. This led to a period of Asian exclusion resulting in the infamous Chinese Head Tax legislation in Canada and anti-Asian legislation in the United States, which fuelled systemic racism and the breakup of families due to limits on immigration and work visas.

Other U.S. cities enacted legislation to criminalize smoking opium in dens, and in 1883 Congress began to increase tariffs on opium prepared for smoking.[24] Initially, where the smoking of opium by foreigners was condemned, the many patent medicines, tonics, and elixirs that White people consumed were ignored by moral reformers. However, that was to change too. Drugs that had been heralded as positive were now being questioned, especially patent medicines. The newly emerging medical profession argued that patent medicines were dangerous because there was little control over ingredients and potency and those who sold them. In Britain, physicians lobbied to have laws enacted so that patent medicines were properly labelled and to curtail recreational opium use and "infant doping" by the poor (giving soothing syrups containing opium to infants).[25]

Perceptions began to shift about some drugs. Moral reformers, citizen groups, politicians, and the media claimed that Asian men used and sold drugs like opium in smoking form to White people. They were seen as a danger and a threat to White womanhood, the family, and the nation. In the United States, Black men were represented as becoming violent, criminal, and sexually aggressive towards White women after using cocaine.[26] Early on, White upper-class and middle-class users were constructed as morally weak; and if they sought to break their habit, they did so with the help of doctors or stayed at a private asylum. Following drug prohibition, the poor and working-class and racialized people discovered that they would be seen as criminals and sent to prison or hospitals for the criminally insane.

MORAL REFORM MOVEMENTS

Silent films emerged during the late 1800s and early 1900s, when significant historical, political, economic, and social shifts, including drug prohibition, were occurring in Western nations, and these events shaped film representations. Both silent films and talking films include narratives and imagery about drugs. In Britain, Canada and the United States, industrialization, social unrest, and immigration of Roman Catholics threatened White Protestant hegemony, and it was against this backdrop that temperance and antiopiate movements emerged. The antiopiate and temperance movements of the nineteenth century overlapped and intersected with moral-reform and social-purity movements (i.e., the eugenics movement). Moral-reform movements were both national and religious. Antiopiate and temperance groups claimed that controlled use of opium (in smokable form) and alcohol was impossible,[27] and by the early nineteenth century, self-control, morality, and sobriety became the template of White, Anglo-Saxon, middle-class respectability and the model for the imperial subject. Western Protestants adopted religious dedication and temperance as symbols of social status and self-control, and labour and material wealth were viewed as signs of "God's favour." As Max Weber commented, the capitalist system "so needs this devotion to the calling of making money."[28]

During this period, protecting the family and the border from foreign Others became a nation-building theme, one that supported Anglo-Saxon morality. In speaking about the master narrative of Canadian nationhood, which can also be applied to the British and American narratives, scholar Sunera Thobani notes that "differences between nationals and outsiders are exaggerated, even as the commonalities within these grouping are inflated." The nation's outsiders are represented as those "who have been constituted as 'non-western' and 'non-modern and, therefore, not in possession of the exalted qualities of 'western' nationalities."[29] Because drug use is racialized, White women's drug use was represented as a failure of nation building and moral and religious transformation. Laws criminalizing drugs such as opium and cocaine were enacted in the early 1900s in Canada, Britain, and the United States, and international treaties were signed condemning them. Plants and drugs associated with foreign Others were specifically condemned, regardless of the fact that White Anglo-Saxons used opiates, cocaine, and cannabis in patent medicines and elixirs. Western imperialism and colonization had already been accompanied by the suppression and later criminalization of many of the plants used for healing, spiritual, and social use by indigenous peoples around the world and the use of Western drugs such as alcohol by aboriginal peoples.

Western drug legislation is not premised on science or measures of toxicity. The drug schedules of Western nations assume that some drugs are "essentially damaging,"[30] without providing empirical or cross-cultural evidence. Drug-prohibition ideology erases all evidence that some drug are experienced as positive, such as marijuana and ecstasy, which are normalized youth recreational activities today in Britain, Canada, and the United States,[31] and that some drug use enhances cohesiveness, social health, and well-being.[32] Prohibition ideology generalizes broadly, conflating fears about the nation, racialized bodies, women, youth, epidemics, decay, and crime. Prohibition ideology is quite malleable. Indeed, it is ever ready to be kick-started again, to make claims, and to set out narrow parameters and boundaries about drugs, users, sellers, risks, dangers, and legal and police solutions.

Citizen groups, moral reformers, the media, professional groups, and the state shaped the parameters of drug-prohibition ideology. However, unlike some moral-reform movements, much of drug policy is state sanctioned and initiated. In Britain, Canada, and the United States, the state generates and actively produces, with law-enforcement agencies, professional associations (i.e., medical), and the media, knowledge about drug users, sellers, and producers. Overall, Western views of drug use are also sanctioned in international treaties.[33] Nonstate moral-reform groups, such as Partnership for a Drug-Free America, and self-help groups like Narcotics Anonymous also produce drug discourse.

Although there are ruptures in drug-prohibition narratives, drugs continue to be categorized as "good" or "bad," even though the lines separating drugs are illusionary and not static. Leading up to and following the criminalization of drugs in the early 1900s, the protection of the Western "nation" from the threat of illegal users, traffickers, smugglers, and now terrorists has become central narrative in drug films. Although the demon drug shifts in film narratives and the public imagination, over the last century prohibition narratives are standard in film productions.

A BRIEF HISTORY OF DRUG REGULATION

As noted above, British, Canadian, and U.S. drug laws were shaped by social and political reform movements and moral reformers. Britain's drug-regulation history is also shaped by the Opium War of 1840–42, when the Chinese were forced to open their ports to opium exports by the British. The East India Company earned huge profits from the sale of opium and was reluctant to have its profits threatened. However, by the late 1800s the United States pressured Britain to restrict the opium trade. Domestic drug legislation in Britain culminated in the Pharmacy Act of 1868 to regulate the sale of poison. And in 1908, the Poisons and Pharmacy Act was passed to regulate patent medicines (similar legislation was enacted in the early 1900s in Canada and the U.S.). Historians Berridge and Edwards[34] state that the act was a response to class tensions and the medical profession's growing power and concern about patent medicines. The medical profession was vocal in its concern about working-class recreational opium use and "infant doping" by poor mothers and hired nurses who cared for working-class mothers' infants when they were working, although they had little to say about infant doping by nurses who cared for middle- and upper-class children. The public, including mothers and nurses, believed in the "beneficial properties of opium for a baby."[35] Nevertheless, it was the use of the drug by poor mothers that came under scrutiny.

British drug researcher Nigel South states that "significant drugs legis-lation passed in Britain was less a response to any real domestic problem and more the result of willingness to meet national obligations set by inter-national treaties"[36] initiated by the U.S. government. On the international scene, British representatives attended the Shanghai Commission in 1909, the first meeting by Western nations to set the groundwork for interna-tional drug control. Here again, concern lay with the smoking of opium by racialized and colonized people rather than with patent-medicine use.[37] In 1911, the United States sponsored the International Conference on Opium, formalizing the regulation of opium and cocaine use, production, and sale outside of medical use. In 1914, Britain signed the treaty even though there was no recognized opium smoking problem at home. The Hague conven-tion, which outlines a nation's responsibility to create federal legislation to regulate narcotics, was added on to the Versailles Treaty to end WWI. As well, from 1914 to the mid-1920s, new concerns emerged about flap-pers, chorus girls, actresses, and working-class girls using drugs and being seduced by men of colour. Writer John Kohn writes that concern about the "sexualized menace" of the drug subculture vividly reported in the media also informed efforts to support drug prohibition in Britain. The enact-ment of the Defence of the Realm Act Regulation 40 B in 1916, restricting cocaine possession, is viewed by some as the first step toward criminal-justice control of drugs in Britain. In Britain, doctors retained the right to treat addiction through drug maintenance. Therefore, drug treatment and maintenance options were quite different from those in Canada and the United States. Nevertheless, crime control became central to drug regula-tion. U.S. efforts to create global drug prohibition helped to shape both British and Canadian drug regulation. The signing of the United Nations' Single Convention on Narcotic Drugs in 1961 by Britain and Canada also helped to consolidate U.S. control of drug prohibition.

Early U.S. drug laws were fueled by concerns that Christian, Anglo-Saxon supremacy was threatened. Concerns about White women's moral-ity, in addition to economic and anti-Asiatic tensions, culminated in drug legislation in the late 1800s and early 1900s. By then it was already widely believed that Black men's use of cocaine led to violence and that Chinese men were busy corrupting innocent White women. Thus, federal law to prohibit opium and cocaine was not opposed, even though there has never been any empirical evidence to suggest that these claims were true.[38] The Harrison Act was passed by 1914. Again, U.S. citizens believed that the Harrison Act would be used to criminalize foreign outsiders and problem segments of the population. Harry J. Anslinger, the head of the Federal Bureau of Narcot-ics, took his job seriously, a moral entrepreneur who spread misinformation about marijuana and other drugs. Mexican men who arrived in the United States looking for work in the early 1900s were associated with smok-ing marijuana and introducing it to Americans, and Red-scare ideology conflated drug use with political radicalism and ultimately a threat to the nation.[39] Anslinger, who associated marijuana, narcotics, and cocaine with immorality, sexuality, crime, murder, and insanity, was also instrumental in the making of the classic film *Reefer Madness* (1936), an educational tool to publicize the evils of marijuana. The Marijuana Tax Stamp Act was passed in 1937. As time passed, new laws were passed to criminalize other drugs, and fears culminated again in the 1960s, when drug use increased and reached middle-class consumers.

In Canada, the Opium and Narcotic Act was enacted in 1908 following an anti-Asiatic riot in Vancouver in 1907. The riots were sparked by the economic fears of White labourers towards their Chinese and Japanese counterparts following the completion of the national railway. Mackenzie King, then Canada's deputy minister of labour, was sent to Vancouver, British Columbia, to settle damages for what the federal government had defined as a labour conflict. After discovering that the opium trade was unregulated, and hearing the complaints of several affluent Chinese Canadians about the opium industry, King proclaimed, "We will get some good out of this riot yet."[40] King subsequently submitted a report on the use of smoking opium to the federal government. In response, Parliament passed Canada's first Opium Act.[41] King's report drew heavily from newspaper reports depicting opium as corrupting the morality of White women. In particular, King represented smoking opium as an "evil" that threatens the "principles of morality" that should "govern the conduct of a Christian nation."[42] King also argued that Canada should join the international community to prohibit opium smoking. No evidence is provided to support his claims about the dangerousness of this form of opium use and the subsequent breakdown of morality. Believing the claims that only a small minority group would be affected, there was little public opposition to this early piece of legislation, subsequent amendments, or the related broadening of police powers.[43] Racialized groups were easily targeted, and drugs associated with these groups increasingly came under attack.[44] In the early 1920s, moral reformers, print media, and citizen groups produced anti-drug discourse about Chinese opium users and traffickers and demanded harsher laws.[45] Early arrest patterns in Canada suggest that between 1908 and 1930, Chinese and Black men were singled out by the police for arrest, especially if it was believed that they sold drugs to White people.[46] Changes in drug law in 1922 allowed "aliens" convicted of drug possession and/or selling to be deported, and Chinese residents were soon being deported too.[47] In Canada, no public drug-maintenance or drug-treatment programs were set up for people addicted to narcotics following criminalization.

PROHIBITION

Throughout the era of prohibition, drugs were literally taken away from the people and placed under the domain of doctors and of course the criminal-justice system. One immediate consequence of drug prohibition was the creation of a new criminal class. The majority of drug users in the early 1900s had used drugs like laudanum, morphine, and heroin for medical treatment. Following drug prohibition, Vin Mariana, Mrs. Winslow's Soothing Syrup, and patent medicines and tonics made up of marijuana, cocaine, and opiates were no longer legally available. Although some drugs were now available by prescription from a doctor, they were not available for drug maintenance in Canada and the United States. In the United States, a number of arrests and court challenges made clear that physicians who prescribed for addiction maintenance were breaking the law. In fact, a wide range of drug users were now criminals, but it was the poor who suffered most due to the fact they were more visible to the police and had less access to legal drug sources, economic and social resources, and medical care.[48] Those physicians in the United States who provided narcotic maintenance were eventually scorned and their clinics were shut down.[49]

An illegal market emerged and individual entrepreneurs and organized crime now produced, smuggled, and sold these newly criminalized drugs—narcotics and cocaine—in all three nations, and alcohol during prohibition in the United States and parts of Canada. And whereas tonics and patent medicines were most commonly used by people prior to prohibition, now more potent and concentrated forms of drugs became more widely available, simply because it was much easier and more profitable to smuggle a kilogram of pure powder cocaine than a shipment of Vin Mariana wine or coca leaves. Thus, less potent liquid and tablet forms of the drugs became rarer and more potent, and refined forms of the drugs were sold on the illegal market. In addition, to make more profit, drugs were adulterated with other substances. The unsure quality and potency of drugs sold on the illegal market rendered drug users vulnerable to overdose deaths and other health problems. And whereas drug users tended to use liquid and tablet forms, or even smoked drugs like opium prior to prohibition, routes of administration shifted too. Prior to prohibition, most drug users took drugs by mouth, and a smaller percentage sniffed drugs and injected drugs (like cocaine, morphine, and heroin) under their skin. Following the enactment of federal drug laws in the United States, Canada, and Britain, intravenous drug use (IV) emerged and was first recorded in 1924. Intravenous drug use became popular because of changes in the illegal-drug market. As natural and milder drugs like opium were criminalized, opium pipes were replaced by hypodermic injections (under the skin) or sniffing.[50] Drugs in their natural form, such as raw opium, were no longer available; and more refined drugs, such as heroin and cocaine, became available. Once drug prohibition emerged, drug prices soared and the lives of drug users changed dramatically. Literally overnight, law-abiding people became criminals. As we will see in the following chapters, some of these political and social shifts were captured on the screen.

FILM CENSORSHIP IN THE UNITED STATES

A number of writers have examined censorship of representations of drugs in U.S. films[51] and found that films produced in the late 1800s and early 1900s depicting drug use were popular with the public. During this era, "opium films" utilized the newest film technology depicting users drifting off into elaborate opium-induced dreams. However, moral-reform movements, including the temperance and antiopiate movements, saw films as a site for moral regulation. In the United States, prior to and following the enactment of the Harrison Narcotics Act in 1914, moral reformers sought to censor film. By the early 1920s, Hollywood was seen as a site of immorality and suspicious left-leaning politics. The National Association of the Motion Picture Industry reproached films that showed the use of narcotics and other "unnatural activities thought to be dangerous to social morality."[52]

In the United States, self-censorship emerged when the Hays Commission, created by the Motion Picture Producers and Distributors Association in 1922, created a list of subjects to avoid, including illegal drugs and miscegenation. One of the provisions of the Hays Commission was that all correspondence between the studios and the censors would be confidential and "not open to public scrutiny."[53] Gerald Gardner[54] is one of many researchers who gained access to the movie-censorship letters when the Hays Office turned over the files to the Academy of Motion Picture Arts and Sciences in the late 1960s. The files contain letters outlining censors' demands and directors' responses. It is evident from the files that the censors believed that depictions of immorality in film, if allowed at all, must always be punished. Acts of immorality must never be condoned, and when it came to depictions of illegal-drug use, early censors were adamant that it should not be shown on the screen.

Although there are a number of versions to the following story, film writer James Robertson says that during the filming of the *Valley of the Giants* (1919), the well-known silent film actor Wallace Reid injured his leg.[55] He was in severe pain and it seemed that he might not be able to complete the last few scenes for the film. The Famous Players-Lasky film company feared that their investment in the film would be lost and arranged for a studio doctor to care for Reid until the film was completed. The doctor supplied Reid with morphine to lessen his pain so that he could continue working. When the filming wrapped up, Reid was not able to stop using morphine. Famous Players-Lasky film company refused to grant him time off to withdraw from morphine because they would lose profit by holding up their production schedule. Consequently, Reid was supplied with an ever-increasing amount of morphine by the studio doctor in order for him to continue working, until he collapsed on a film set. Reid died in hospital shortly afterwards.[56]

At the time of Reid's death in 1923, Hollywood was already in the middle of a number of scandals regarding well-known celebrities, the most infamous being the trial of screen comedian Roscoe "Fatty" Arbuckle, originally charged with murder and rape. Immorality and alcohol and drug use were identified in the public mind with Hollywood.[57] Fearing public disapproval and state censorship, the film industry approached Will H. Hays, President Harding's postmaster general, who was ready for retirement at the time, and asked him to head a censorship body. He agreed and presided over the Motion Picture Producers and Distributors Association from 1922 to 1945. Hays was quick to ban all screen representations of drugs in Hollywood films.

A number of film historians note that Reid's death came at the worst time because of public concerns about scandals, drug use, morality, and censorship in Hollywood.[58] However, the U.S. public and Hays were sympathetic to Reid in part because his addiction to morphine was seen as related to an injury rather than to immorality or a decadent lifestyle. Hays responded to the crises by allowing Reid's widow, Dorothy Davenport, a film director in her own right, to produce and star in *Human Wreckage* (1923). The film was produced with the assistance of the Los Angeles Anti-Narcotics League, and apparently the film featured a number of real "police chiefs, anti-drug police," and civic leaders.[59] The film includes a foreword by Dorothy Davenport in which she makes clear that "dope" is the deadly menace confronting the United States.

In 1927, the Code of the Motion Picture Industry created a list of "Do's and Be Carefuls" that included the trafficking of illegal drugs. In 1930, the Code of the Motion Picture Industry stated that "The illegal drug traffic must never be presented. Because of its evil consequences, the drug traffic should never be presented in any form. The existence of the trade should not be brought to the attention of the audiences."[60]

By 1934, the Motion Picture Production Code more formally established itself (it was introduced in 1930) to monitor films produced in Hollywood. Explicit alcohol and illegal-drug use and violence and sexual intimacy were banned from the screen. Yet independent films continued to be produced, and many of them portrayed drug use and linked marijuana with insanity and crime, such as *Reefer Madness* (1936) and *Marihuana, the Weed with Roots in Hell* (1936). *Reefer Madness* was produced with the help of H. J. Anslinger, the U.S. commissioner of narcotics. Both U.S. films (now seen as classic propagandist films that generate gales of laughter from contemporary viewers) educated moviegoers about the horrors of marijuana use and laid the groundwork for criminalization in 1937. Independent propagandist drug films, made in concert with U.S. Commissioner of Narcotics H. J. Anslinger and the Federal Bureau of Narcotics, also inadvertently challenged the Motion Picture Production Code by helping to make films containing explicit scenes of drug use and selling to further their goals to criminalize certain drugs and to depict drug users and sellers as dangerous.

The Legion of Decency, a Catholic group in the United States, also acted to censor films and warn viewers of immoral depictions in film.

From 1934 to 1967, they viewed and censored films that were considered offensive to Catholic viewers. However, times were changing, and the Code was amended in the 1940s, reflecting societal shifts concerning representations in film and what constitutes immorality. In 1946 the code stated, "The illegal drug traffic must not be portrayed in such a way as to stimulate curiosity concerning the use of or traffic in such drugs; nor shall scenes be approved which show the use of illegal drugs, or their effects in detail."[61]

Changing attitudes about drugs also occurred following the recommendations of the National Committee for the Education on Alcoholism, which began to lobby Hollywood to produce movies that depicted their principles: "Alcoholism is a disease; the alcoholic is treatable and deserves help; and alcoholism is a public heath problem."[62]

The film *The Man with the Golden Arm* (1955) is often cited as the first Hollywood film to explicitly depict heroin addiction and challenges to the Hays Commission in the 1950s. In the film, directed by Otto Preminger, Frankie Machine, played by Frank Sinatra, is a young man who is recently released from prison and ends up addicted to heroin once again. The film vividly portrays his struggles with the drug (and his unhappy marriage, his struggle to find work, and his relationship with his wife and girlfriend). Originally the screenplay was rejected by the Hays Office censors, who in 1950 stated:

> The unacceptability of this story stems from the fact that it violated the following provision of the Production Code: 'The illegal drug traffic must not be portrayed in such a way as to stimulate curiosity concerning the use of or traffic in such drugs; nor show scenes . . . which show the use of such drugs or their effects and details.'
>   In view of the fact that this dope addiction problem is basic to the story, we suggest that you give careful consideration to this material. . . .[63]

Nevertheless, MGM persisted, and Pandro Berman, a senior producer, approached the Hays Office a month later. Once again the Hays Office rejected the proposed film and a representative wrote back stating: "I told Mr Berman we can see no possibility . . . of handling this subject of dope addiction. . . ."[64] About four months later, the screenplay was sent once again to the Hays Office. Their response, on June 21, 1950, was " . . . it is our considered and unanimous opinion that this story is totally in violation of the Production Code. . . ."[65]

Five years later, Otto Preminger sent a revised screen adaptation of *The Man with the Golden Arm* to the Hays Office. Once again the film was rejected due to its violation of the Production Code. Without the approval of the Hays Office, Otto Preminger and United Artists (who distributed the film) decided to go ahead anyway and they produced the film. The Hays Office responded after screening the movie by stating that it was still in violation of the Production Code; however, instead of banning it outright, they only recommended two minor changes for it to be approved.[66]

In response to the rigid censor code, United Artists resigned from the Motion Picture Association of America (MPAA), which housed the Hays Office. Worried that other studios might resign, the MPAA called a meeting of the studios to discuss the Production Code. By then, *The Man with the Golden Arm* was playing to sold-out theatres in the United States. The studios agreed to some amendments to the Production Code, and illegal-drug use was no longer banned. It was argued instead "that drug addiction and narcotics traffic were national problems" that required public attention.[67]

Social shifts in the United States, including the 1960s counterculture movement, culminated in the liberalization of censorship and the U.S. Motion Picture Production Code was abandoned and replaced by the Code and Rating Administration (CARA) in 1968. A rating system for each film was developed, such as *R* for restricted or *G* for general audiences. Today, film producers can show scenes of violence, sexual intimacy, and explicit drug use and trafficking in their films. However, Starks argues that the current system can be more restrictive than the code, and now directors are often forced to sign contracts to stay within specified ratings; thus, censorship begins prior to production. Drug films in the United States are usually given an *R* rating if CARA deems that representations of drug use or selling in the movie fail to condemn the activities.[68]

Today, producers of both film and television productions keep in mind the "conservative U.S. broadcasting climate." Canadian shows, such as *The Next Generation*, which has shown scenes of illegal-drug use, teen sex, and abortion, have been edited, and scenes have been cut out by The N (a U.S. teen-oriented TV cable channel) so that episodes can be shown in the United States. Episodes of *The Next Generation* have also been restructured so that deviant behaviours lead to immediate consequences. Other episodes, such as one depicting a character contemplating having an abortion, were not shown at all.[69] The producer of *The Next Generation* states that she now "collaborates more closely with The N to anticipate incidents that might cause anxiety south of the border, and shoot scenes in such a way that adults more nervous than her can cut out the bad bits."[70] Thus, self-censorship, especially for foreign producers wanting to have their work distributed and shown in the United States, is alive and well and possibly more insidious than previously thought.

In the United States, the government is also in the business of censorship. In 1989, the Office for Substance Abuse Prevention (OSAP) created guideline materials about alcohol and drugs for health professionals and television and film writers.[71] Film and TV scriptwriters who wish to assure their scripts will meet with approval with the U.S. government can refer to *Spotlight on Depiction of Health and Social Issues*, published since 1997 by the National Institute on Drug Abuse (NIDA), in partnership with the Entertainment Industries Council (EIC), and the Robert Wood

Foundation to educate and encourage them to be more responsible in their portrayal of drug, alcohol, and tobacco use.[72] The authors state that "The entertainment industry can make an enormous contribution in changing public perceptions about substance abuse and addiction. Its products reach and influence millions, and incidents and themes of alcohol, tobacco, and illegal drug use, abuse, and addiction are already commonly found in storylines."[73] Similarly, the director of the National Institute on Drug Abuse states that "accurate depictions of drug abuse and addiction in entertainment productions can strongly counter public misperceptions."[74] Although tobacco and alcohol are discussed in *Spotlight*, there is no mention of the marketing of these products in television and film.

U.S. television networks that write scripts with antidrug messages are also rewarded with government advertising deals for accurately portraying drug issues. The entertainment Industries Council offers full service from "script-to-screen" guidance for television and film writers. Their depiction selections for cocaine include inserting "occasional lines of dialogue with people reacting negatively to someone's" cocaine use and other illegal drugs in order "to cast a shadow" on use, and they instruct screenwriters to show that illegal-drug use is very addictive.[75]

CENSORSHIP IN BRITAIN

In Britain, the Cinematograph Bill of 1909 marks the first federal law to regulate movie houses. The bill sought to safeguard the public from fires at cinematograph entertainments. The act responded to the rapid growth of unlicensed "picture palaces" to show films. The act required that all picture palaces be licensed by country and county borough councils and that they abide by safety regulations established by the secretary of state. Following the act, "local authority licensing of cinemas began."[76] Censorship of film was not given any serious consideration when the original bill was enacted. However, as Williams notes in the 1979 *Report of the Committee on Obscenity and Film Censorship*, the act had the potential for a wider application, and it was not long before local authorities began to attach conditions to their cinema licences.[77] In 1910, the London County Council banned cinemas from operating on Sundays and other Christian holidays. A cinema was prosecuted for showing films on Sundays, and on appeal, the judgement by the lord chief justice stated that the county councils regulating licenses could impose conditions as long as they were not unreasonable. Williams and others note that if it were not for this judicial decision, film censorship in Britain might have been played out differently.[78] The new interpretation of the act meant that the power of the local licensing authorities was not limited to public safety and fires. Following the lord chief justice's judgement, in the same year the London County Council banned films from the United States showing the heavyweight title fight between

Jack Johnson and James Jeffries in London. The ban on public viewing of the fight film represents the first case of official censorship by the local councils in Britain.[79]

Over the next year, controversy grew about whether film representations and the story line of some movies were "wholesome" and appropriate for family viewing. Similar to the United States, the British film industry decided it would be better to self-censor than to be censored arbitrarily by local councils or the state. In 1912, the independent British Board of Film Censors was created and began to review films in 1913. The BBFC is a self-regulating, nongovernmental body that attempts to create uniform standards; however, local councils can still overrule BBFC decisions. Major film distributors agreed to voluntarily submit films for review before their release. Local censorship authorities began to rely on the BBFC. Although film studios are not required to submit their films for classification, and many independent filmmakers do not, local councils today most often follow the BBFC, making it legally binding. The board has been labelled overzealous by its critics in its crusade in censoring film; however, compared to Canadian censorship of film, this claim may be up for debate.

Film censorship in Britain was also shaped by early debates about drug regulation, race, and women's morality. In Britain, new public fears about drugs emerged in 1916 and peaked in 1921, centred on young working-class women and women who worked as chorus girls, flappers, and actresses. At the centre of the debate were concerns about women's independence, drug use, and possible seduction by racialized men. As early as 1915 the BBFC annual report recommended censorship of drug use depicted in film.[80] The report states:

> Another question has however come to the fore, namely the drug habit and the use of morphia, cocaine, and other narcotics. It is claimed for such films that they serve to warn the public against the dangers of the abuse of such drugs, but the Board decided that there being no reason to suppose that this habit was prevalent in this country to any serious extent, the evils of arousing curiosity in the minds of those to whom it was a novel idea far outweighed the possible good that might accrue by warning the small minority that indulged in the practice.[81]

By 1916, the British National Council of Public Morals established the Cinema Commission of Inquiry, and the BBFC argued that depictions of "the drug habit, e.g. Opium, morphia, cocaine, etc." were banned.[82] In 1919, the film *The Case of a Doped Actress* was banned because it was based on the overdose death of the well-known actress Billie Carleton in 1918.[83]

In 1922, the film *Cocaine* was rejected by the BBFC censors. The film depicts a cocaine kingpin and his daughter who is being supplied cocaine by another man; once discovered, the father murders him. The producer of *Cocaine* challenged the BBFC decision, and when it was shown in

Manchester, the public and critics supported it, claiming that it clearly warned against drugs. The BBFC then backtracked and reversed their decision, and the film was allowed to be viewed in Britain in 1922 under a new title, *While London Sleeps*.[84] Starks notes that a number of film titles were changed so that viewers were kept ignorant of the substance of the movie.[85]

The U.S. film *Human Wreckage* (1923) is significant in drug-film history for revealing the intersection of personal tragedy, Hollywood, the star system, censorship, and government. The film was also banned in Britain in 1923–24 for its depiction of drug use and a scene that depicts Bessie Love preparing to inject morphine. In response, the director and star of the film, Dorothy Davenport, arranged for private viewings of the film, but the BBFC remained steadfast in their ban and issued a statement to the Home Office supporting their decision: "There have been few, if any, films, submitted to the Board since its inception which the examiners look upon as more dangerous than this film '*Human Wreckage*' and we see no possibility of altering it so as to make it suitable for public exhibition in this country."[86]

Jeffery Richards and others argue that the BBFC's ban on *Human Wreckage* was not consistent with its earlier certification of *While London Sleeps* in 1922.[87] Nevertheless, the BBFC continued to ban films that depicted drugs even though two Sherlock Holmes series (1939–46) contain references to Holmes's "needle habit."[88] Movie viewers would have to wait until Otto Preminger's *The Man with the Golden Arm* (1955) was released in Britain to see explicit scenes of drug addiction and selling on the screen again.

The Man with the Golden Arm was submitted to the BBFC for review in December 1955. BBFC censors and two representatives of the Home Office and Sir Austin Strutt, the Home Office assistant under-secretary, viewed the film. They stated that they had no objections and that the film was consistent with BBFC certificates about drug addiction and more specifically that the film's "moral value" was sound and the taking of drugs was not represented as "attractive" or "financially profitable" by dealers.[89] The BBFC justified their decision to allow the film to be viewed by the public: "Sordid and grim though the story is and concerned as it is with the serious vice of drug addiction, the film throughout consistently stresses moral values and would certainly have the effect of deterring anyone, in the most powerful manner, from any temptation to drug addiction."[90] The film was screened and the public did not oppose it. Robertson notes that although *The Man with the Golden Arm* shook the foundations of the censorship code in the United States, it left the "British system untouched."[91]

The Obscene Publications Act of 1959 was continually challenged by film productions in the 1960s, and the BBFC became in many ways a more liberal board reflecting shifting social changes. Although the BBFC claimed that it could not be the "guardian of public morality" and films became more explicit during this time, censorship was still practiced and scenes were cut and edited. Rather than a concern for explicit scenes, the BBFC began to more closely examine and censor screen representations that encouraged corruption and glamorization of sexual violence. Quite a number of films were censored in the 1970s, especially U.S. films (including Andy Warhol's *Trash* [1970]), that were seen as featuring graphic drug use, sex, and violence.

In 1984 the BBFC changed its name from the British Board of Film Censors (BBFC) to the British Board of Film Classification (BBFC), which assumes that their function is to classify rather than censor film. The BBFC current guidelines still identify drugs as a subject area that may be censored by editing or cutting the scene altogether. They state that "No work taken as a whole may promote or encourage the use of illegal drugs. Any detailed portrayal of drug use likely to promote or glamorize the activity may be cut."[92]

CANADA

In Canada, the history of film censorship is shaped by its early status as a colony of Britain and the absence of a local or national film industry. Hollywood, British, and French films dominated the Canadian market rather than Canadian productions. Similar to the United States, film arrived in Canada in the late 1890s in the form of Kinetoscope or peepshows, first developed by Thomas Edison and his assistant W. K. L. Dickson. On April 14, 1894, two Canadian businessmen from Ottawa opened the first Kinetoscope parlour in New York. In December of the same year, the Edison Kinetoscope was displayed in Toronto. Two years later, in 1896, a new machine marketed by Edison, called the Vitascope, was shown in Canada. *The Kiss*, which lasted less than a minute, was included in the public performance.[93] Although there was praise for these early inventions, there were also misgivings and worry about the moral content and sensationalism depicted in the visual imagery of film.

Canada's participation in the film industry shifted slightly with the emergence of the Canadian Film Board in 1939, which helped produce "educational" documentaries and later fictive films. In 1967, the Canadian Film Development Corporation was established (now named Telefilm Canada) and supported by the federal government to promote Canadian-owned and -controlled film industry. Although French-Canadian film culture preceded it, 1965 is cited by some as the date that marks the beginning of English Canada's feature-film culture.[94] Similar to local authorities in Britain, each province in Canada has separate power to censor and classify films.

Right up until 1959, Canadian film was subject to federal censorship (drawing on the *Hicklin* test from Britain) to determine whether material was considered an obscenity and a criminal offence.[95] However, unlike the United States and Britain, few films were produced in Canada in the early 1900s. Thus, censorship of films centred on reviewing films that had already passed through a censorship process in their country of origin. On arrival in Canada, films were once again reviewed by provincial boards, the first set up in 1911. In 1911, Ontario, Quebec, and Manitoba passed acts to license and censor film shown in public. British Columbia and Nova Scotia followed by creating statutes for censorship of film in 1913 and 1915, respectively. In Ontario, the initial law, The Theatres and Cinematographs Act of 1911, was carried out with a vengeance. In its first few years of operation, the Ontario Board rejected 75 percent of the films it reviewed.[96] A film might be banned outright and/or sections eliminated or cut from the film. Depictions of sexuality and violence were central concerns, as were representations of drug use and selling.

Criminologist Neil Boyd points out that censorship was not consistent throughout Canada, since censorship boards were made up of eclectic groups of people with no film background. Malcolm Dean, the author of *Censored! Only in Canada*, notes that the boards were liberal scene cutters and regularly banned films that they considered to be immoral. Early provincial film-censor boards were also "guardians" of nationalism; thus, U.S. flag-waving in film was censored and eliminated. Early censors also worried about the absence of the Union Jack, the British flag, in film.[97] By 1913, the British Columbia film censor board made U.S. flag-waving in film the third leading cause for film censorship, following seduction and infidelity, respectively.[98]

Dean describes one of the first contemporary Canadian film productions that pushed the boundaries about cinematic representations of drugs.[99] The film, titled *High* (1967), was directed by Larry Kent, his first film to document illegal-drug use in a Canadian context. Kent's early films, including *High*, offer a critique of the socially conservative era of the 1950s and the 1960s in Canada. His films take on gender relations, class, the work ethic, and sexuality. *High*, a black comedy that delves into free love, criminality, gender relations, and illegal drugs, was banned prior to its anticipated screening at the Montreal International Film Festival in 1967. Dean outlines some of the history behind the censoring of *High*, including an Ontario censor's note that stated that the board members found *High* to be "violating common standards of decency." Another board member commented that "Evil, sin, crime and wrongdoing shall not be justified."[100] The Ontario board eliminated offensive scenes—culminating in a footage cut of 162 feet.[101]

The Canadian public had to wait until 2003 to view *High*. For about 20 years the film director, Larry Kent, searched for a copy of the uncensored film. The original negative of the film was finally found in 2002 and subsequently restored and made available to the public in DVD and video format in 2004 (the DVD has special features including an interview with Kent). Today, Larry Kent is seen by many as Vancouver's and Canada's first "indie" filmmaker.

During the 1960s, many critics argued that Canada was one of the most film-censored populations in the world.[102] In the 1970s, film censorship relied on "community-standards" tests. The province of British Columbia set out policy for films to be classified and censored and similar acts were enacted in Ontario, Quebec, and Nova Scotia. The Ontario Theatres Act is much more sweeping in its regulation and censorship than British Columbia's Motion Picture Act. The Ontario Film Review Board had created a list of images that can be censored, including drug use.

In Canada, film censorship continues to be challenged by filmmakers and viewers. Neil Boyd notes that in the province of Ontario for the years 1982–83, of 1,050 films viewed by the censor board, 109 films had deletions and 46 were banned.[103] The struggle continues between freedom of expression and censorship in Canada, Britain, and the United States. These struggles coincide with our relationship to drugs and illegal-drug films in all three nations.

2 Illegal-Drug Users and Addiction Narratives

The Early Film Years

Moral-reform movements and changing attitudes towards some drugs and the people who used them provided provocative story lines for the print media and early films. Cautionary and temperance stories about weak-willed people, drug-scare tales, and later addiction-as-disease narratives became familiar plot lines that movie viewers have come to recognize. It took very little effort by moral reformers, law enforcement, politicians, the medical profession, and the media to convince citizens of Britain, Canada, and the United States that some drugs were bad and others beneficial. It also took surprisingly little effort to convince citizens that people associated with specific drugs like opium in smoking form were deviant and criminal and responsible for spreading addiction and degradation. In Western White-supremacist nations, drug use is racialized and associated with the poor and the working class, and fears related to the Other are continually inflamed.

As noted in chapter 1, by the early nineteenth century, temperance became the template of White, Anglo-Saxon, middle-class respectability and the model for the imperial subject. The philosopher Michel Foucault suggests that in the eighteenth and nineteenth centuries, White bourgeois citizens of the state distanced themselves from the poor and other marginalised populations.[1] The self-regulated subject "had to be spatially separated from degeneracy, abnormalcy, and excess that would weaken both him and the bourgeois state."[2] Marginalised bodies were identified, categorized, and segregated through surveillance and moral regulation. The newly emerging professions sought to delineate addicted bodies and criminal bodies from normal bodies.

Until the nineteenth century, traditional use of the word *addiction* was not connected to drug use; rather, it might refer to being addicted to reading or other positive pursuits.[3] Right up until the late 1800s, drug taking (whether drinking alcohol or ingesting laudanum) and addiction had no "scientific definition."[4] Rather, alcohol addiction was perceived as afflicting those "who loved to drink,"[5] and similarly, opium addiction afflicted only those who loved to use opium. Social and cultural shifts shaped the definition of "addiction" rather than an "independent medical and scientific discovery."[6] Sobriety and self-control became the template for the White, middle-class, Christian citizen, and people who drank too much or used other drugs habitually were "othered" and constructed as weak-willed (powerless over their drug). The drug itself was also seen as a culprit, luring innocents into addiction. The temperance and antiopiate movements linked addiction to "habitual drunkenness and habitual opium use."[7]

Moral weakness and personal responsibility have long been a central component of medical theories of addiction; however, concepts of the disease model are also old, dating back to the temperance writings of Benjamin Rush in the late 1700s, as are concepts about "free choice and moral culpability."[8] It was not until the twentieth century that habitual use of drugs was more uniformly transformed into addiction discourse; however it would be a mistake to see addiction discourses as linear. Discourses related to the will, self-control, and the soul sit comfortably side by side with addiction-as-disease ideology. Drug-research historians Charles Terry and Mildren Pellens note that, from the 1800s on, doctors made clear that treating narcotic addiction was part of their field of expertise. The researchers also note that physicians played a part in generating discourse and misinformation about narcotic addiction, especially the notion that withdrawal and abstinence lead to a cure.[9] Today, the state, and a wide range of groups, including the medical profession, law-enforcement, social-work, nonprofessional groups like Narcotics Anonymous, and drug-user groups create discourse about drugs, drug users, and addiction. The media, including print, the Internet, and the film industry, are significant contributors to illegal-drug discourse. However, not all discourse is equal or readily accessible to the public.

Drug researchers Brecher et al. state that since the enactment of the Harrison Narcotic Act and the arrest of a number of physicians for prescribing to addicted patients, the medical community and law enforcement in the United States have held "deeply entrenched" ideas about the criminal nature of people addicted to illegal drugs.[10] "Addiction" was believed to be less important than the "criminal" tendencies of illegal-drug users. Law enforcement was a significant player in perpetuating "criminal-addict" discourse. These deeply entrenched ideas also shaped Canadian drug policy and treatment.[11] Addicted and nonaddicted bodies and criminal and noncriminal bodies were delineated. Where there was sympathy for medical professionals and "therapeutic" addicts, there was little sympathy for "criminal addicts." Law enforcement became the primary profession to control and regulate illegal-drug user's lives in Canada and the United States. Control of illegal-drug users and the emerging black market became one of law enforcement's primary "tasks" and poor and working-class illegal-drug users, especially narcotic users, were arrested and sent to prison for long lengths of time.[12] Early on, the police profiled Chinese opium smokers and later Black men who were thought to use cocaine. Later, the police focussed on White people who used narcotics, including heroin and morphine. New drug laws and court interpretations discouraged maintenance (at that time the law prevented doctors from providing "narcotics" for self-administration). Doctors became active in helping the police in prosecuting other doctors who they believed were prescribing maintenance doses of narcotics.[13]

Both Canadian and U.S. law enforcement played a significant role in advising about drug treatment and policy.[14] Then, as now, they made sure that their stories and "construction" of the illegal-drug user was supplied to journalists and politicians.[15] Following drug prohibition, law-enforcement officials argued that maintenance programs would not deter "criminal addicts" from preying on society.

In Britain, as in Canada and the United States following prohibition, debate centred on whether or not there was a "cure" for addiction and whether or not "addiction" could be contained. In Britain, physicians (and later psychiatrists) retained the right to prescribe narcotics.[16] The Rolleston Report, made public in 1926, was written by a committee of physicians, many professing to being experts in the field of addiction. They made clear that people addicted to narcotics were sick, maintenance was legitimate, and it enabled people to lead stable "normal" lives. Their recommendations were adopted and doctors were not persecuted for prescribing drugs to addicted people.[17] And though drug control was now under the mantle of criminal justice, British physicians retained more control over treating addiction than their counterparts in the United States and Canada.

THE FILMS

In this chapter I discuss the films *For His Son* (1912), *The Mystery of the Leaping Fish* (1916), *Human Wreckage* (1923), *Narcotic* (1934), *The Cocaine Fiends (1935)*, *Assassin of Youth* (1936), *Marihuana, the Weed with Roots in Hell* (1936), *Reefer Madness* (1936), *The Man with the Golden Arm* (1955), and *Monkey on My Back* (1957). These films and others serve to illuminate themes, myths, shifts, and ruptures in film discourse about drug users, addiction, and treatment.

The early films: *For His Son* and *The Mystery of the Leaping Fish*

Quite a number of early short silent films depict opium and cocaine use, including D. W. Griffith's early U.S. film *For His Son*, produced in 1912. *For His Son* depicts the descent of a physician's son into cocaine addiction. Similar to many silent films of the time, characters in *For His Son* do not have names; instead, they are given general labels such as the "good physician." In the film, the "good physician" is represented as an elderly upper-class White man who creates a soft drink containing cocaine. He has a college-age son who is depicted as dependent on his father's goodwill and money. Fearful of his son's wrath when he is unable to provide him with any more ready cash, the "good physician" creates a soft drink to market.

He calls it dopokoke. He sells it at the local pharmacy and it becomes quite popular. Without knowing the contents of the soft drink, the good physician's young college-age son tries it and soon he is hooked and so too is the physician's secretary from the dopokoke warehouse. The son and his father's secretary soon discover that cocaine is the central ingredient of dopokoke. After their initial horror, they are shown adding powdered cocaine to their soft drink to give themselves a bigger lift. The caption reads: "A victim of dopokoke." Soon the son is depicted carrying a hypodermic needle in a case, and we are led to believe that he is now injecting cocaine. "Bound by their common vice," the son elopes with his father's secretary, leaving behind his upper-class, moral, and upstanding fiancée. In the next scene, both the son and his new wife are depicted looking sick, bedraggled, and hunched over. They are living with his wife's mother in a bleak apartment. The son is barely able to walk and he is shown trying to grab a vial with cocaine in it out of his wife's hands. They fight and he grabs his chest and collapses onto the floor. His father, the good physician, is called for, but it is too late: his son is dead.

In the film *For His Son*, all of the characters are represented as White and upper and middle class, except for the secretary, who works at the dopokoke warehouse. Thus, the son falls from his class position by running away and marrying her. Cocaine is depicted as compelling, leading weak-willed people into addiction, degradation, and death. The son is represented as weak and selfish, and the good physician is ultimately depicted as blinded by his need for money to help support his son. In the end, his disregard for the health and well-being of dopokoke users leads to his own son's death.

For His Son captures tensions in the United States about tonics, beverages, patent medicines, and elixirs that contained unknown ingredients like cocaine and opiates. Originally, in the mid-nineteenth century cocaine was heralded by physicians in the United States and other Western nations as a wonder drug for a host of ailments. It was also consumed recreationally in tonics and beverages such as Vin Mariani wine and Coca-Cola.[18] Concern about the ingredients of tonics and beverages led to laws to regulate drug use in these forms. In the early 1900s, legislation was enacted in the United States, Britain, and Canada to regulate opium and cocaine in patent medicines and tonics. The 1908 Poisons and Pharmacy Act was enacted in Britain, and in the same year in Canada, An Act Respecting Proprietary on Patent Medicines was passed.[19] By the late nineteenth and early twentieth centuries, further concerns about the harmful effects of drugs and unsubstantiated fears related to southern Black men using powder cocaine and becoming violent led some states to pass legislation to curtail the use of the drug.[20]

A number of other short silent films depict cocaine use; however, these films are comedies rather than dramas, and they capture societal acceptance of the drug and fermenting tensions about it. A number of short films drew from the Sherlock Holmes series by Arthur Conan Doyle. In these short films (i.e., *A Squeedunk Sherlock Holmes,* 1909), Sherlock is portrayed as using cocaine to comic effect.[21] *The Mystery of the Leaping Fish* (1916) is credited with being the first full-length-feature drug film. It is a silent comedy that features a Sherlock Holmes character who uses cocaine, among other drugs. The film begins with the following text: "The story concerns a professional incident in the life of the world's greatest detective Coke Ennyday."

Coke Ennyday is a copious drug user. The police ask him to help them with an investigation of a smuggling ring run by an Asian opium gang. When Coke consumes drugs he is depicted as happy and energetic, but he is a little despondent when he is not using drugs. In his office, which resembles a bunker, he has a large clocklike sign on his wall that spells out his activities for the day: "dope, eat, sleep, and drink." Every time Coke consumes a drug, the hands on the clock swing to the appropriate activity. Coke Ennyday inhales huge amounts of powder cocaine from a container on his desk labeled in large letters, COCAINE. He also jabs himself with a hypodermic needle every once-in-a-while in all parts of his body, although favouring his forearm. He drinks laudanum, an opium derivative, by injecting it into his mouth from a huge container that looks suspiciously like a bug repellant container. His male helper looks like someone straight out of an S/M movie. He is dressed in a black undersized bellhop-looking outfit decorated with metal studs. Coke Ennyday has energy to spare after using drugs and he dances and laughs throughout the movie.

The film does not condemn drug use, since Coke Ennyday is depicted using some drugs with abandon; however, he uses drugs (cocaine and laudanum) that are still approved in the West, even though they are contested, rather than smoking opium, which is condemned and associated with racialized people and foreign others, specifically Asian people. Coke Ennyday's drug use is not presented as negative, and there is no addiction narrative in the film. In fact, his copious drug use does not stop him from functioning normally; rather, it appears to help him to investigate the case. Although Coke Ennyday's drug use is not problematized, the film captures tensions about legal and approved drugs and those condemned by moral reformers of the time. Asian men in the film are vilified and they are represented as the source of smoking opium. A Chinese man called Fishy Joe is represented as not only criminal and trafficking in opium but also as a sexual threat to White womanhood. He threatens and kidnaps Bessie, the heroine in the film.

In the late eighteen and early nineteenth centuries, U.S. exclusionary laws were enacted to restrict Asian immigration, property ownership, areas of residence and work, and intermarriage with Anglo-Saxons.[22] Similar legislation was passed in Canada.[23] In Britain, Canada, and the United States, the opium den was seen as the site of corruption, where a "cunning Chinaman wreathed in opium fumes"[24] seduces moral White women. A number of researchers have pointed out how racialized people from the silent era on have been represented as evil and sinister characters in film.[25] Edward Said brought our attention to how institutions, scholarship, texts and films, and other media sources reinforce cultural stereotypes.[26] Western representations in films of Asian, Black, Aboriginal, Latino, and Oriental people and culture are most often constructed through the lens of the White Protestant Western upper- and middle-class imagination, as are representations of Irish Catholics and Italian people.

Where *The Mystery of the Leaping Fish* condemns opium smoking, the silent film *Broken Blossoms* (1919), produced by D. W. Griffith, is more sympathetic to the practice. Interestingly, D. W. Griffith also produced the short film discussed above, *For His Son* (1912), which condemns cocaine use. In *Broken Blossoms* (subtitled *The Yellow Man and the Girl*), a young Chinese man immigrates to London. The caption states, "The Yellow Man holds a great dream to take the glorious message of peace to the barbarous Anglo-Saxons, sons of turmoil and strife." The Yellow Man in the film is played by a Caucasian actor and is depicted as a peaceful man who worships the teachings of the Buddha. In contrast, a group of young White English sailors are depicted as violent and disruptive.

Following his immigration to the Limehouse district of London, we see The Yellow Man some years later. The captions reads, "Limehouse knows him only as a Chink store-keeper." His dream of bringing the teachings of the Buddha to the West has been deterred. In a following scene, The Yellow Man is depicted in an opium den. The caption reads, "Chinese, Malays, Lascars, where the Orient squats at the portals of the West." The opium den is portrayed as a sitting room with people from different ethnic backgrounds and genders gathered there. A White woman is depicted lying on a lounge couch. A Chinese man is sitting cross-legged on the floor smoking from an opium pipe. A man wearing a turban sits next to a White woman, and a small petite blonde-haired White woman sits primly next to a very large Black man who is dressed in working-class garb. The caption reads, "In this scarlet house of sin, does he ever hear the temple bells?" Even though The Yellow Man is portrayed as a kind, vulnerable man who takes up the opium pipe to ease the pain of his thwarted dreams, the racialization of danger and excess are a dominant narrative in the film.

Lucy, the other main character in the film (played by Lillian Gish), is depicted as a young woman in her teens. Her father is characterized as a brute, "a gorilla of the jungles of East London." He drinks alcohol to excess and he terrorizes and brutally beats Lucy in their rundown and barren home. In the film, her little body is covered in bruises. The Yellow Man sees Lucy on the street and he watches her from his store. He falls in love with her from afar. One evening, in a fit of rage, Lucy's father beats her almost to death. After her father leaves the room she struggles to get up. Her dress is torn and she walks out on to the street. She collapses against the doorway of The Yellow Man's store. He is walking home from

Broken Blossoms. Source: United Artists/Photofest. © United Artists.

the opium den. At first he thinks he is having an opium dream when he sees Lucy in his doorway, but he quickly realizes that it is really her. The caption reads, "The first gentleman she has ever known." He brings her into the store and upstairs into his living quarters. He lays her down on his bed and he cares for her. He gives her a silken robe to wear and he arranges flowers in the room for her. Sitting next to her he holds her hand all night. She asks him, "What makes you so good to me, Chinky?" Their idyllic time together is cut short when her father finds out where she is, "A Chink after his kid! . . . Above all . . . he hates those not born in the same country as himself."

The captions make clear that The Yellow Man's "love remains a pure and holy thing." Lucy's father is unacquainted with any such sentiment. He barges into The Yellow Man's home when he is out buying more flowers for Lucy. He grabs Lucy and drags her home. There her father beats her with a whip. She screams for help but no one comes. Her father is shown drinking alcohol as Lucy dies. The Yellow Man arrives at her home and shoots Lucy's father when he threatens him with a hatchet. The Yellow Man leaves the gun on the bed and picks up Lucy and carries her to the bed and lays her down. He places the doll that he gave her in her hands and covers her with a blanket. He lays down the flowers he bought and then he returns to his own home. The next scene shows him lighting incense and praying to Buddha. The film ends as he stabs himself and dies.

In the film notes that accompany the CD version of *Broken Blossoms*, the movie is called the "first tragic poem on film." The film firmly condemns alcohol use and links it to male violence and the breakdown of the home. Even though The Yellow Man is portrayed as a kind and caring person, in contrast to the brutish English working-class White men he encounters in London, he has a bowed appearance and he shuffles and squints throughout the film. He represents Western appropriation and misrepresentation of Chinese people and culture. In response to White Western fears related to Asian sexuality and the mixing of the races, the Hays Code restricted film depictions of interracial romance and sexual relations.[27] Similar to casting of The Yellow Man in *Broken Blossoms*, film producers during this era cast White actors to play Asian characters.[28] The Yellow Man is represented as effeminate and his unrequited love is juxtaposed against the film's depiction of the mixing of the races in the opium den and its implication of sexuality. The film plays on fears related to the "mixing of the races" drug use, and moral White women's proximity to foreigners and Black men. The Yellow Man's opium use is clearly depicted as a response to his loneliness and lost dreams. The film captures many of the concerns of moral reformers and temperance advocates about alcohol and working-class vices, and its condemnation of male violence against young women is quite powerful.[29]

Broken Blossoms and *The Mystery of the Leaping Fish* touch upon White moral reformers' concerns during this era. The temperance movements in the United States, Canada, and Britain during the early 1900s regarded sobriety and morality as innate in the female gender; yet it was thought that women could be easily corrupted because of their fragile character. Alcohol and the smoking of opium were constructed by temperance and antiopiate reformers as two of the main culprits of many of society's ills—such as poverty, criminality, and violence. Moral reformers in Britain, Canada, and the United States were concerned that drugs like alcohol and opium in smoking form contributed to the "breakdown" of the nuclear family and the project of nation building.[30]

British, Canadian, and U.S. conventional views on certain drugs, and individuals and groups who used and sold drugs, would shift dramatically by the early 1920s, partially due to the efforts of moral reformers, law enforcement, film representations, and print media. In each country, local newspapers led antidrug campaigns calling for action against drug users and traffickers.[33] Temperance leaders and citizen groups, along with well-known moral reformers such as Canadian Emily Murphy, a juvenile court judge and the author of the 1921 book *The Black Candle*, and Sara Graham-Mulhall, former employee of the Department of Narcotic Drug Control in New York and the author of *Opium the Demon Flower*, produced new discourses about opium, drug users, and traffickers. Antidrug discourse was intended to educate uninformed Anglo-Saxon citizen about the "drug problem."[34] Discourse about the "yellow menace" and sexualized and violent Black men were central to their arguments.[35] Writer Marek Kohn writes that concern about the "sexualized menace" of the drug subculture vividly reported in the media from 1914 to the mid-1920s informed efforts to support drug prohibition in Britain.[36] White-supremacist and imperialist discourse, colonization, the institutionalization of racism, and the legacy of slavery also contributed to identifying and categorizing groups associated with opium smoking and cocaine use. White moral Christian women are constructed as the moral barometer of Western society; their downfall, especially related to unsanctioned drug use and proximity to racialized men, is linked to the breakdown of the family and the nation.[37]

Coupled with fears about women s drug use and foreign Others were Western concerns related to what is referred to as the first "Red Scare," the period from 1917 to 1920. Following the Russian Revolution in 1917, fear of communists and anarchists, especially those labelled "foreigners" like Emma Goldman, led to a number of laws being enacted in the United States and Canada to deport "political agitators" and strike leaders. The Palmer Raids in the United States from 1919 and 1921 and the Winnipeg Strike in Canada in 1919 led to the deportation of thousands of labour organizers. Drug historian David Musto explains that WWI and the "Red Scare" of 1919 brought about changes in attitudes about addiction. Addiction was now being constructed as a threat to the war effort and nationalism.[38] It was believed that narcotic use was associated with antisocial behaviour and moral degeneration. Illegal-narcotic use and public narcotic maintenance was seen as an "indulgence . . . [that] tended to weaken the nation and was associated with other un-American influences which would dissolve the bonds of society."[39] In the United States, federal alcohol prohibition was also enacted in 1919. There was considerable pressure to effect a ban on all drugs at this time not only because drug use was seen as a threat to the war effort and the nation but because it was thought that those who drank alcohol would switch to other drugs.[40]

Human Wreckage: addiction and family breakdown

Following World War I, U.S. illegal-drug films like *Human Wreckage* (1923) displayed little sense of humour about narcotics. Responding to WWI and early "Red Scares," anti-Asian moral panics, and temperance and antidrug campaigns against opium, morphine, and cocaine use, public attitudes had shifted and harsh legislation prohibiting possession, sales, and production of these drugs was enacted. In addition, societal fears about women s independence (which seem to emerge following their greater participation in the workforce during times of war) surfaced in film representations.

Human Wreckage (1923), as discussed in chapter 1, is interesting because it was produced by the actress Dorothy Davenport, the wife of the silent-film star Wallace Reed, who died of complications related to his morphine addiction. The film was produced when offscreen scandals by actresses and actors were threatening to damage Hollywood's image and profits. Following her husband's death, Davenport became a vocal antidrug advocate. Until the 1960s, with its exploration of psychedelic experiences and other drug-induced states represented in film, *Human Wreckage* is one of the last films to employ "fantasy sequences," double exposures, and shifts in lighting to re-create the "addicts" world.[41]

In *Human Wreckage*, a well-off lawyer is depicted becoming addicted to morphine after it was prescribed by his doctor following his nervous breakdown. His wife also becomes addicted. Unfortunately, only stills exist of *Human Wreckage*. One still shows a young White woman injecting drugs into her upper arm with a hypodermic needle (although not into her vein) as Mrs. Reid, holding her baby close to her, looks on. This classic shooting-up scene—which has become fetishized—is one that movie viewers now recognize and attach meaning to. Unlike the comedic pantomime of Coke Ennyday administering his drugs, *Human Wreckage* represents morphine and other narcotic drugs as dangerous and leading White men and women to moral degradation and the breakdown of the family and society. The film can be viewed as a morality tale, produced with the assistance of the Los Angeles Anti-Narcotics League and chief of police.

By the early 1920s and 1930s, considerable shifts had occurred in relation to drug law and the regulation of drug users. As mentioned earlier, opium in smoking form and cocaine were criminalized in all three nations, and marijuana was criminalized in 1924 in Canada and 1928 in Britain. Police powers expanded and harsh laws were enacted to regulate those drugs deemed illegal. Censorship of depictions of drug use and trafficking began to limit what movie viewers could see in Britain, Canada, and the United States. In the United States, federal alcohol prohibition (1920–1933) was in effect, and temperance ideology had become mainstream. In Canada, as part of the war economy, national alcohol prohibition was enacted in 1918. However, unlike the United States, it only lasted for one year.[42]

U.S. films produced in the 1920s and 1930s are morality tales[43] and antidrug propagandist films that seek to educate viewers about the evil of drugs and addiction. These early films also advocate police intervention, criminalization, and drug prohibition as a solution to addiction. Drug treatment is not really explored to any extent in these early films; yet they set the stage in "educating" viewers about some drugs, users, drug addiction, and its consequences. In 1927, sound films were produced, and by the 1930s, partially in response to alcohol and drug prohibition, a number of new films focussed on criminal gangs.[44] However, films that focussed on the plight of illegal-drug users remained popular.

Narcotic: "You can't get it out of the mind"

The black-and-white film *Narcotic* was produced in the United States in 1934 by Dwain Esper. Contemporary viewers enjoy it for its camp value, similar to later films like *The Cocaine Fiends* (1935) and *Reefer Madness* (1936). *Narcotic* captures concerns expressed by the medical profession about patent medicines and "quack doctors." Although there were some legitimate concerns expressed by the medical community in Britain, Canada, and the United States about the unknown quality of patent medicines, the regulation of "legitimate" medicine was one strategy employed by physicians to consolidate their own power and influence.[45] The film also highlights the shift from opium smoking to injection use of heroin. *Narcotic* is presented as a true "case study" and it opens with the following text: "This picture is presented in the hope that the public may become aware of the terrific struggle to rid the world of drug addiction."

The film then shifts to a scene of a lightning storm, and we see a car speeding as if being pursued. The scene shifts to a suicide note. The letter reads: "Dwain: It's four o'clock . . . dawn is here . . . the devil's trumpets are bellowing, 'You can take it out of the body, but you can't get it out of the mind' . . . but I have found a way. Will." Will is the main character of the film. He becomes addicted to narcotics and commits suicide at the end of the film. The letter above is his suicide note. The camera quickly cuts to the following text, which reads: "This is the astounding biography of Dr. William G. Davies. With his captivating speeches, from wagon and tent, he made his notorious cure-all 'Tiger-Fat,' one of the best known of all quack-medicine names . . . These facts are presented to you, not as a romantic story, but as the actual case-history of one of the millions of narcotic addicts."

The camera shifts to a dorm room at William's college, established through a brief montage of still photos. William is shown arm wrestling with another medical student (both played by White men apparently well into their 40s). Here, the narrative really begins. A man named Gee Wu sits in the corner of the room. He looks like he is smoking opium in a pipe, but he says it is tobacco. He is a Caucasian actor made up to look "Oriental." In the film, William and Gee Wu are presented as friends. Outside of Gee Wu, William and his other friends are depicted as middle- to upper-class White "Americans." At the beginning of the film, William is introduced as an up-and-coming doctor who finds his work stressful and he is unable to sleep. The film records William's moral degradation and drug addiction and his transformation from being a respectable community doctor to a "quack" hawking patent medicine in a carnival setting.

Throughout the film, Gee Wu provides cultural references and juxtapositions to "Oriental" and "Western" opium use. In reference to opium, he states, "Yes, we Orientals do indulge, but due to character . . . it is a harmless diversion to us." He claims that Westerners are "overwhelmed

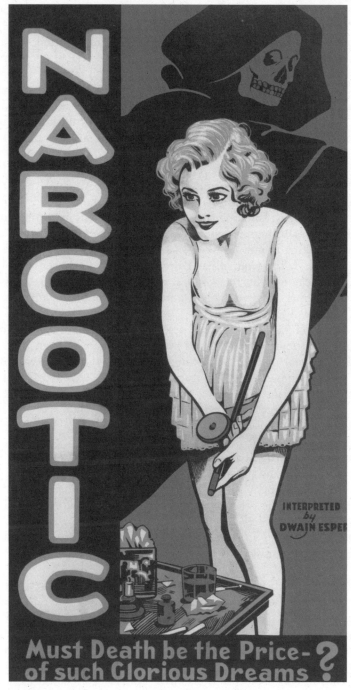

Narcotic. Source: Roadshow Attractions/ Photofest. © Roadshow Attractions.

with progress and speed which make any diversion a vice." A common perception in addiction discourse at this time was that progress and speed contributed to drug use and addiction.[46] Today we have similar discourse about cocaine, methamphetamine, and Prozac use. In the film, opium use is racialized and heroin is introduced as a "new" drug that is even more dangerous and addictive than opium. We also come to know cocaine and heroin users as criminals who endanger their health in pursuit of their (newly criminalized) drugs. In one scene, the police bring an illegal-drug user to William's medical office. The police officer tells William, "You don't know anything about these snowbirds. They're all thieves. When they get hooked, they have no feeling to eat. The only dough they spend is on the stuff."

William is introduced to opium by Gee Wu. Gee Wu believes that William needs a "diversion" from his stressful work, and he brings him to an opium den. Initially, smoking opium provides relief from stress and overwork. However, William is depicted as quickly becoming addicted, and he is shown smoking opium by himself. Later, an opium-den scene shows a blonde-haired, White woman passed out on a bed. Less then a foot away from her, the camera cuts to a Chinese man, who is depicted leering at her. The opium den is depicted as dark and impoverished, in contrast to later party scenes of White drug users.

Following William's descent into opiate addiction, he begins to surround himself with Oriental artifacts, and he smokes opium in front of his wife. He begins to wear "Oriental" clothing, a silk smoking jacket with dragon symbols on it. He is called a "disgrace to society" as well as a "mental and moral coward." Concerned about his addiction, his wife and Gee Wu visit a "federal narcotic agent" to seek help for him. The White agent is depicted as a reliable and authoritative source of drug knowledge. He says:

> You see, the drug always finds the *weakest spot in character* for its attack. The daring or wayward type start using it to satisfy their craving for adventure. While the moral coward takes the drug to get the courage which he otherwise does not possess. In either case, it soon *subordinates the will*. . . . Hope for a *cure lies in the individual*. *It cannot be accomplished by redrugging*. The only cure is the will to be cured (my emphasis).

Thus, the drug itself is granted agency and it is depicted as powerful and able to attack willpower and moral character, leading one into addiction and degradation. Those susceptible to the drug are constructed as morally weak. Drug maintenance is discouraged and the onus for recovery is placed on the individual. Recovery entails discontinuation (abstinence) and willpower.

The film briefly depicts a Division of Narcotics Hospital as a site of treatment and recovery; however, this is not dramatized. It is made clear that William stays there for a couple of weeks as he recovers from opium addiction. Little is shown of his time there outside of a brief scene at the hospital with his wife. The hospital is set against a serene rural environment, and William visits with his wife while sitting on a bench with flowers and lawn in the background.

Although William successfully stops using opium and returns to his home, after being hurt in an auto accident he is given heroin in the hospital and he quickly becomes addicted to it. Throughout the film, therapeutic drug use is easily transformed into addictive use. The syringe is shown as a visual indicator of heroin use. An extreme close-up of heroin being injected is shown, and opium pipes and "cocaine spoons" are depicted, visual signifiers of deviant drugs that we recognize.

William's moral degeneration and descent into heroin addiction is characterized by the following scenes. A party scene depicts William and other White men and women using an array of drugs. They are gathered together in an opulent-looking suite. The women wear long evening gowns and the men are in suits. Cocaine, marijuana, and heroin are all neatly displayed on a cocktail tray. Regardless of which drug is consumed, it is depicted coupled with disinhibition and titillating scenes of sexuality, especially by the women at the party. The women at the party are depicted loosening up, giggling, and dancing after they use drugs. A White, blonde woman states, "It takes a needle for me to get a bang." When a woman pulls up her dress and shows her slip and a bit of her upper thigh, one of the men cries out, "Ladies, ladies, let's not get vulgar yet!"

In another scene, William's wife enters his study at home and he explains to her that he wants to sell medical remedies directly to the public. She is alarmed and responds, "But Will, that would not be ethical. Selling medicine like a common huckster." He argues, "Well, supposing the profession does look at it that way. It can be done in a dignified manner. Think the good I would be doing solving health problems in a simple way."

However, William does not sell his remedies in a dignified manner. Eventually we see him hawking his remedies at carnivals. In the film, carnivals are depicted as a site of suspect morality and a marker of lower-class status. William is shown at carnivals making large amounts of money pushing his remedy, Tigar-Fat. He pays people to sit in the audience to deliver fake testimonials. William is now addicted to heroin and no longer living with his wife. Another scene shows the image of the Hippocratic oath written on a piece of paper as it flutters to his office floor, representing a visual sign of his moral decline and downfall.

By the end of the film, William is destitute and aged. He is wild-eyed and his hair is unkempt. He no longer wears a suit; now he is dressed in long underwear with his pants held up by suspenders. He has missing teeth and he is shaking uncontrollably. He is shown in his rundown apartment, alone, searching for a stash of heroin. He finds it and sits down in a chair. Next to him is a table with a gun on it. Next to the gun is a small glass vial of white powder labelled "heroin." William picks up the gun. A loud shot is heard and William's arm falls limply over the side of his chair. The camera cuts to the words "*Out of Body. . . . Out of 'Mind.'* "

Although the character Gee Wu is represented as intelligent and a friend of William's, he is also represented as the Other, being culturally different from William, asexual, and introducing his friend to narcotics. All things represented as "Oriental" in the film are associated with degradation and descent into addiction. *Narcotic* also highlights, inadvertently, the shift from opium smoking to injection heroin by users following the criminalization of opium and the closing down of opium dens and availability of the drug.

In the film, addiction is largely represented as incurable, a state in which there is little chance of recovery once one is addicted. Recovery is temporary and fleeting, and drug addiction is depicted as leading to "mental deficiency," as well as physical and spiritual degradation. Ultimately, suicide is the only available means of redemption and escape from heroin addiction. The clinic that William attends offers him only temporary relief from addiction.

In the late 1800s and early 1900s, drug treatment as we know it today did not exist in Britain, Canada, and the United States. There was no need for drug-maintenance prescribing or clinics prior to criminalization. The rich could afford the cost of doctors and private sanatoriums to treat addiction and care for the patient during drug withdrawal if it was deemed necessary. The poor managed at home. Following drug prohibition, poor users were especially hard hit in the United States and Canada because visits to family doctors or private sanatoriums were out of their reach and not available in many rural areas. In order to provide some relief, narcotic maintenance programs were established in the United States from 1912 to 1924. These public clinics served as a mechanism to provide legal narcotics to those people addicted to narcotics following criminalization. According to drug researcher David Musto, the clinics (with the exception of the New York clinic) did a good job of providing narcotic maintenance. About 44 clinics opened between 1912 and 1924, and up to 12,000 people received help. Some of the clinics actually dispensed morphine and heroin; others provided legal prescriptions. The clinic population was overwhelmingly White.[47] Ignoring their success, the narcotics unit of the Treasury Department (later the Federal Bureau of Narcotics) campaigned to have the clinics shut down. They argued that "addicts" registered at the clinics were also selling some of their drugs on the black market. The press publicized a number of cases and eventually the clinics were discredited and closed down. The Harrison Act was strengthened in the 1920s, and the importation of heroin even for medical use was banned and physicians who attempted to prescribe opiates to people to maintain their addiction were arrested in the United States.[48]

With the closure of the clinics, people addicted to narcotics in the United States had few supports, especially poor users. In response to the number of people addicted to narcotics and the lack of services, in 1935, the first federal public hospital to house people addicted to narcotics opened in Lexington, Kentucky. It was a large hospital with "1,000 beds and 500 employees."[49] The large staff composition was due to the fact that, unlike other hospitals, people addicted to drugs were *incarcerated* there and treated for addiction. Treatment largely consisted of detox and abstinence. A couple of years later, another hospital was opened in Forth Worth, Texas. From 1935 to 1952, federal "narcotics farms," as these hospitals were referred to, imprisoned and treated narcotic users. At the farms, drug users were expected to be drug free. This was the primary treatment option. Yet a "cure" for addiction was not discovered and follow-up studies showed that once released the majority of "prisoners" became readdicted and reimprisoned.[50] In the film *Narcotic*, it is most likely that the narcotics hospital he goes to for help was modelled after the one established in Lexington. In Canada, no provisions were set up for people addicted to narcotics following criminalization (i.e., public drug-maintenance or drug-treatment programs).[51]

The Cocaine Fiends: female degradation

A year after *Narcotic* was released, *The Cocaine Fiends* (1935) (a remake of the earlier film *The Pace That Kills* [1928]), hit theatres in the United States and later in the United Kingdom. *The Cocaine Fiends* is also a morality tale. In the film, cocaine use is central to the story. *The Cocaine Fiends* begins with a "timeless quote" rolled out on the screen. It warns about the destruction of civilization and the "tragic problem" that may conquer "our race." Then it asks:

> What is this octopus—this hideous monster that clutches at every heart. Creeping slowly, silently, inexorably into every nook and corner of the world?—It is the demon *DOPE!* In its slimy trail follow misery, degradation, death; and from its clutching tentacles no community, no class no people are immune regardless of birth, training or environment.[52]

The Cocaine Fiends features an innocent White girl, Jane Bradford, who is lured from the country by a corrupt and lying man, a drug peddler named Nick. She is seduced by him and his promises of marriage and a rich life in the city. He offers her medicine, which he calls "headache powder," for her headaches. It works well, but she does not know that it is cocaine. She eventually runs away with Nick, leaving behind her kind elderly mother and brother. Once she arrives in the city with Nick, she realizes that the rich life he offered her is a lie and she wants to go back home, but when she expresses her concerns she is told that the headache powder Nick has been giving her is cocaine. She shouts out that she hates Nick, but as soon as he takes out a small white packet, which we now recognize as cocaine, on seeing it she cries out, "I'll do anything, only give it to me." Addicted, she is trapped into a life of degradation (and possible prostitution). She is now depicted as a "mobster's moll," and she changes her name to Lil so that no one will connect her to her old life.

Her brother Eddie comes to the city to find her, but he gets caught up in the jazz scene, represented as wild and immoral. He is introduced to cocaine by a fellow carhop named Fanny. She is a young, White, blonde-haired woman

The Pace that Kills. Source: Willis Kent Prod/Photofest. © Willis Kent Productions.

with whom he becomes romantically involved. After being fired from their jobs, Eddie and Fanny are shown quickly descending into a life of addiction and degradation. They live together in a one-room tenement apartment, although they are not married. The camera follows Eddie as he paces in their small room. Fanny arrives home and he cries out, "I got to have a shot. I'll sell my soul for just one shot." Fanny replies, "All right Eddie, you need it that bad I'll get it for you." She goes out into the night (it is implied she works in the sex trade now) and later returns and hands Eddie some drugs. He hesitates, but then he takes it from her and leaves their apartment.

After leaving Fanny, Eddie goes to an opium den run by an Asian man. He lies on a rough bunk and an Asian woman prepares his pipe. He yells at her, "Hurry up! Can't you!" It is here that his sister Jane finds him. She enters the den and the same Asian woman tries to stop her. Jane snaps at her, "Oh, beat it you. This is my brother." Jane tells Eddie that, unlike herself, he can put his addictions behind him and start all over. "No," he says. "I'm a hophead." She argues, "You're just in the first stages; you can snap out of it!" Eddie says he has no money. She tells him she will get him lots of money and they arrange to meet later. When Eddie returns home, the landlady and the police are in his apartment; they do not see him in the doorway. Fanny is dead. "Accidental," the policeman says. However, the movie viewer knows better because we are shown a scene in which Fanny commits suicide after Eddie left their apartment (she leaves the gas stove on).

As we will see in more detail in chapter 5, in illegal-drug films, women must pay for their drug use, and there is rarely any escape from their destiny—sexual immorality, pregnancy, suicide, and drug overdose. While men in illegal-drug films suffer too, they are granted more agency and their fate is less determined. In *The Cocaine Fiends*, the jazz scene is the site of immorality. Addiction is portrayed as quick, and treatment and recovery are not explored outside of "snapping out of it" and "going home" to White rural America. Women in the film cannot be redeemed, but the possibility of recovery is imagined through the character of Eddie, even though it is not realized on screen. Although the ending is ambiguous, Eddie has a chance to leave the racialized opium den and the immoral city behind him.

Assassin of Youth, Marihuana, The Weed with Roots in Hell, and *Reefer Madness:* depravity and violence

Assassin of Youth was also produced in 1935. Whereas the films *Narcotic* and *The Cocaine Fiends* focussed on opium, heroin, and cocaine, *Assassin of Youth* (1935), *Marihuana, the Weed with Roots in Hell* (1936), and *Reefer Madness* (1936) focus on marijuana as the evil, luring young White youths into addiction, depravity, insanity, and murder. All three films were produced as "educational" with the help of H. J. Anslinger, the U.S. commissioner of narcotics. These depression-era cautionary tales depict White rural America and middle-class youths who are lured into using marijuana by unscrupulous dealers and women's drug use is sexualized. In *Assassin of Youth*, addiction treatment is represented in the film as the domain of White male doctors who provide expertise and care in the home. An early party scene in *Assassin of Youth* depicts the home of two unscrupulous White middle-class drug dealers, a couple, who supply the youth of the town with marijuana. The wife oversees their marijuana parties. There we see young White innocent youth smoking marijuana. The drug-dealing man attempts to seduce Joan, the lead character, by drugging her. Her sister Marjorie suffers too. After smoking marijuana at one of the parties, she picks up a knife in a fit of jealousy and murderous rage and attempts to stab another woman. She is rescued in the nick of time, dropping the knife. She is brought home and the local doctor, an elderly White man, is called in to see her. We see Marjorie lying in bed looking sick and pale. The doctor says to Marjorie's mother, "Your daughter is a psychopathic case. She is on the verge of insanity. She has much symptoms of drug addiction and I strongly believe she has been using marijuana." The mother replies, "What's that?"

Doctor: A cigarette made out of a narcotic weed.
Mother: Where did she get anything like that?
Doctor: It's easy enough to obtain. Your daughter is the fourth case I have examined today. All young people with similar symptoms.
Mother: What will happen to her, doctor? She'll get well, won't she?
Doctor: With proper care, we may be able to help her. I'll send you a competent nurse. In the meantime, if you note any changes, call me immediately.

The narrative above between the concerned mother and the doctor perpetuates myths related to marijuana and places the medical profession as the primary caretakers for wayward middle- and upper-class youth who experiment with the drug. In the film, we are told that with proper medical care there is a chance that Marjorie will recover from marijuana addiction and insanity. Moral middle-class youth are presented as vulnerable to the evil of marijuana and susceptible to drug dealers. Marijuana is represented as a threat to moral White families and communities.

Marihuana, the Weed with Roots in Hell (1936) was also produced by Dwain Esper, with the help of federal, state, and police narcotic officials, including H. J. Anslinger, the U.S. commissioner of narcotics. The film begins with dramatic music in the background and black-and-white sketches of nude women surrounded by swirling clouds of smoke and the following foreword:

For centuries, the world has been aware of the narcotic menace. . . . But—did you know—the use of Marihuana is steadily increasing among the youth of this country? Did you know that the youthful criminal is our greatest problem today? And that—Marihuana gives the user

Assassin of Youth. Source: BMC Roadshow/Photofest. © BMC Roadshow.

false courage, and destroys conscience, thereby making crime alluring, smart? That is the price we are paying for our lack of interest in the narcotic situation. This story is drawn from an actual case history on file in the police records of one of our large cities.

The foreword is followed by a "note" that states that marihuana's "most terrifying effect is that it fires the user to extreme cruelty and license."

The story line and visuals of the film are actually quite risqué for the times. In the film, we are introduced to a spirited young White blonde woman named Verna. She comes from a middle-class family whose social standing is contingent on their elder daughter Elaine's upcoming marriage to an established and wealthy man named Morgan. Verna feels left out and ignored by her mother and sister and she goes out with her friends. She is introduced to marijuana at a party at Tony's home. Tony is an older, unscrupulous dealer, and he works with his partner Nicky, who has a thick accent. It could be inferred by their names and accent that they are Italian. Tony comments that the youth are "not suspicious and easily hooked." At the party, all of the young women try smoking marijuana. They are depicted giggling and ripping off their clothes to swim nude in the ocean. The men stay in their suits even as they pursue the women on the beach. Verna makes love with her boyfriend on the beach, and later she finds out that she is pregnant. One of the young women, Jennifer, drowns at the beach party, and Tony threatens all of the youth that they will become "wards of the court" if they do not help to cover up Jennifer's death. Later, Verna threatens to tell the police about the cover-up. She calms down and reconsiders after Tony gives her a drink into which he has poured white powder. Tony helps her to get away to have her baby (the father has been killed). After the baby is born, Tony and Nicky convince her that she has little to offer the child. They tell her they know a well-off couple who would like to adopt it. She finally agrees because she believes her baby will have a better life with different parents.

The film cuts to a few years later. We see Verna drinking and smoking a cigarette while leaning back on a couch. The film constructs a "gateway" discourse as Verna graduates from marijuana to heroin use. She is shown "shooting up," although it is mostly left up to the viewers' imagination, unlike shooting-up images shown in films today. Verna becomes a drug dealer, and she comes up with a plan to kidnap her socialite sister Elaine's young three-year-old daughter for a ransom of $50,000. She insists that Elaine would never go to the police and tell on her own sister. Verna, with the help of Tony and Nicky, kidnap the child. Verna meets with Elaine's husband to pick up the ransom. He tells her that the child is not his, that she is the daughter of Elaine's sister; thus, Verna inadvertently discovers that the child she kidnapped is actually her own. Meanwhile, the police raid her apartment and find the child. They arrest Nicky and Tony. Verna returns and administers a shot of heroin in her upper thigh. She walks unsteadily into the apartment and sees her daughter next to a police officer; her head rolls back and she collapses on to the floor; marijuana cigarettes fall all around her. At the film's end, Verna is dead and Tony and Nick are in custody.

More familiar to contemporary viewers is the film *Reefer Madness* (1936), which was released in the same year as *Marihuana, the Weed with Roots in Hell*. In the film, people who use marijuana and heroin are depicted as morally weak and antisocial. *Reefer Madness*, similar to *Assassins of Youth*, portrays marijuana use as causing addiction, sexual immorality, insanity, violence, and murder. The film opens with a foreword warning that a new drug, marijuana, is destroying the youth of America in record numbers. It warns that marijuana is a "violent narcotic" and that it is *Public Enemy Number One!* The following text scrolls down the screen outlining the effects of marijuana use and the purpose in producing the film:

> Its first effect is sudden, violent, uncontrollable laughter; then come dangerous hallucinations—space expands—time slows down, almost stands still . . . fixed ideas come next, conjuring up monstrous extravagances—followed by emotional disturbances, the total inability to direct thoughts, the loss of all power to resist physical emotions . . . leading to acts of shocking violence . . . ending often in incurable insanity. In picturing its soul-destroying effects no attempt was made to equivocate. The scenes and incidents, while fictionalized for the purposes of this story, are based upon actual research into the results of marijuana addiction. If their stark reality will make you *think*, will make you aware that something *must be done* to wipe out this ghastly menace, then the picture will not have failed in its purpose.

The script then warns parents that their son or daughter could be the next victim. Then the camera cuts to a series of newspaper captions with alarming headings like "Dope peddlers caught in high school," followed by a scene portraying a parent association meeting at Truman High School. The lecture for the night is titled "Tell Your Children," and concerned parents and teachers have come out to hear Dr. Carroll speak about "narcotics and marijuana in particular." The doctor and the audience are depicted as White and middle class. Dr. Carroll speaks about the Department of Narcotics fight against drug traffickers who are corrupting innocent youth. He talks about heroin and cocaine, but he quickly turns to the main focus of his lecture—marijuana. He says: "And the more vicious, more deadly, even than these other soul destroying drugs, is the menace of marijuana." He then proceeds to provide some "real facts" about cases. We hear about a 17-year-old girl who smoked marijuana and was "found in the company of five men." He tells the audience about a 16-year-old boy who killed a family with an ax after smoking marijuana. He then introduces his main story, a sordid tale about unscrupulous marijuana dealers (Mae and Jack) luring innocent youth into depravity and murder. Youth depicted in the film come from "decent" homes (or even wealthy homes, given the film's depression-era setting). The youth are depicted as victims of predatory drug pushers.

In the film, respectable youth are lured into marijuana use by Jack and Mae, the two drug dealers. Bill, one of the characters in the film, is described by Dr. Carroll as being "a fine upstanding American boy, a good scholar, a good athlete" prior to using marijuana. Mary is Bill's girlfriend. She is constructed as moral and innocent. She goes to Mae's apartment to look for her brother Jimmy. At the apartment she is offered a cigarette, but it is not tobacco and she accidentally smokes "reefer" at Ralph's (a local youth who has a crush on her) urging. He then attempts to sexually assault her. She escapes, only to be accidentally murdered by Jack. Jack pins the murder on Bill, who is depicted as having no memory of the night because he is under the influence of marijuana.

In the film, drug treatment is not portrayed, although Ralph's marijuana use is depicted as addictive and leading to "criminal insanity." He is memorable for his demonic behaviour in the film, as he sits on a couch listening to the character Blanche play the piano. He smokes reefer and demands that she play "Faster! Play faster! Faster!" He clenches his hands spasmodically as Blanche plays faster. She too is smoking reefer. Jack comes into the room. Ralph is convinced that he has come to murder him so that he will not tell the authorities that he killed Mary (Bill has been blamed for the murder). He picks up a fire poker and starts brutally hitting Jack. At this point the police arrive and take him and everyone else into custody. Blanche is overcome with grief due to her descent into marijuana use and her complicity in the events that unfolded at the parties. After confessing her guilt and admitting to "fostering delinquency," she jumps out of a window at the police station and commits suicide. Later in court, Ralph's lawyers argue that he is "insane," a "condition caused by his marijuana use." The judge sentences him to be incarcerated in a hospital for the criminally insane for the rest of his life. Similar to *Assassin of Youth*, insanity is linked to marijuana use, yet where Marjorie is cared for by a kindly doctor in the home, Ralph is represented as criminally insane, and mandatory treatment in a mental asylum will be his destination. Here we become acquainted with the popular law-enforcement representation following prohibition—"criminal addict."

The films discussed above, made with the help of H. J. Anslinger, supported criminalization of recreational use of marijuana in 1937. Although whiteness dominates in these films, movie viewers were becoming well aware through the print media and law enforcement, especially H. J. Anslinger, that marijuana was associated with violent crime and racialized peoples, including "Greeks, Turks, Filipino, Spaniards, Latin American, and Negroes."[53] These films serve to "educate" White America about the racialized threat. Originally, marijuana was associated with Mexican labourers who immigrated to the United States to find work during the Great Depression and with the jazz scene.[54] H. J. Anslinger is responsible for producing a wide range of racialized antidrug discourse during his reign of 32 years as the U.S. drug czar.

From the 1920s onward, state and federal officials moved to enact increasingly harsh state and federal drug laws to prohibit the use of specific drugs. H. J. Anslinger was integral to this process. By 1924, the Harrison Narcotic Act was strengthened. Anslinger used the media, both print and film, to "educate" White Americans about the "horrors" of drugs, drug users, and dealers. For most American viewers, the morality films and news reports produced with the help of Anslinger and other law officials were their only source of information about addiction and the "depraved" lives of drug users. In these early morality films, drug use is linked to criminality, violence, and sexual immorality. The films are presented as "true case studies" from police files. In these films, law enforcement is represented as the ultimate authority on drugs. White middle-class families and communities are portrayed as under threat by criminal gangs, drug epidemics, and unscrupulous dealers. Addiction is accompanied by degradation, suicide, murder, and insanity. Weak-willed upper- and middle-class users are cared for by physicians, sometimes to no avail.

Early films made with the help of law-enforcement agents, along with sensationalized print media accounts of drug use, served to divert attention away from political, social, and economic factors that were shaping the lives of people during the depression era. The focus on drugs as the culprit, and sobriety, legislation, and more police powers as the cure, coloured temperance literature and alcohol prohibition from 1920 to 1933 in the United States. Drugs were linked to the breakdown of morality, families, communities, and ultimately the Anglo-Saxon nation. Outside of these independent films, few other U.S. and British illegal-drug films were produced in the 1930s and 1940s. Starks[55] notes that the depression, the lead-up to World War II, the war years, and its aftermath, probably limited the production of drug films. Of course, censorship of depictions of illegal-drug use and trafficking also shaped film representations.

The Man with the Golden Arm: heroin addiction

From 1934 to 1948, no Hollywood film depicted heroin use and/or trafficking as the central story line, even though the Federal Bureau of Narcotics supported the production of a number of films outside of the Hollywood system. The postwar years were generally conservative in terms of drug policy and treatment and drug laws in both Canada and the United States. In Britain, Canada, and the United States, the state made concerted efforts to drive women back into the home following their participation in the war economy. The home, the private sphere, was once again depicted as the domain of White middle-class women and children, and the public sphere, the world of paid labour, the domain of men.

The 1955 film *The Man with the Golden Arm* is often cited as the first contemporary Hollywood film to explicitly depict heroin addiction and to challenge movie censors, who were set up in the 1930s. It also vividly depicts heroin withdrawal. In the film, Frankie Machine, a young, White working-class man, played by Frank Sinatra, is recently released from prison. The opening scene of the movie highlights Frankie leaving a prisonlike place, which might be the federal mandatory treatment centre (narcotics farm) in Lexington, Kentucky. Although the scene only lasts for a few seconds, it is significant because it shows Frankie sitting with a man who appears to be a doctor. The doctor advises him to "Keep busy to keep mind off craving. One fix. Hooked again." This scene reinforces the myth that one fix will lead to immediate addiction. It also confirms addiction as the domain of the medical profession and prison as the appropriate site for abstinence and mandatory treatment.

Frankie is released from prison after doing six months. He dreams of being a drummer in a jazz band, but his scheming wife has other plans for him. His wife Sophia drinks beer, has a noticeable accent, and she is confined to a wheelchair. We learn that she was permanently disabled in a car accident. Frankie was driving the car. Sophia hides his drumsticks because she hates the sound of his drums and encourages him to take a job as a "card dealer" because it is more lucrative. She does not understand his passion for music. She yells at him, "Take them [drumsticks] down to your girlfriend if you want to make noise and practice." Luckily for Frankie, his girlfriend lives in the same apartment building and he visits her and sets up his drums there. His girlfriend Molly is White, blonde, and nurturing. She is pictured drinking milk, not beer, and she encourages Frankie to follow his dream to play drums in a band.

Later, we see Sophia alone in their apartment. She gets up from her wheelchair and walks unaided to the window. The viewer begins to suspect that Sophia is scamming Frankie so that he will continue to support her. He is constructed as a sensitive man who experiences guilt and remorse about her "disability" and his role in it. Frankie starts working as a card dealer and he becomes involved in petty crime. He is also using heroin again and quickly becomes addicted. At one point in the film, he pleads with Molly to give him some money because he is so dope sick. Molly responds, "Get the cure . . . with help, medicine, doctors." Frankie says that is impossible now because he is wanted by the police for murder (which he did not commit). He tells her, "You don't understand. All I need is one shot." She says all right and hands him some money and says: "Why should you hurt, like other people hurt? Yes. So you had a dog's life, with never a break. Why not try to face it like other people do? No, just roll all your pains into one big hurt, and than flatten it with a fix."

Molly informs us that Frankie can be cured with the help of a doctor. Here the narrative also informs us that heroin users are no more sensitive than nonusers and that they need to just stop wallowing in their pain and get on with life.

At the end of the movie, Frankie pleads with his girlfriend Molly to help him stop using heroin. He says: "But kicking it, a guy can't do it by himself." Representing the pure and nurturing girlfriend, Molly replies, "I'll help." He warns her:

> You don't know what you're getting yourself into. It ain't pretty and it could be dangerous. I mean dangerous for me. *Sometimes a junky will kill, to get away from the treatment.* Understand? So if you have any knives or scissors in the house, you got to put them away for awhile and don't let me out of the room. No matter what I say or promise, or how much I beg. Because if I get out it will only be to find a fix. That's the way it is you understand? *Just lock me in a room and if I try to make a break for it, stop me any way you know how.* And no matter how much you see it hurting me, don't try to help me with pills or dope or anything like that. You think you can handle it? (author's emphasis)

She responds by locking the door.

"Here we go, down and dirty," he says. Today we recognize the story line—people addicted to drugs or going through withdrawal must be locked up against their will—and they will kill to get away from treatment.

Later in the film we see Frankie trying to open the door. He drinks copious amounts of water. He holds his stomach with his arms and wraps a belt around his arm (mimicking preparing to "shoot up"); he shivers and lies on the floor in a fetal position. He then goes to the door and screams, "Let me out!" and bangs on the door. He pleads, shakes, and we see his hands clenched. He then opens the window of the room and is stepping out to commit suicide when Molly returns to the room. He screams at her, "Can't stand it! I gotta get out and get a fix, I'll kill ya!"

Here, Molly deceives him. She tells him she has something in the closet that will help him. Frankie goes over and walks into the closet. Molly slams the door and locks him in. Frankie bangs on the door repeatedly, but finally he is quiet and she later opens the door. He asks to be killed. "If you love me, kill me," he says. He eventually lies down and she covers him with blankets, saying out loud, "God, God, God." Frankie falls asleep.

The next day, Frankie wakes up and looks outside. He says. "Most gorgeous day I've ever saw. I feel all the things inside me settled into place." We see Molly empty a bag filled with razors and knifes. And when Frankie asks for a razor to shave, she asks him, "Can I trust you again?" They are later shown walking down the street admiring consumer goods in store windows portraying kitchenettes and gleaming fridges and stoves—symbols of domestic middle-class family life—with Molly representing conventional

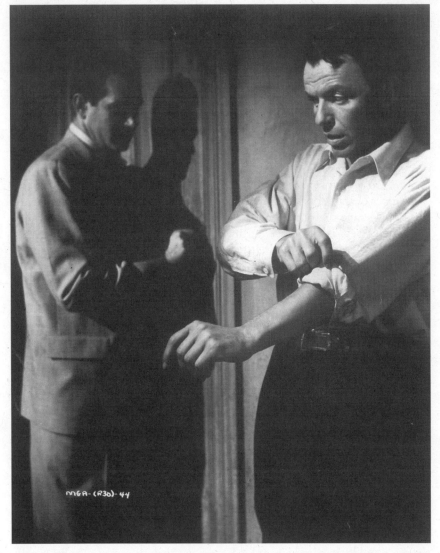

The Man with the Golden Arm. Source: United Artists/Photofest. © United Artists.

White middle-class womanhood. She supports Frankie in his endeavours and his quest to put his addiction behind him. Most important, she is looking forward to her domestic home life with him.

In *The Man with the Golden Arm*, addiction is once again depicted as quick and inevitable. The doctor warns Frankie at the beginning of the film that one fix would send him spiralling into addiction again. Drug users are constructed as dishonest, willing to lie and cheat. They are also willing to kill for a fix, especially when withdrawing from drugs. It is clearly laid out that they cannot be trusted. Withdrawal is represented as terrible, causing unbearable emotional and physical pain. So terrible is withdrawal that people addicted to drugs are represented in film as needing to be locked up against their will, whether it is their own bedroom, in mandatory treatment, or in prison.[56] Withdrawal myths reinforce mandatory treatment and prison as the primary site for treatment. As well, it reinforces practices that infringe on the human rights of drug users. Yet by the end of the film, Frankie makes it through withdrawal, and he is cured without the aid of a doctor (although it is made clear that he is wanted by the police and he can no longer get professional medical help). He has a loving girlfriend at his side. He looks forward to a conventional family life with her (now that his scheming wife is dead). The causes of Frankie's addiction are dismissed, and he is framed as being "weak-willed" by Molly because, as she states, lots of people have a hard life and they find ways to cope without resorting to heroin addiction. In the film, Molly represents conventional gender-role expectations for women following WWII where government and film imagery exerted pressure for women to move from the workplace into the home.

From the 1950s on, changing attitudes about the nature of addiction and addiction-as-disease ideology informed fictional film narratives. The medical profession in the United States and the National Committee for the Education on Alcoholism began to lobby Hollywood to produce movies that depicted their principles: "Alcoholism is a disease; the alcoholic is treatable and deserves help; and alcoholism is a public health problem."[57] *The Lost Weekend* was produced in 1945, and it can be viewed as the first modern alcoholism film. The film director consulted with Alcoholics Anonymous (AA) members and depicted "alcoholism" in the White upper-middle-class home.[58] Whereas illegal-drug movies were also situated in White America, representations of addiction as disease were slower coming. Even though psychiatric and addiction-as-disease perspectives were beginning to inform medical treatment and public attitudes, the notion of the "criminal addict" was still firmly entrenched in law-enforcement and medical discourse and practice in the United States and Canada. This is interesting, given that alcohol is associated with crime more often than illegal drugs; yet public sentiment and official practice still see alcoholics as more "deserving" of medical care and treatment for their "disease" than illegal-drug users.

Although concepts of addiction as disease, especially in relation to alcohol, can be traced back to the writings of Benjamin Rush, a temperance advocate in the late 1700s,[59] it was not until after World War II that the model became well known. Following World War II, with the rise of psychiatric and medical perspectives about treatment and rehabilitation, and addiction as disease, attitudes about drugs and treatment shifted, especially in the United States. In the mid-1930s, Alcoholics Anonymous groups were established in the U.S. AA's founders considered alcoholism to be a disease.

The group's philosophy was published in 1939, and they challenged both medical and scientific discourse about alcohol use.[60] The founders of AA were deeply impacted by the work of Carl Jung. Spirituality and conversation were therapeutic cornerstones of the model.

In the United States, E. M. Jellinek is credited with popularizing the perspective in his own work by providing a "scientific footing" for the AA model.[61] The AA model, Jellinek's book, *The Disease Concept of Alcoholism* (published in 1960), the Yale Center for Alcohol Studies, and the National Council on Alcoholism (NCA) provided a scientific "setting" for the disease concept of alcoholism.[62] Jellinek argues that alcoholism is a physical disorder and not the result of being weak willed or of immoral character. Addiction is constructed as a biological, progressive, and permanent disease; thus, total abstinence is required. Unlike temperance ideology or alcohol prohibition that condemns all alcohol use, AA advocates claimed that only those persons with the disease should cease drinking. Self-help, sobriety, regular support meeting, and, since the 1950s, working through the twelve steps became the template for AA meetings. Most important, meetings were voluntary, free, and run by peers who were nonprofessionals. Sobriety is achieved by working through the twelve steps. The twelve steps have little to do with drugs; rather, they work as a guide for stressing one's powerlessness over alcohol. Testimonials and taking it "one day at a time" are intrinsic to AA philosophy. Later, twelve steps and AA philosophy were applied to other addictions, including drugs such as morphine, heroin, and cocaine. Abstinence from alcohol and all illegal drugs became integral to the program. Interestingly, tobacco, tea, coffee, and prescribed drugs are not included on the list of drugs to abstain from.

AA philosophy was instrumental in shifting the emphasis from the drug to the individual. Criminologist Mariana Valverde states that AA turned a "disease into a full fledged, life-long social identity."[63] Rather than alcohol being the cause of addiction, alcoholism is viewed as a disease that is life-long. Yet societal consensus and medical practice related to alcohol, illegal-drug use, and addiction remains contested. Illegal-drug films capture some of these contradictions. Illegal-drug addiction is represented as a vice, a crime, immoral, lack of self-control, and, following the 1950s, as a disease. Yet addiction-as-disease representations are coupled with narratives about crime, risk, and self-control. The film *Monkey on My Back* (1957) introduces movie viewers to some of these representations and narcotic addiction as disease.

Monkey on My Back: addiction as disease

A number of U.S. movies produced in the 1950s depict addiction as instant and painful. However, they do not portray drug-treatment scenes. *The Cool and the Crazy* (1958) and *High School Confidential* (1958) construct a "gateway" discourse of drugs and addiction (a propagandist theme that emerged in *Marihuana, the Weed with Roots in Hell* (1936). Marijuana is depicted as a gateway drug to heroin and other "hard" drugs. In *High School Confidential*, one young woman is able to quit using marijuana with the help of her schoolteacher, symbolically represented by breaking a marijuana joint in two. However, for the rest of the drug users in the film, once addicted to hard drugs, it is "too late" for them. In contrast, the earlier film *The Man with the Golden Arm* depicted withdrawal and even recovery from heroin (a "hard" drug) use. Two years later, the film *Monkey on My Back* (1957) portrays a man who recovers from morphine addiction; however, it provides a slightly different narrative about addiction than *The Man with the Golden Arm*. In this film, addiction to narcotics and other activities such as gambling are represented as a "disease," and the film includes lengthy scenes at a mandatory-withdrawal unit in a federal hospital. The film begins with the caption "The story of Barney Ross. One time world's lightweight champion. Twice world's welterweight champion. Ex-Corporal, U.S. Marine Corps. Awarded Silver Star for gallantry in action." In the background we can see the U.S. federal hospital behind a large gated metal fence. Barney Ross, once known as the "Pride of the Ghetto," is shown walking out of the locked gates.

Through flashbacks, the viewer learns that Barney is "addicted" to gambling. His girlfriend is concerned and she says that his gambling is "a disease. And he's incurable." He loses all of his money and later joins the Marine Corps in hope of starting all over. He is shown in a fierce battle in which he fights off Japanese soldiers, derogatorily referred to as "Japs" in the film. By the time he is rescued, he is delirious and screaming. He suffers greatly from "malignant malaria" and nightmares. He is treated with opiates by a field doctor. Barney informs us in a voice-over, "That was the start. Morphine. The only thing that could drown out the guns . . . and sing me to sleep." Barney's descent into addiction and degradation is swift. He steals morphine from the military clinic and says, "I needed the stuff more than I'd needed anything. It didn't make no difference what I had to do to get it." Yet on returning home he quits using morphine for a while. He marries his girlfriend, who has a little girl from a previous marriage. Soon he begins to buy morphine on the illegal market. His addiction and cravings are depicted by his looking desperate, sweating, holding his neck with his one hand, and doubling over and holding his stomach with his other hand. He hooks up with a local dealer and soon he is in debt to him. When he runs out of money, he threatens his dealer, telling him, "I'll kill you if you don't give me a fix!" Later he is depicted shooting up morphine, and he is asked to leave his job because of his erratic behaviour and his growing debt to his employer. His wife is suspicious of his behaviour, but she does not know what is wrong until one night she wakes up to find Barney smashing open her daughter's piggy bank in order to steal the money inside of it. With her support, Barney seeks help.

Barney eventually becomes a voluntary patient in the mandatory-withdrawal ward at the U.S. federal hospital. He is treated by a doctor and assigned a room. Rather than cold turkey, for a week he is given injections of morphine, smaller doses each day. He is depicted lying on a single bed tossing and turning. In a voice-over he says, "This is what they meant when they talked about kicking the habit. No control of myself. A thousand little, hot, branding irons at the end of every nerve in my body." Barney starts to hallucinate that the ceiling and lamp above him crack. The ceiling opens and rocks come tumbling down on him. He screams.

Later, we see Barney pacing in his hospital room. He lives in fear that the "craving will come back." He spends over four months at the hospital. Finally, the doctor tells him that it is time to go home. Barney asks him if he is really cured and the doctor responds, "So far as we're concerned. But you have to know it. You have to remember it every waking hour of the rest of your life." Barney reaches for the phone to let his wife know that he is coming home, and the doctor quickly reprimands him: "No outgoing calls. You know the rules." The film ends as the camera cuts to Barney walking out of the mandatory-treatment hospital gates and the caption "The Beginning" rather than "The End" appears on the screen.

Except for a boxing opponent and Japanese soldiers depicted in one scene, all of the main characters in the film are represented as White. Barney is characterized as a man who has worked his way up from the ghetto to become a famous boxer. However, we never see his life prior to his celebrity as a boxer. In the film, his working-class background is represented by his rough manner and poor grammar. His addiction to morphine is swift and all encompassing, and he is willing to steal and kill for a fix (just as Frankie is in *The Man with the Golden Arm*). Yet Barney is also portrayed with sympathy, given that he is a sports and military hero. With the support of his wife and the professional "care" by the White doctors at the mandatory-withdrawal ward, he is able to become abstinent and rejoin his family. The film clearly depicts doctors as experts on addiction. It also more clearly depicts addiction as disease than did previous illegal-drug films. A disease that is lifelong. Yet the film also emphasizes Barney's vices, especially his addiction to gambling and his struggles to stop gambling. In the film, Barney's wife is completely supportive once she finds out that his erratic behaviour is due to morphine addiction.[64] When Barney tells her that the "dope's stronger than me," she replies, "Is it stronger than we are?" She represents moral White womanhood, unselfish, caring, and giving. The White heterosexual nuclear family is reaffirmed as the site of strength and support for family members. In the film, mandatory drug treatment is not problematized; rather, it is represented as the site of recovery. Giving up one's freedom is the price one has to pay to gain treatment and to achieve sobriety.

Although the disease model of addiction was applied to alcoholics, it was not automatically extended to illegal-drug users. It might be difficult for some readers to remember a time when treatment was not available to illegal-drug users and when addiction was not considered a disease by the medical profession and by society at large. In the 1950s, poor and working-class illegal-drug users continued to be framed as "criminal addicts," and there was little sympathy for them in Canada and the United States. By the 1950s, harsh drug laws, including life sentences for drug trafficking in Canada and the death penalty for trafficking to minors in the United States, were enacted. Incarceration for drug possession was all too common in Canada and the United States.[65] Drug-treatment services for illegal-drug users were not available outside of federal mandatory facilities like Lexington. In Canada, no public treatment or maintenance programs were available. Therefore, the situation for illegal-drug users, especially those addicted to heroin or other narcotics, was quite dire. The situation in Britain differed because doctors could legally prescribe heroin for detox and maintenance.[66]

Slowly, the medical community and drug users themselves embraced addiction as disease, and both have been active in "redrawing" its boundaries (which are quite elastic). Yet still "the complexities of drug using behaviours continue to defy rigorous categorization under the heading of addiction-as-disease," largely because the concept still suffers from a lack of scientific validity.[67] Drug researcher Craig Reinarman argues that the "biological basis for addiction-as-disease remains elusive."[68] Nevertheless, from the 1950s on, addiction-as-disease ideology informs policy, research, debate, practice, and film narratives about illegal drugs.

CONCLUSION

Early illegal-drug films were quite diverse and some drug use was depicted as comedy and not problematized (such as Coke Ennyday's laudanum and cocaine use in *The Mystery of the Leaping Fish* [1916]). However, from the start, drug use was racialized. Smoking opium was demonized as an Asian vice, whereas early on opium-based patent medicines were seen as positive and therapeutic for White women. Later films reflecting moral reformers' concerns and societal anxieties represented some drugs and the people who used them as dangerous. In films, opium in smoking form and cocaine were depicted as dangerous to White moral society, associating the drugs and the people who sold them as luring innocent women and youth into a life of addiction. Drugs like opium, heroin, morphine, cocaine, and marijuana were depicted in film as being instantly addictive, and users were represented as descending into a life of degradation (and sexual immorality if female), crime, insanity, and ultimately death. Fantastical film dialogue such as, "I'll sell my soul for a fix (or kill to avoid treatment and withdrawl)," becomes part of drug and popular discourses. The drug epidemic was represented as spreading into White America, affecting middle- and upper-class moral youth and destroying the fabric of the family, communities, and, ultimately, if left unchecked, the nation. White enforcement agents and doctors are the favoured authority about illegal drugs in early films.

Early films had no or little reference to drug treatment outside of leaving the city to go to the country or discontinuing visiting opium dens (located in the city). Abstinence and separating the user from the drug were the most popular form of treatment (as they are today). Although movie viewers were introduced to fictionalized, crazed, and immoral "addicts" on the screen, it was not until the 1950s that movie viewers were shown "horrific" scenes of drug withdrawal in film. Controlled-use and nonhorrific withdrawal were absent from film narratives. Films began to depict locked bedrooms, hospitals, and asylums as the site for drug withdrawal and detox from drugs. Eventually, reflecting changing medical, psychological theory and practice, and societal attitudes, addiction was presented as a medical problem to be treated by physicians and psychiatrists. By the 1950s, addiction as disease is adopted by the medical profession, and a number of films on alcoholism are produced; yet illegal-drug users are still represented as weak willed and immoral. The film *Monkey on My Back* (1957) introduced film viewers to addiction as disease; however, twelve-step and Narcotics Anonymous meetings are absent from the narrative.

Illegal-drug-use representations in film and drug-use patterns in all three nations were about to change, for the 1960s brought with it unparalleled recreational illegal-drug use by youth. The 1960s would bring with it a host of new films that ruptured addiction narratives about illegal drugs and challenged conventional perspectives about drug use, abuse, and addiction.

3   The 60s On

Counterculture, Addiction-as-Disease, and Mandatory-Treatment Narratives

In this chapter I continue to discuss addiction-as-disease narratives, treatment, withdrawal, and alternative representations of illegal-drug use from 1960 on. The 1960s brought about a significant shift in illegal-drug film representations and illegal-drug use, and altered states of consciousness are represented as positive; however, as we will see, a number of films produced in the 1970s can be considered "backlash" films to the liberal 60s. In the 1980s, illegal-drug films focus on cocaine and crack-cocaine use and its "addictive qualities." Narcotics Anonymous and twelve-step programs are represented as commonsense treatment models. White and upper- and middle-class users are shown in voluntary drug-treatment centres; however, mandatory treatment is shown as the site for treatment of poor and racialized illegal-drug users. As we will see in this chapter, where and how drug treatment is represented is instructive about class and race politics. I discuss several films as examples of shifting narratives about illegal-drug use, addiction, and drug treatment.

THE SIXTIES

Many of the illegal-drug films produced in the 1960s are startling in their rejection of earlier narratives about "demon" drugs. As noted in the previous chapter, from the 1930s to the 1950s the U.S. drug czar, H. J. Anslinger, was a significant producer of antidrug discourse, including films. During these years, drug laws became increasingly harsher. Drug historian David Musto notes that the federal budget was quite modest; thus, a significant portion of the U.S. campaign against drugs was centred around "popular imagery—the more fearful the better."[1] Musto interviewed H. J. Anslinger in 1972. The 60s youth culture and increased illegal-drug use caught Anslinger totally by surprise. Anslinger was convinced that his campaign of negative drug imagery, harsh mandatory sentences, and the support of the professions and institutions against illegal-drug use would counter illegal-drug use in the United States.[2] Musto proposes that Anslinger did not count on the fact that youth saw through antidrug-war discourse and the ignorance of its producers. They found antidrug propaganda to be so "extreme as to be laughable."[3] Illegal-drug films produced during the 1960s counter antidrug-war propaganda, especially in relation to marijuana and LSD use.

Influenced by the Beat writers of the 1950s, the civil-rights and Black Panther movements, the Vietnam War and peace movement of the 1960s, a number of counterideological films were produced in Britain, Canada, and the United States from the early 1960s to the early 1970s that illuminated societal shifts about drug use, addiction, and treatment. This era is often referred to as the 1960s countercultural movement. Experimentation with criminalized drugs expanded and a generation of White middle-class youth adopted marijuana and psychedelic drugs as their drugs of choice. However, it would be a mistake to assume that only middle-class youth participated in drug use; in fact, youth drug use increased in all stratas of society in Britain, Canada, and the United States.[4] Many members of the Beat and 60s movement used marijuana, LSD, and other psychedelic substances like peyote and mescaline. Illegal-drug use skyrocketed during this time, and youth associated recreational use as positive.

Although LSD was discovered in the 1940s, it was not until the 1950s and early 1960s that it was used as a legal therapeutic tool. LSD was heralded as a breakthrough for therapeutic use with chronic alcoholics. Legal therapeutic accounts were positive, and soon people were using the drug outside of therapeutic settings. The drug was associated with political dissent and altered states of consciousness.[5] For many youth and the not so youthful, shifts in states of consciousness were seen as positive, leading to mystical experiences, cultural revolution, and a challenge to "rational consciousness."[6] When middle-class youth began to experiment with LSD outside of therapeutic settings, anti-LSD propaganda emerged in the 1960s linking use to traumatic experiences, suicides, birth defects, and permanent psychological damage.

Following WWII, all three countries experienced tremendous economic growth, and a completely new generation of youth was free from wartime concerns and conscription. Economic expansion and the emergence of a postwar generation of "baby boomers" to young adulthood also contributed to social and political shifts, including drug consumption.[7] At the same time, what is referred to as the "psychopharmaceutical revolution" occurred in Western nations. A number of researchers point out that the pharmaceutical industry and drug consumption were transformed from the 1950s on.[8] With the discovery of Thorazine and minor tranquillizers in the 1950s and 1960s, such as Milltown, Librium, and Valium, to deal with the stresses of everyday life, drug use shifted dramatically. Rather than using these drugs for purely medicinal purposes, Milltown parties sprang up in the suburbs. Films like *Valley of the Dolls* (1967) capture these phenomena. In 1965 only 300 prescription drugs were available; by 2002, over 9,000 were available.[9] Later, the discovery of selective serotonin reuptake inhibitors (SSRIs; i.e.,

Paxil and Prozac) contributed to the trend to medicalize "modern anxiet-ies."[10] Although moral reformers tend to focus their attention on natural drugs like opium, marijuana, and heroin (a semisynthetic drug), synthetic legal drugs do not stay neatly tucked away or used in ways recommended by doctors. From the 1950s on, doctors proclaimed the virtues of specific drugs (i.e., Milltown, Seconal, Librium, Valium, Prozac, and Oxycontin). Scores of drug users agreed and filmmakers in Britain, Canada, and the United States incorporated representations of these drugs, explorations of states of consciousness, withdrawal, and treatment on the screen.

Chappaqua: psychedelic cinema and treatment

Social and political shifts during the late 1950s and 1960s were reflected in a number of movies that challenged conventional ideology that criminal-ized drugs were bad. The U.S./French film *Chappaqua* (1966) is often seen as the first full-length film to be labelled "psychedelic cinema."[11] *Chap-paqua* (1966) is an exception to earlier addiction and withdrawal narra-tives following prohibition. The narrative is loosely based on the director's personal experience. Addiction as disease is explored very briefly in the film; however, it is not explicit. The central focus of the film is on surreal-ism and spirituality. *Chappaqua* focuses on Russell Hardwick, a young upper-class White male who has been using alcohol and drugs since his early youth. The film opens with scrolling text, written by Hardwick. He writes that he started drinking alcohol when he was 11 years old and by the time he was 15 years of age he was experiencing delirium tremors. At 19 years of age he discovered marijuana, cocaine, and heroin. He writes that his life became a shifting pattern of addictions until he was introduced to LSD and peyote, which enabled him to put his addictions behind him for a while. The film shifts from urban scenes in New York City to the Ameri-can West, using double exposures to juxtapose the American West and aboriginal imagery with scenes of neon signs in New York City. The city is contrasted with rural spaces throughout the film. The city is depicted as decadent in contrast to the pure countryside.

The film follows the process of treatment that takes place at a large cha-teau like clinic in rural France. Hardwick, the only patient there, is informed that he is suffering from addiction. Treatment consists of an experimental "sleeping cure" and speaking with a doctor, possibly a psychiatrist. Sur-realism is used to depict drug use and withdrawal. In the film, Hardwick is depicted hallucinating and the film is quite psychedelic. However, unlike the horrific withdrawal scenes in *The Man with the Golden Arm* (1955) and *Monkey on My Back* (1957), Hardwick's withdrawal focuses more closely on the subjective experience. The surrealistic imagery in the film draws on aboriginal, Eastern, and Christian spirituality. There is ambigu-ity between spiritual and addictive use of drugs. The film provides a narra-tive of how peyote was first brought to the people.

The film includes a number of significant musicians and writers of the time. The music of Ravi Shankar accompanies the film and he has a small part in it. The Fugs are also shown playing at a club in New York city, where Hardwick eats LSD-soaked sugar cubes. Beat writers Allen Ginsberg and William Burroughs also appear briefly in the film. Following his withdrawal, Hardwick is warned by the doctor to never use drugs again once he is cured because relapse will endanger his life. However, it is interesting to note that the film does not provide a confessional narrative or the narrative of "fall and redemption," which had become common in drug films. Nor do we see Hardwick "hit rock bottom" before entering the clinic. Rather, drug use and spirituality are fused in the film. In addition, Hardwick is not constructed as criminal, evil, or weak willed, and he is not shown striving to or wanting to reenter or join mainstream society following his time at the clinic. Women are not central to the narrative of *Chappaqua*, although the few times they appear they are represented as sexualized objects. For example, in a scene where Hardwick hallucinates, the clinic nurse is portrayed as sexually enticing. In addition, a White woman is represented as the aboriginal "peyote goddess." However, the representations of aboriginal imagery and narrative are grounded in White America fantasies rather than specific aboriginal practices. Thus, the filmmakers contribute to colonial misrepresentation and appropriation of aboriginal and Eastern spiritual experience.

The Trip and *Easy Rider*: normalized, counterculture representations of illegal drugs

The Trip was produced by Roger Corman in 1967, and the script was written by Jack Nicholson. It begins with a comic take on earlier morality films; the opening scene is in black and white and the script reads:

> You are about to be involved in a most unusual motion picture experience. It deals fictionally with the hallucinogenic drug, LSD.
>
> Today, the extensive use in black market production of this and other such "mind-bending" chemicals is of great concern to medical and civil authorities.
>
> The illegal manufacture and distribution of these drugs is dangerous and can have fatal consequences, many have been hospitalized as a result.
>
> This picture represents a shocking commentary on a prevalent trend of our time and one that must be of great concern to all.

The next scene is in colour and we are introduced to the main character, Paul, a young White upper-class man, played by Peter Fonda, who works filming commercials. He is portrayed filming a commercial for perfume on the beach. His wife Sally arrives on the set, upset because he missed their appointment with their divorce lawyers.

The Trip. Source: American International Pictures/Photofest. © American International Pictures.

Paul is shown visiting a home where sitar music plays and young White people are shown seated, passing around a joint. Psychedelic art hangs on the walls. A woman approaches Paul and asks, "Here for some acid?" He responds, "Why?" She says, "Why? Insight. Find out something." "About myself?" he asks. He takes the LSD offered to him and as the film unfolds we watch his transformation. The film portrays psychedelic images similar to shapes shown through a kaleidoscope. Paul's LSD trip is represented as evoking death, awakening, self-transformation, and cultural revolution. The camera cuts to stills of the U.S. flag, dollar bills, a Valentine heart, President Lyndon B. Johnson, rows of new stores, and TV commercials. Paul is also depicted watching the news on TV, a segment in which the announcer talks about Saigon and 113 wounded soldiers. Through this imagery, the film critiques consumerism, commercialism, the Vietnam War, and U.S. nationalism.

During his LSD trip, Paul is depicted having sex with a young blonde woman; however, in an out-of-body scene he sits with his wife Sally and watches himself having sex. In the film, Sally is represented as "straight," unliberated, and sexually uptight as contrast to the themes of transformation and rejection of conventional life. Yet the characters' Whiteness and upper-middle-class representations serve to erase the history of other segments of society then struggling for social change.

Whereas *The Trip* popularizes LSD, the narrative of *Easy Rider*, produced in 1969, celebrates the 60s counterculture; yet it is stripped of innocence. Like *The Trip*, it explores themes of materialism, freedom, and drugs and it is accompanied by a terrific 60s sound track. Yet the film is also critical of the counterculture. In a naturalistic style, Dennis Hopper, Peter Fonda, and Jack Nicholson team up in *Easy Rider*, a popular film in and beyond the United States. Dennis Hopper, the director of the film, states in the DVD special features that *Easy Rider* is an "outlaw narrative." The films characters, two white males, Billy (the Kid; played by Dennis Hopper) and Wyatt (Earp; played by Peter Fonda) are depicted as freewheeling motorcycle-riding drug dealers. Wyatt is also known as Captain America (the name of a Marvel superhero comic-book character). Billy and Wyatt are also recreational drug users, and throughout the film we see them consume cocaine, LSD, and marijuana. The film chronicles their journey to pick up cocaine from a small Mexican village and deliver it to a dealer in Los Angles. From there, their destination is Florida, where they plan to retire. The landscape in the film speaks to the narrative of freedom. Panoramic scenes of the country, mountain ranges, desert plateaus, blue sky, flowing rivers, nude swimming, campfires at night, and the soundtrack complement the film narrative. Nature and counterculture lifestyles are depicted as freedom from conventional society.

In *Easy Rider*, taking LSD is represented as a surreal spiritual experience, showing religious iconography of a graveyard and the reading of a biblical passage. The scenes of the "trip" are open to interpretation, for it is not presented as positive or negative. Yet the film makes clear that the trip brings users face-to-face with their inner selves, and the experience is portrayed as both enlightening and frightening.

In the film, marijuana use is recreational, and its use is seen as part of socializing and philosophizing among the characters. Alcohol use is also problematized. In one scene, Wyatt introduces George to marijuana. George is depicted as a hard-drinking American Civil Liberties Union lawyer whom they meet in jail after being arrested for "parading without a permit." George is drinking alcohol and Wyatt passes him a lit joint. George exclaims, "Marijuana. Lord have mercy; is that what that is?" He is reluctant to try it initially, stating that he "has enough problems with the booze" and he "can't afford to get hooked, leads to harder stuff." Wyatt assures him that this will not be the case, and he teaches him how to inhale the smoke. Wyatt gives George a fresh joint to smoke first thing in the morning and says, "Gives you whole new way of looking at the day."

The men camp at night because they have been refused at hotels during their journey due to their counterculture personas. Wyatt comments on this discrimination and George replies, "They scared of what you represent. Freedom. Don't ever tell anyone they're not free. They'll get busy killing and maiming to prove to you that they are. . . . It makes them dangerous." Later that night, men depicted as White rednecks attack them at their campsite, killing George. Lyrics in the background, "All he wanted was to be free," can be heard.

Easy Rider highlights normalized recreational illegal-drug use. In the film, illegal-drug use does not lead to violent or deviant behaviour or LSD-induced freak-outs. Nor does the film have an addiction-and-treatment narrative. Rather, the film celebrates altered states of consciousness and recreational illegal-drug use is represented as positive and alcohol as dangerous. The film explores concepts of freedom, idealism, and materialism. In many ways its violent ending represents the defeat of idealism rather than a promise of radical change and a contranarrative about the meanings of freedom associated with illegal-drug use. The film's critique of White America is represented partially by its stereotypical and demeaning depiction of southern White maleness as embodying ignorance and violence.

Chappaqua, The Trip, and *Easy Rider* are only a few of the films made during the 1960s. Jack Nicholson, Peter Fonda, and Dennis Hopper were significant producers of alternative narratives about illegal drugs during this era. Andy Warhol also made a number of underground films that depicted small scenes of normalized LSD use or references to LSD. Youth during this era rediscovered the book and film production, *Alice in Wonderland* (1951), a psychedelic film, partially spurred on by Jefferson Airplane's song "White Rabbit," which was released on their 1967 album *Surrealistic Pillow*. The British production *Yellow Submarine* (1968) is also viewed as a psychedelic LSD film. It is an animated film that depicts the Beatles and "Lucy in the Sky with Diamonds" and other songs are

Easy Rider. Source: Columbia Pictures/Photofest. © Columbia Pictures.

on the soundtrack. Drug-film expert Michael Starks claims that *Yellow Submarine* is "often regarded as a paean of praise to LSD" and it "led an entire generation through acid."[12] These films bring to the screen images of positive drug use and the value of altered states of consciousness and mind-expanding drugs. *Psych-Out,*[13] *I Love You, Alice B. Toklas,* and *Skidoo* were produced in 1968. All three films can be seen as Hollywood productions that attempt dramatic and comic explorations of the "hippie" drug-using culture in the 1960s. Unlike the more naturalistic films discussed above, illegal-drug use and youth are represented as stereotypical and constructed from the gaze of conventional society rather than the counterculture.

Alice's Restaurant (1969) also depicts normalized marijuana use, but this comedy's main focus is on the counterculture lifestyle, a critique of law enforcement, the Vietnam War, and Arlo Guthrie's music. It is more successful in portraying counterculture life and recreational illegal-drug use during this era. In one moving scene, both Arlo and Pete Seeger play Woody Guthrie's song "Car Car Song" to Woody as he lies in his hospital bed. In the film, a distinction is made between marijuana and heroin use. An underlying narrative in *Alice's Restaurant* centres on the plight of Shelly, an artistic and sensitive young White man and recovering heroin user who has just left the hospital. He stays with Alice and Ray at the church they have bought and renovated. However, soon he begins to use heroin again, and he is confronted by Ray and Alice. Ray is confrontational and he hits Shelly. Distressed, Shelly leaves his friends and returns to the city, where he dies all alone from a heroin overdose. Heroin is not demonized; rather, Shelly's relapse is viewed as stemming from his depression and psychological angst. The hospital is depicted as the "appropriate" site for treatment for addiction, and confrontational intervention is depicted as "backfiring."

These 60s counterculture films normalize recreational marijuana use, Whiteness, and middle-class and counterculture lifestyles (although *Alice's Restaurant* does have an ethnically diverse cast). They are a contrast to later films that celebrate excessive use, such as comedic "stoner flicks" and alternative films that challenge the war on drugs. Sixties counterculture films offer ruptures to official addiction and redemption narratives. Illegal drugs, especially marijuana, LSD, and cocaine, are taken for pleasure in these films without permanent harm. Conventional society rather than drugs is represented as dangerous and misguided. Film directors and scriptwriters during the 60s era associated the use of drugs like LSD, peyote, and mescaline with transformational and mystical experiences. On the screen, we understood, as in real life, that these experiences might not always be enjoyable. Yet they could be a source of understanding, transcendence, and social change. LSD and marijuana consumption did not cause the 60s counterculture movement. Nor is ecstasy the cause of the dance culture that emerged in Britain in the 1990s; rather, in both instances, specific drugs "contributed to one element" of the " 'emotional community' of those involved."[14] These drugs also contributed to the political community of those involved.

Of course, not all illegal-drug films produced in the 1960s depicted illegal drugs as positive. *Alice's Restaurant* (1969), for example, shows the dangers of heroin overdose, and a few films were much more intent on linking sex and illegal-drug use with excess and problematic legal-drug use (See *Valley of the Dolls* [1967]) and with violence. The film *High* (1967) is a black comedy that captures an emerging White youth culture pushing against the barriers of conservative Canada. However, it also perpetuates myths about the intersections of illegal-drug use, criminality, violence, and sexual freedom. In the film, marijuana use is associated with murder. *Riot on Sunset Strip* (1967) provides a template for the later production *Joe* (1970), for it too depicts an avenging father who goes after "hippies" after his daughter is supplied with LSD and sexually assaulted. Other films, such as *Come on Baby, Light My Fire* (1970), linked drugs with sex, violence, and trouble.[15]

In the United States, supporting his law-and-order mandate, a backlash occurred with the election of Richard Nixon for president in 1968. Nixon declared a "War on Drugs" and passed the Controlled Substance Act in 1970. In order to carry out his administration's more punitive drug-prohibition initiatives, the Drug Enforcement Administration (DEA) was formed in 1973. In Canada, youth optimism in some quarters of Canada was expressed in "Trudeaumania," helping to bring about the election of the Liberal candidate Pierre Trudeau as prime minister in 1968. His government supported the federally funded Le Dain Commission in 1969 to examine youth drug use. The final report recommended the decriminalization of marijuana (although to date the Canadian government has failed to carry out these recommendations). However, law enforcement (especially the RCMP), the Canadian Medical Association (through divisions among members), and the Council on Drug Abuse (created by the pharmaceutical industry) successfully opposed decriminalization.[16] In response to increased recreational drug use by youth in Britain, the second Brian Commission published in 1965 sought changes in drug policy in which special psychiatrists rather than general practitioners would be allowed to provide maintenance in special treatment clinics. In 1967, the Dangerous Drugs Act and the subsequent Misuse of Drugs Act brought British drug policy more in line with the United Nation's Single Convention on Drugs, which it had signed in 1961. The United States was instrumental in pushing forward "a global drug prohibition regime" through the signing of the United Nation's Single Convention on Drugs.[17] The United States, Canada, and Britain are signatories. The list of criminalized drugs expanded as synthetic drugs such as LSD and amphetamines were discovered and later criminalized. In all three nations, LSD possession and sale were criminalized in the 1960s.

Performance and the end of the 60s

The British film *Performance* (1970) provides a lens through which to explore the excesses of the London counterculture scene and the end of the 60s through the character Turner (played by Mick Jagger), characterized as a reclusive ex-rock star, and Chas, an East London gangster who is on the run from his bosses following a violent and bloody hit that was a mistake. Chas ends up hiding out at Turner's home. The film brings together the British gangster genre with rock and roll and counterculture aesthetics. The cast is almost entirely White. The producers exploited Mick Jagger's reputation as a young man whose music and reputation were viewed as being on the edge, and they capitalized on his musical talents in the film.

It was reported that vast quantities of drugs were taken on-screen and offscreen during the production of the film.[18] Drug use is normalized in the film, and double exposures and blurred images capture states of consciousness and Chas's psychic and physical transformation after ingesting magic mushrooms. We see him being dressed in "Middle Eastern" dress and Turner's rooms are filled with "foreign" artefacts from Morocco, including a hookah in the corner of his bedroom. We are also introduced to two White women living with Turner, Pherber and Lucy. In a number of scenes, the women are nude and they are represented as willing partners in free love. Although drug use is central to the film, not all drug use is depicted equally. In one scene, Turner's girlfriend Pherber is shown injecting drugs into her backside; she does this by standing nude with her back to a full length mirror as she turns her head to see where to inject herself. Turner admonishes her, saying, "You shoot too much of that shit, Pherber."

The following morning, after Chas experiments with mushrooms, his hideout is discovered by the gangsters looking for him. Several tough-looking men arrive to take him away. Chas walks into Turner's room, and as Turner lowers his head, Chas shoots him in the head. This key scene is interpreted by many, similar to the murders at the end of *Easy Rider* (1969), as the end of the counterculture. Violence rather than peace prevails. Yet the final scene in *Performance* is ambiguous; as we see Chas being driven away, he looks out the window and we see the face of Turner.

Similar to other illegal-drug films, Pherber is depicted as more involved with "bad" drugs than Turner. The women in the film are also represented as sexually more aggressive. The film does venture into some gender bending in relation to heterosexual and bisexual sexuality, but it never strays far from its sexualized gaze on the women in the film. Illegal-drug use is also associated with the Other, achieved through the use of hookahs and foreign lands like Morocco.

The British production *Performance* (1970), the Canadian production *High* (1967), and the U.S. productions *The Trip* (1967), *Skidoo* (1968), *I Love you, Alice B. Toklas* (1968), and *Easy Rider* (1969) exemplify normalized illegal-drug use without an addiction or treatment narrative. Whereas

The Trip, Skidoo, I Love you, Alice B. Toklas, and *Easy Rider* support exploring altered states of consciousness, *High* (1967) eventually associates marijuana use with prostitution, theft, and murder. *Performance* is more ambiguous, as is its last scene. Altered states of consciousness are not condemned, excepting drugs that can be injected, such as heroin; however, where drugs lead one is questioned in the film. The innocence and hopefulness represented in the narrative of *The Trip* is problematized to a certain extent in *Easy Rider* and *Performance.*

BACKLASH FILMS: ADDICTION AND DEGRADATION

A host of what may be seen as backlash movies also emerged in the 70s, such as *Joe* (1970), *The French Connection* (1970), *Panic in Needle Park* (1971), and *Coffy* (1973). Their message was loud and clear: the summer of love is over. In these films, illegal-drug use is a criminal matter. Men who use and sell illegal drugs are constructed as criminal and violent. Rather than represent illegal drugs as positive, these films focus on illegal-drug use as negative, even though their central narrative is on the drug trade. For example, the heroin users depicted in *The Panic in Needle Park* (1971) are portrayed in an endless, inescapable cycle of heroin addiction, arrest, and imprisonment. At the beginning of the film, viewers are introduced to Helen. She is a young White, middle-class woman from Indiana who is now living in New York City. She looks quite sick, and we learn that she has just had an abortion and that she is bleeding heavily. Her artist boyfriend, Marcus, is indifferent to her plight; however, his drug dealer Bobby is not. He tenderly covers her with a blanket, offers her his scarf, and later visits her in the hospital.

Bobby is depicted as a poor White hustler (played by Al Pacino). He is also a heroin user and small-time dealer who has been in and out of jail all of his life, including two times in Lexington, the mandatory-treatment prison. In the film, Helen represents innocent White middle-class America. She tells Bobby that grass brownies at her university are the extent of her drug experience. It is implied that she left Indiana because something traumatic occurred. Bobby represents the urban poor and family dysfunction. His older brother is depicted as a burglar and we never learn about his parents. Helen hooks up with Bobby even though she knows he is using heroin. She and Bobby are shown living in Needle Park in single rooms in rundown hotels that house the poor. Both Bobby and Helen are likable characters and we sympathize with them in the film. Bobby is depicted as tender and nurturing. When Helen first sees Bobby preparing to inject heroin, she tells him, "You'll kill yourself doing that." He replies that he is not "hooked. I'm just chipping." When Helen meets Bobby's associates, they want to know if she is "feeding his arm." When Helen comments that she likes Bobby's life and his friends, he warns her, "Some friends, I've been beat by half the people out here." Bobby's friends are multiethnic. This characterization stands out because the majority of illegal-drug films prior to the 1970s, with the exception of anti-Asian and Latino representations, are notable for their Whiteness.

In several scenes the camera lingers on a needle as it punctures the skin, drawing blood into the needle before injecting heroin into the vein. However, in many ways, rather than contributing to the iconic heroin symbolism in other illegal-drug films, the makeshift needles in the film remind viewers how clean hypodermic needles were rare commodities in the 1970s for poor users (and they remain illegal and unobtainable in many U.S. states today). The camera also lingers on heroin boiling in bottle caps (rather than spoons). There is a heroin drought, a panic on the streets, and the film portrays a number of Bobby's associates hanging out on a park bench in Needle Park, many of them dope sick. In one scene, Helen and Bobby are lying in bed, and Bobby is shown nodding out, fully clothed. Helen is shown being amorous towards Bobby, but he is not interested. He tells her, "When I'm doing junk, I can't."

Soon Helen is also using heroin and she quickly becomes addicted. Fearing for her, Bobby tells her that "I'm a germ. You should split." Helen stays and her heroin use escalates. When Bobby is arrested, she visits him in jail. She tells him that when he gets out they will go to the "country" and start afresh. They profess their love for each other. Once Bobby is back home, he learns that she has been working in the sex trade to support her heroin habit. Bobby is furious. He hits her for "peddling her ass." Helen no longer looks innocent, and it is made clear that she has even prostituted herself to Bobby's brother and a young adolescent boy. The film shows a number of scenes in which Bobby's friends shoot up, and heroin consumption is followed by nodding out to such an extent that needles are left hanging in the users' arms.

Bobby and Helen finally go to the country for a day. They buy a little puppy there and the camera follows them as they walk in a field of green trees and grass. Bobby says, "This what you want," referring to their happy little "family" in the country where change and renewal seem possible. They talk about ending their drug use and making a "fresh start." Helen suggests that they move away from "Needle Park," but Bobby argues, "That is where I live." On their way home from the country, Bobby prepares one last hit for Helen in the washroom of the ferry that they are travelling on.

Bobby and Helen's attempts to get clean are never realized. Needle Park is inescapable. Shortly after they arrive back in the city, Helen is arrested for "pushing pills," and a young cop who has taken an interest in her asks her if she has ever been in jail. He tells her it is "like a zoo . . . [they] see a cute chick like you, take your brains and scramble them for breakfast." He tells her that she is going to get one to three years' prison time, but if she rats on Bobby, she can go free. Bobby has finally been able to secure himself a job with a local heroin supplier. He is employed regularly and

The Panic in Needle Park. Source: Twentieth Century Fox/Photofest. © Twentieth Century Fox.

his fortunes have finally turned around. Fearful of prison time, Helen rats on Bobby. When the police arrest him, Bobby sees Helen with them and he yells out at her, "I was gonna marry you!" By the end of the film, it is clear that there is no hope for Helen's redemption. When Bobby is finally released from prison, Helen is at the gates waiting for him. At first he is depicted ignoring her, walking away from her. Then he looks back and says, "Well?" and they are shown walking away together. At the end of the film, we are left with the impression that Helen and Bobby will continue on their downward descent in the city and that betrayal and heroin addiction will continue to characterize their relationship.

In this film, Helen's drug use is sexualized, and addiction is depicted as a life of degradation, prostitution, and an appetite for drugs that surpasses Bobby's. In contrast, Bobby's drug use is not sexualized; in fact, he is portrayed as lacking any interest in sex when he uses heroin. Bobby is the prototype of the recidivist "criminal addict." The subtext of this film, and others discussed in this section, is that harsher drug laws are needed to contain the "epidemic" and narratives about "criminal addicts" rather than "addiction as disease" prevail. Drug "treatment" is mostly absent from the film narrative, similar to later films such as *Scarface* (1983), *Clockers* (1995), *The Supergrass* (1985), *Go* (1999), *Narc* (2002), and *25th Hour*

(2002). In *The Panic in Needle Park*, the country is represented as pure and a site of renewal, while the city is represented as corrupt. The film makes clear that vulnerable White women are at risk in the city to the lures of poor men and illegal drugs.

In *The Panic in Needle Park*, Bobby's friends are characterized as multiethnic, and he eventually works for a Black man who is depicted as a high-level supplier. Although Whiteness continues to be the normative representation in British, Canadian, and U.S. film, in the 1970s, a number of U.S. illegal-drug films included Black and Latino actors and actresses. However, not all of these representations are positive. The 1972 U.S. film production *Lady Sings the Blues* is very loosely based on Billie Holiday's life from 1915–1959. Diana Ross plays Billie in the film, and her narcotics addiction is linked to sexual assault, racial oppression, and the pressures of living on the road as a singer. The film follows her rise to fame and her troubles with narcotic addiction. When Billie uses narcotics, she is represented as childlike, unaware of her surroundings, talking to herself, and barely able to function. In one scene, when her boyfriend attempts to keep her from using, she picks up a razor and threatens him with it: he says, "You'd kill me for it, wouldn't you?" Billie tries to stop using and she enters a private sanatorium where, gradually withdrawing from narcotics, she is shown reclining in a lawn chair on the grounds with a blanket over her. Ignoring her doctor's protests that if she "stops cold the shock to her system could kill her," two police officers from the narcotics division walk up to her and arrest her for an earlier charge of possession of narcotics and take her to jail. One of the police officers says to the doctor, "Don't give us any trouble. It's still illegal and you know it." Next we see Billie being booked and thrown into a padded room. She is depicted going through withdrawal, screaming and slamming herself against the walls. Matrons enter the cell and put a straitjacket on her. Her hair is wild, she mumbles, trembles, and makes retching motions. She seems catatonic and unaware of her surroundings. Through a montage of black-and-white photos, her time in prison is briefly shown. Following her release from prison, Billie is shown using narcotics again due to the pressure of being on the road. The film does make clear that, due to her felony charge for narcotics, Billie was unable to get a license to play in clubs in New York. She dies at the age of 44 from cirrhosis of the liver.

The actual inclusion of Black, Asian, and Latino actors in film, rather than White actors playing racialized characters, speaks to some of the social and political shifts in U.S. society and elsewhere for marginalized peoples, including the civil-rights and Black Power movements, aboriginal, Puerto Rican, Chicana/o movements, and other Third World liberation movements around the world. Along with these shifts came heightened policing of these groups, especially in the United States.[19] Following challenges to White hegemony in political, social, and economic spheres, racialized people were often represented by conventional filmmakers as urban, poor, criminal, violent, addicted to and/or trafficking in illegal drugs. However, representations are not static, and a number of film producers in the 1970s, including Black film producers, produced counterhegemonic representations that challenged conventional film representations.

The blaxploitation film *Cleopatra Jones* (1973) is exceptional for depicting a strong, beautiful young Black woman as the main character. In many ways the character Cleopatra Jones (played by Tamara Dobson) represents Black power and women's independence. Her ability to defend herself and others, and her Afro hairstyle and stylish clothes, appealed to movie viewers, especially Black audiences. Yet, rather than directly challenging the state, Cleopatra Jones is a law agent. However, Cleopatra is also represented as subversive because she sets out to protect Black people from a corrupt and violent drug-trafficking family headed by a White woman. In this film and other blaxploitation films, the White criminal-justice system is portrayed as corrupt and complicit in brutalizing both innocent and criminalized Black people.[20] *Cleopatra Jones* (1973) includes one of the first film depictions of a community-run rehab centre in the inner city, run by Black men and women. Outside of a very brief depiction of a young Black man going through withdrawal, the rehab process is not shown, although moral support by treatment workers is emphasized in the film. Nevertheless, it is important to note that the centre is community-run, is linked to Black Power politics, and seems to be administered and run by nonprofessionals. In a similar vein, the blaxploitation film *Coffy* (1973) also depicts a rehab centre, and it is represented in the film as a legitimate and sympathetic response to drug use and addiction. However, unlike the rehab centre in *Cleopatra Jones*, the centre in *Coffy* is in a medicalized institutional setting. In both films, we see the emergence of representations of illegal-drug use (cocaine and heroin) situated in the inner city and its impact on poor White and Black people living there. As mentioned earlier, and just as significant, we begin to see the emergence of Black men represented as illegal-drug dealers. Although these films represent Black Power politics, they are not serious endorsements for fighting the system. Rather, in *Cleopatra Jones*, the main character is depicted as the arm of the state, a secret agent, and *Coffy*'s main character, of the same name, is depicted as a lone vigilante who goes on a rampage killing drug dealers who have infiltrated the inner city after her sister is exposed to illegal drugs. Both films speak to the failure of the White criminal justice system to protect Black people and communities against crime, violence, and illegal-drug use, addiction, and drug trafficking.

A number of researchers note that the population of heroin users in the United States shifted following World War II. Whereas most heroin users were White males confined to large urban centres, following the war, Black and Hispanic use increased.[21] However, this was not the case in Britain and Canada, where White use prevailed. During and following WW II, Black and Hispanic people moved to urban centres throughout the United States looking for work. Both Hispanic and Black people experienced institutionalized racism, but Jim Crow laws and ideology and legal segregation shaped the lives of Black people. Agar and Reisinger state that during the civil rights movement a "powerful mix of hope and degradation" shaped the lives of Black urban youth during this era. They state that there was hope that the walls of institutional racism would crumble, yet youth were fully aware of their very public position of "social marginality."[22] The authors go on to explain that most people do not become addicted to heroin, or other drugs, because they are marginalized or poor; yet the circumstances of hope and open marginalization culminated in urban Black people being a "risk group" for heroin addiction and shifting international distribution patterns made the drug more available,[23] especially in inner cities in the 1960s and 1970s.[24]

In addition, some U.S. soldiers were exposed to and used heroin in smoking form in Vietnam. However, nine out of ten soldiers who used heroin in Vietnam did not use again after they returned home.[25] The small percentage that continued to use found that buying heroin in the United States was much more difficult than in Vietnam, where it was cheap, readily available, and culturally acceptable. Their return and subsequent use of heroin at home probably contributed to shifts in drug-use patterns and selling and film representations. Yet unlike the characters portrayed in films like *The Panic in Needle Park*, studies of returning Vietnam vets made clear that addiction is not inevitable and is often situational.

I am not suggesting that visible heroin use in inner cities in the United States during the late 1960s and early 1970s did not contribute to social discord; it did. Similar social discord emerged again when crack cocaine emerged in the 1980s in inner-city neighbourhoods. Low prices, availability, and initial lack of user knowledge or drug "norms" to curtail problematic use presented a number of personal and social problems for families and neighbourhoods, including highly visible addiction linked to lack of access to private spaces, increased police surveillance, and drug-trade violence. These social problems affect a number of inner-city communities today. Researchers have brought our attention to the racialized nature of police profiling and U.S government complicity in the drug trade.[26] These social and political events are touched on in illegal-drug films representations from the 1970s on (e.g., *The Panic in Needle Park* [1971]). Films labelled blaxploitation, such as *Superfly* (1972) and *Cleopatra Jones* (1973), speak to some of these themes.

COCAINE AND CRACK SCARES: WHITENESS AND ADDICTION

Whereas a number of films in the 1970s focused on heroin use and trafficking, illegal-drug films produced in the 1980s and 1990s brought their lens to cocaine use and trafficking. In the United States, cocaine use increased during the 1970s. Early on, due to its high price, powder cocaine use was mostly confined to middle- and upper-class people, and it was seen as the party drug of the rich. In 1984, a new form of cocaine became available, called "crack."[27] Cocaine powder can be turned into crack by a fairly simple chemical procedure that produces "hard, smokable pellets" or rocks.[28] Inhaling smoke, rather than sniffing cocaine powder, provides a route of administration that delivers the drug more rapidly to the bloodstream. Smoking the drug provides a "quicker, more intense" effect, yet crack is not purer or stronger than powder cocaine or freebase forms; rather, crack usually contains between 10 and 40 percent cocaine.[29] Freebase is quite pure, and powder cocaine can range in purity from 100 percent to as low as 10 percent. Crack is easy to make and it can be sold in small quantities, making it especially appealing to poor users who cannot afford to buy powder cocaine, which is traditionally sold by the gram at much higher prices. Given the racialization of poverty in the United States, poor inner-city crack users were most often Black and Latino/a, and middle- and upper-class powder-cocaine users were associated with Whiteness.

Drug researchers Craig Reinarman and Harry Levine point out that although the media and all political parties in the United States helped forge the "crack scare," which began in the mid-1980s, New Right conservative ideology focused on crack as an all-purpose scapegoat for the "worsening conditions in the inner cities."[30] Cocaine in crack form was vilified and blamed for a host of social problems, its effects depicted as being immediately addicting, in which users lose all control. Crack was portrayed by the media and politicians as an epidemic destroying individuals, homes, and communities. In 1989, President George Bush Senior warned Americans that crack was "murdering our children,"[31] and crack continues to be associated with racialized poor inner-city users.[32]

It took a while for film representations to capture this phenomenon. Early film narratives centred on powder cocaine and those most associated with the drug, White middle-class users. In films like *Bright Lights, Big City* (1988), *Clean and Sober* (1988), and *Postcards from the Edge* (1990), we are introduced to White, privileged characters who use cocaine. In *Traffic* (2000), an affluent young White adolescent who uses crack is depicted.

In *Bright Lights, Big City* (1988), the main character is a young White man named Jamie (played by Michael J. Fox), an aspiring writer who works as an editor for a prestigious magazine. He uses cocaine to party and to numb his feeling after the death of his mother and his abandonment by his wife. It is made clear at the beginning of the film that the cocaine depicted in the film comes from Bolivia, and it is the drug of choice by White privileged partygoers in Manhattan. Jamie's cocaine use escalates and interferes with his work and family relationships until he has an emotional epiphany. In the film, cessation from problematic cocaine use is treated as a matter of willpower and moving through trauma and grief. Drug treatment is not depicted and Jamie's loss of employment is not shown as "hitting rock bottom." Compared to earlier and later depictions of cocaine users, he suffers little due to his cocaine use. Jamie's cocaine use is similar to that of Syd in the film *London* (2005). He is also a young White man who hangs out with affluent friends in New York City. Syd consumes huge amounts of cocaine and alcohol; however, treatment narratives are absent and he does not suffer greatly for his use. In contrast to *London* and *Bright Lights, Big City, Clean and Sober, Postcards from the Edge,* and *Traffic* explore cessation from illegal-drug use in drug-treatment centres. *New Jack City* (1991) and *Losing Isaiah* (1995) introduce viewers to addiction as disease and mandatory treatment as the site of treatment for poor and racialized people.

Bright Lights, Big City (1988), *Clean and Sober* (1988), *London* (2005), and *Postcards for the Edge* (1990) are good examples of the dichotomy ever present in media representations of upper-class White powder cocaine users in contrast to poor Black crack users. Although diverse films depict drug treatment and AA/NA meetings, as we will see in this chapter, where and how they are represented is instructive about class and race politics today. In the film *Clean and Sober* we hear a phone ringing. Darryl, a not so young White man, wakes up in bed. He answers the phone and speaks to Martin—a coworker—who is heard asking him about some money that is missing from an escrow account. We understand now that Darryl is well-off financially. There is a naked woman lying next to Darryl. After getting off the phone, Darryl picks up a mirror and snorts a couple of lines of cocaine on it. He passes the mirror to the woman; however, she does not respond. He kisses her and then realizes that she is dead. She has overdosed.

In *Clean and Sober*, Darryl is depicted as "addicted" to cocaine. He is portrayed as in denial even though he has gone into debt and embezzled $90,000 from his real-estate company to pay for his drug use. Darryl does visit a clinic, and here we see drug withdrawal linked with aggression, as demonstrated by a Black male patient at the clinic who smashes the television and tries to escape while going through withdrawal. In a similar vein, when Darryl leaves the clinic, he goes on a violent rampage in his office in an attempt to find his cocaine stash.

In the film, Darryl finds redemption through honesty and sobriety. He enters another treatment facility that is highly regulated and controlled. Patients are required to have urine testing and phone calls and visitors are restricted. Patients are encouraged to adopt an AA/NA construction of an "addict" identity, and after his release we see the continuing importance of AA/NA and the relationship between the recovering "addict" and the "sponsor." In the film, addiction is constructed as physically dangerous, as seen by the death of the young woman at the beginning of film who overdoses from cocaine use, and the death of Charlie, Darryl's love interest, who dies in a car accident during her relapse into drug use. In the film, abstinence and embracing the disease model of addiction are depicted as the only route to salvation.

Postcards from the Edge (1990) also depicts AA/NA-style meetings. The film, set in Los Angeles, features the fictional character of Suzanne, loosely based on the life of Carrie Fisher. In the film, Suzanne is characterized as addicted and out of control, and her drug use is jeopardizing her fledgling film career. At the beginning of the film she is shown taking cocaine and prescription pills, and she blacks out and overdoses while in bed with a man she does not know and whose name she cannot remember. Here we see Suzanne hit "rock bottom," a concept that emerged in the 1950s addiction discourse. She enters a drug rehab centre where an AA/NA model of treatment is offered and she sees a counsellor. The rehab scene is brief, however, because the film focuses on her life outside of rehab, especially her dysfunctional relationship with her celebrity mother, who is depicted as a well-known film star who drinks heavily. In a passing reference, her father is said to be worse than she is.

After her overdose at the beginning of the film, Suzanne is shown relapsing once. She takes some pills from her mother's medicine cabinet, but she forces herself to vomit them up moments later. After that there are no other relapse scenes, and it is implied in the film that Suzanne successfully ceases using drugs. There is one interesting bit of dialogue that deconstructs the legal/illegal divide. After leaving rehab, Suzanne stays at her mother's home, and her mother asks her if she minds if she has a drink.

Suzanne responds, "Do you mind if I drop acid?"

M: "Dear, I drink socially."

S: "I took acid socially"

Although the dialogue above disrupts notions about illegal and legal drugs, it also positions LSD in a similar category as alcohol. LSD "addiction" is highly unlikely.[33] In the film, we see a shift to addiction as disease rather than a particular drug being the source of addiction. All substances in the film are conflated and abstinence is required. Female sexual immorality, overdose, and loss of employment are some of the risks associated with Suzanne's cocaine use. In order to continue working in the film industry after she leaves rehab, Suzanne must undergo urine tests, and she must remain under her mother's guardianship. However, outside of these infringements on her freedom, she is not shown as having any long-term effects from her cocaine use.

As discussed briefly in the Introduction, in the U.S. film *Traffic* (2001), viewers are introduced to an upper-class teenaged illegal-drug user, Caroline; however, she smokes crack instead of using powder cocaine, and this makes all the difference in relation to how she is portrayed in the film. Crack use is racialized and associated with the urban poor, and it is depicted as instantly addictive by filmmakers and some researchers.[34] Caroline is the daughter of the U.S. drug czar, a young, innocent, White, blue-eyed, blonde, high-achieving student in a private high-school uniform. She is introduced to crack by her boyfriend Seth, but unlike her boyfriend, when Caroline smokes crack she is depicted as physically transformed on the screen: her head rolls back, she sweats, her eyes roll, and she looks disoriented. We watch Caroline's rapid descent into crack addition and moral decline until she is confronted by her father and sent to a private residential drug-treatment centre. At an NA meeting at the treatment centre, a man speaks about his "powerlessness over alcohol; my disease says I don't have a disease. It's a disease, allergy of the body and obsession of the mind." However, Caroline rejects treatment and her father's wishes and she runs away and goes to the black inner city. Caroline goes to the home of a young Black man who is a drug dealer. Later we see them lying naked on a bed and the camera zooms in as he injects drugs into a vein in her foot.[35] She lays back and closes her eyes and the black man resumes having sex with her. In keeping with the addiction narrative, Caroline's sexual encounter with the Black dealer in the inner city is constructed as "hitting rock bottom." Later we see Caroline in a hotel room with an older White man. It is made clear that she is now prostituting herself. In a dramatic scene, taking the law into his own hands, her father kicks down the hotel room door and rescues her.

In class-biased, sexist, White-supremacist America, a White girl's downfall and degradation is constructed as addiction and sexual corruption at the hands of a Black man. This is an old story, one that has historically supported the lynching of Black men and harsher drug laws. Film representations, from the early 1970s on, represent poor urban Black men as violent predators who traffic drugs.[36] Drawing from old representations of the "yellow menace" in earlier film representations, containing the racialized drug "epidemic" takes on new significance in *Traffic*.

It is not until Caroline is later rescued by her father that she finally comes to terms with her "addiction." The final scene of the film depicts the drug czar and his wife watching their daughter Caroline speaking at an NA meeting. She looks quite drab compared to earlier representations of her. Her blonde hair is pulled back and her clothes are no longer stylish. She tells the people at the meeting that she is just taking things a day at a time. As she leaves the podium and sits down beside her parents, a man asks the drug czar if he has anything to share. He replies, "My name is Robert, and my wife Barbara and I are here to support our daughter Caroline. And we're here to listen." The narrative affirms the White upper-class nuclear family as a site of support and addiction narratives as central to the recovery process.

In *Traffic*, White fears about crack and inner-city crime and Black men and White women's sexual morality are represented through the character of Caroline. Unlike Seth, who is able to control his crack use, Caroline is not. The Black dealer that Caroline runs to after she leaves treatment is depicted as capable of violence when he holds a gun to Seth's head when he comes looking for Caroline with her father. Caroline's crack use is sexualized and her rapid descent and degradation, and abandonment of White upper-class values and space, is dramatized in the film.

The film *Traffic* (2000) and other films, such as *Clean and Sober* (1988), include scenes of "escape" from drug-treatment institutions and failure to comply with rules. These representations are constructed as individual failure to comply with treatment policy and evidence of denial about one's addiction and "disease." The fact that "escape" or failure to complete a treatment program may be a rejection of institutionalized policy and practice, rather than individual failure, is not explored (see *Curtis's Charm* [1995], *Trainspotting* [1996], *Gridlock'd* [1997], *Protection* [2000], and *A Scanner Darkly* [2006] for some critique of drug treatment). The political implications of rejecting rigid rules and addiction models and human-rights infringements (such as urine tests, lockdown facilities, and aggressive group therapies) are not often explored to any degree in illegal-drug films. Rather, these disciplinary techniques are normalized and represented as natural and necessary components of treatment. However, the degree of infringement and discipline shifts, depending on who is being treated.

New Jack City and *Losing Isaiah:* mandatory treatment

In contrast to the affluent White powder-cocaine and crack-using characters depicted in *Clean and Sober* (1988) and *Traffic* (2000), the films *New Jack City* (1991) and *Losing Isaiah* (1995) focus on poor racialized crack users in the inner city. These films, similar to *Bright Lights, Big City* and *Clean and Sober,* are set in Reagan's presidency, in which conservative ideology and law and order, rather than social support, prevail. Nancy Reagan was author of the simple mantra "Just say no to drugs," and she became a leading antidrug crusader by visiting schools and recruiting prominent politicians to support her cause. Her husband and his administration provided the means to carry out the other legal, social, and political aspects of the war on drugs. Reported by the media, President Reagan and his wife, along with a number of politicians of all political stripes, claimed that crack cocaine was destroying the nation and killing generations of children. However, crack was never widely used in the United States or elsewhere; instead, its use was confined to a small percentage of the population, and claims about rising crack use mostly occurred when drug-use rates had stabilized.[37]

In *New Jack City* (1991), a blaxploitation film directed by Mario Van Peebles, the "crack crisis" is depicted on the screen. The film is set in New York in 1986, during the Reagan era. Crack is represented as dangerous and addiction to it is inescapable. Urban poverty and Black-on-Black violence is represented as the norm. Instead of representing the ethos of Black Panther and other liberation groups that sought to challenge the "system" and the "man," in this Blaxploitation film, and others, Black-on-Black fighting and becoming the "man," or the agent for the man, dominates the narrative.[38]

In *New Jack City*, Pookie (played by Chris Rock) is depicted as a poor young Black crack dealer who becomes addicted to the drug. He is shown acting manic and sweating profusely every time he smokes crack. We see him attack a young woman in an alley, punching her uncontrollably. Scotty (played by Ice-T), a Black undercover police officer, pulls him away, but

Pookie resists, crying out, "Crack shit got a hold of me!," associating crack use with random violence. Scotty brings him to a mandatory drug-treatment centre where we see Pookie being dragged away by two men as he resists.[39] Later, we see him in a crowded room with a diverse group of people. As Pookie leaves the room, we hear the drug treatment facilitator say: "Simple program. Only ask that you don't use or drink one day at a time. Don't leave before the miracle happens. This program has revolving doors. Just because you go out doesn't necessarily mean you can come back in." In this line the script writers, reflecting treatment practice, subvert the original AA/NA philosophy that users are always welcome back. Film representations make clear that racialized crack users have only one chance in treatment, and if they relapse they are thrown out of the program (unlike White powder-cocaine users depicted in *Clean and Sober* and White crack users in *Traffic*, who are shown entering treatment more than once, being welcomed back, and not punished for their relapses).

Pookie is depicted lying in bed shivering. Later, we see him sitting on a kitchen counter, crying and shaking. His withdrawal from crack is represented as agonizing and lasting for many days, even though in reality there is no physiological withdrawal. During his time at the mandatory-treatment centre, there are a number of NA-type meetings in the same room. During one meeting, the camera zooms in on two women, one White, one Black. They recount how they were powerless to stop using crack, even how pregnancy and motherhood could not deter them from the drug.

Scotty watches over Pookie's progress and helps him in his recovery. Pookie is shown again in an NA-type group, and he says, "When I get out, just take everything one day at a time." His fellow inmates cheer him on. Pookie begins to work under cover with Scotty, but he succumbs to crack use again, and his fall back into addiction leads to his murder by a drug gang. At the end of the film, a White policeman says to Scotty, "This whole drug shit, it's not a Black thing, it's not a White thing. It's a death thing. Death doesn't give a shit about colour." In fact, the outcome of drug use and selling is all about "colour" and class. In the United States, it is poor and racialized users who have less access to better quality drugs (legal or illegal), health care, and addiction services. Increasingly, criminal-justice initiatives like drug courts, family courts, and prison are the favoured point of entry for drug treatment, rather than health and addiction services outside of it. Poor and racialized users and sellers are vastly overrepresented in prison in the United States, Canada, and Britain, even though their overall drug-use rates and participation in the drug trade are no higher than their White counterparts.[40] Because *New Jack City* does not highlight White crack use to any extent, the narrative could be construed as heightening fears that addiction and the "ghetto epidemic" will soon be encroaching into White middle- and upper-class space.

In the film *Losing Isaiah* (1994), we are introduced to a Black homeless woman named Khaila (played by Halle Berry). She is depicted as wild-haired, dirty, and using crack, living in an abandoned building in the inner city. Men hang around outside the building, and it is made explicit that she sells sex for crack when they yell at her, "Trade you some good stuff!" She has a newborn baby whom she abandons in a cardboard box. The camera quickly cuts to a close-up of her lighting a crack pipe: we see her puffing, and she blows out smoke, moaning softly in appreciation. Her eyes close and her head rolls back. Later, we see Khaila lying on a filthy bare mattress, bruised, her eye swollen. She runs outside looking for her baby, but the cardboard box is gone. She is wild-eyed and disoriented, and she is later arrested for stealing food in a store. We then see her on a bus filled mostly with other Black women wearing prison uniforms. They enter a building where a "tough" Black woman talks to the other prisoners from the front of the room. She says, "There are those of you who elected this program to cut your time. Well, if that's why you're here, you better turn around and get back on that bus. Because you won't last a day. This is work. Hard work. One mistake. One! And you're out on your based-head, pill-popping, alcoholic asses, back in the general population quicker than you can blink your eyes. Understand?" Similar to *New Jack City*, the original premises of AA are stripped from these film representations of mandatory treatment, except for the focus on abstinence. In U.S.-produced films, poor, racialized users are punished and required to undergo harsh mandatory treatment outside of and in prison. State-run boot camps, diversionary programs, prison, expulsion back to the general prison population, and punishment are represented as the route to redemption. Relapse is punished and participation is no longer voluntary.

Khaila stops using crack and eventually reunites with her baby, but prior to reuniting with her son she is shown working as a nanny caring for White children. She is now depicted as neat and tidy, and in the court scenes her hair is tied back and she appears modestly dressed in conventional "wasp" clothing and small pearl earrings. Throughout the film, Khaila's life is juxtaposed with the life of an affluent White female social worker who has custody of her child (see chapter 6 for a fuller discussion). It is made clear at the end of the film that, even though Khaila is sober and living a conventional lifestyle, she is not capable of raising her child without the support of the White family.

Early in the film, Khaila's crack use is sexualized. She represents White fears related to Black women's sexuality and reproduction and the crack epidemic. Media representations of "crack babies" and Black "welfare queens" draining already strained resources became familiar narratives as Reagan implemented cutbacks to social-welfare programs and drug use was constructed as "individual choice." The films *New Jack City* and *Losing Isaiah* perpetuate myths about cocaine and crack use and infants exposed to the drug. Neither film seriously examines U.S. drug-war policy or punitive federal and state responses to social problems, including harsher drug laws. In fact, *New Jack City* calls for harsher policy. From the mid-1980s on, new mandatory sentencing, harsher penalties for crack than for powder cocaine, the elimination of parole for federal drug offences, and police and DEA race profiling led to rising incarceration rates and drug-trade violence in the United States.[41] Illegal-drug use and addiction and other social problems were constructed as "individual moral choices" by conservative politicians and institutions.[42] Incarceration and state apprehension of infants of mothers who were thought to use crack also served to break apart families, especially poor Black and Latino/a families.[43] These illegal-drug films do not problematize these factors in any great depth. Nor is the contradrug scandal under President Reagan and the government's complicity in drug trafficking of cocaine explored; rather, it is erased from history in these films (see *Clear and Present Danger* [1994] for an examination of state complicity in the illegal-drug trade).

Representations of how illegal-drug users are induced to become and remain sober are diverse in film; however, poor and racialized users like the characters Khaila in *Losing Isaiah*, and Pookie, in *New Jack City*, are most often depicted in mandatory treatment and boot camps, and White middle- and upper-class users are depicted at drug-treatment centres. Since the 1970s, twelve-step, AA, and its counterpart Narcotics Anonymous models were adopted by drug-treatment institutions, jails, prisons, and the new drug courts, especially in the U.S. and Canada. Here the medical profession, addiction specialists, and self-help groups work with the criminal-justice system, and the original intent of AA meetings has been subverted. The value of open conversation without condemnation is compromised when confidentiality no longer exists and "relapse" is punished. Court and probation orders, and criminal justice diversion programs, have also subverted the voluntary model that was advocated by early AA advocates as a necessary component of healing. Today, AA/NA meetings are held throughout the world, and in the United States approximately 40 percent of those in attendance are there involuntarily.[44] The idea that the addiction-as-disease model would curb criminal-justice intervention has proved faulty. The fact that people who are believed to be suffering from a disease are criminalized and incarcerated to protect society is riddled with irony.

The disease/criminal model of addiction remains a prevalent representation in contemporary illegal-drug films. Although U.S.-produced films appear to be most attached to depictions of addiction as disease and "criminal addicts," British and Canadian films have contributed to this genre too. Furthermore, since the 1970s, individualistic psychological theorizing about the roots of addiction inform drug films: distant fathers, violent fathers, sexual assault, grief, absentee fathers, cold mothers, single-parent mothers, alcoholic moms, crack moms, progress and technology, stress, death, low self-esteem, thwarted dreams, thrill seeking, peer pressure, and subcultural deviance serve to catapult subjects into problematic illegal-drug use in these films. Psychological perspectives about addiction (which began to emerge in the 1950s but did not make their way into illegal-drug films until later), coupled with the addiction-as-disease paradigm, serve as a template for addiction narratives in illegal-drug films. Yet even when addiction as disease prevails in film, drug use is often represented as a matter of choice, an individual's moral responsibility, and as a crime. Furthermore, the drug and/or drugs are represented as dangerous and impossible to resist. Occasionally, economic and racial inequality are taken up in addiction narratives, but even when it appears, it is up to the individual illegal-drug user to break through these constraints and to redeem himself or herself through abstinence and redemption and, in some cases, prison time. Nonprofessional groups like NA, the state, the war on drugs, and prohibition are rarely scrutinized as shaping drug-use patterns and outcomes. Nor is drug prohibition seen as contributing to the harms associated with illegal-drug use.

ADDICTION NARRATIVES

Depictions of drug use and addiction in film are not homogeneous, nor do ideologies and myths about addiction and drugs progress in a linear fashion. In the 1960s, numerous films represented illegal-drug use as positive and addiction narratives were rare. Many films produced in the 1960s provided a critique of the illusionary divide separating legal and illegal drugs. These films explore LSD and altered states of consciousness. They provide a rupture in official drug discourse by presenting positive representations of illegal-drugs use, especially marijuana and psychedelics. Pleasure, transcendence, mystical experience, and healing are central themes in alternative-film narratives about drugs.

In the 1970s, community clinics and methadone maintenance are represented in illegal-drug films, in some ways mirroring new treatment options available at that time. By the 1980s, AA/NA and twelve-step programs, as well as ideas about addiction as disease, became the template for representations of drug treatment in illegal-drug films. Characters representing lay counsellors, social workers, and addiction-treatment workers began to appear in film. Behaviour-modification techniques and punishment are also portrayed (such as denial of privileges in treatment centres and the threat of expulsion) in depictions of drug-treatment centres in and out of prisons. Individualized psychological treatment appears in film but mostly for the rich (e.g., *Postcards from the Edge* [1990]). Stress, alcoholic parents, cold mothers, "crack" mothers, distant fathers, subcultural conflict, counterculture ideology, an alienating world, addictive personality, criminality, dysfunctional families, and the death of a loved one are all referenced as the root of addiction. The cure: treatment, counselling, abstinence, and, in most illegal-drug films, AA/NA. Drugs themselves, whether heroin or cocaine, are represented as instantly addicting. Nevertheless, individual choice and self-control are emphasized too, and film representations of twelve-step programs and AA/NA are depicted as the "commonsense" form of recovery. Separating the "addict" from drugs still remains the most popular form of cure in drug films. Yet addiction narratives are not linear, and, just as the criminal/disease model of addiction is rarely problematized in Western drug policy, often more than one addiction ideology is represented in the same film.

A number of writers have discussed the emergence in the 1970s and 1980s of drug-treatment programs. It is a billion-dollar industry,[45] and private paying customers do not have to put up with long waiting lists before receiving care. Contemporary films capture representations of drug treatment, especially the two-tiered system in the United States (representing a lack of universal health care and race and class inequality), in which mandatory treatment and prison provide "tough" punitive treatment regimes for poor and racialized people and private residential drug-treatment centres are reserved for the affluent. Criminal justice then becomes the entry point for drug treatment and the arbiter of states of consciousness. The emergence of drug courts in the United States, Canada, and the United Kingdom, with their emphasis on mandatory treatment situated within the criminal-justice, retribution, and punishment matrix, exemplifies how acceptable it has become to force people to abstain from drugs and states of consciousness not sanctioned by the state.

In addition, except for 1960s films and later stoner flicks and alternative films (discussed in chapter 7), "controlled use" is rarely depicted. It is usually all or nothing, especially in relation to cocaine (crack), heroin, and methamphetamine (see the meth users in *Drugstore Cowboy* [1989], *The Salton Sea* [2002], and *Spun* [2002]). Few illegal-drug films examine normalized drug use, especially when the narrative focuses on drug trafficking, nor do they examine to any extent social and cultural factors that shape drug use.

In many illegal-drug films, withdrawal is depicted as a cinematic climax of the film. Contrary to representations in films like *The Man with the Golden Arm* (1955), *H.* (1990; which wins the prize for the most boring drug film viewed), *Basketball Diaries* (1995), and *Trainspotting* (1996; discussed in chapter 4), heroin withdrawal is not necessarily horrific or hallucinatory. In fact, there are a number of drugs to help manage withdrawal. Withdrawal symptoms can be mild to severe. People's experiences are very diverse and some people claim that they do not experience negative effects when they stop using (although it is highly recommended that they cut down use slowly), or they experience mild flulike symptoms. Cold turkey is not recommended (for narcotics), although drug users have been (and continue to be) subjected to it upon entering most jails. Furthermore, it takes many weeks of sustained and regular use to become physically addicted to heroin and other narcotics.[46]

Cocaine is not physically addictive, as are narcotics, alcohol, SSRIs, barbiturates, and antidepressants. However, cocaine users can feel irritable and tired when they stop using after sustained use. The problem for movie directors is how to visually show cessation of drugs and withdrawal. Showing people going about their daily life, lying quietly in bed, or watching a video, as one might do when stopping drug use, is hardly dramatic. Nor is it dramatic or comedic to depict ex-users after withdrawal from drugs, and the scenes following withdrawal are usually brief. Similarly, how do you depict addiction on the screen? People who go about their life, who work and interact with friends and family, have no dramatic appeal. As well, how can we recognize illegal-drug users from nonusers? In film, illegal-drug use and addiction are depicted by physical deterioration (unkempt bodies and wild hair, smeared mascara), sexual degradation (prostitution, rape, promiscuity), violence and crime (theft, drug trafficking, murder), moral decline (stealing from loved ones, betraying loved ones, overdose death), and bleak, dirty, and rundown space. Other visual signifiers include circles under characters' eyes, weight loss, eyes rolling back, heavy sweating, a belt wrapped around the arm ready for a fix, close-ups of fetishized drug paraphernalia, including, spoons, lit matches, hypodermic needles (as if there are no other routes of administration), crack pipes, suitcases overflowing with stacked money, packets of white powder, and neat white lines on a mirror. As viewers, we have come to understand what these visual representations mean, thereby reproducing meaning once again.

Representations of retribution and punishment narratives prevail in illegal-drug films through depictions of painful drug withdrawal, infection, HIV, drug overdose, insanity, sexual, moral, and physical degradation, arrest and imprisonment, and death. Only a small number of illegal-drug films make reference to drug prohibition itself contributing to harm, including drug trade and violence associated with it (see *Withnail and I* [1987], *Drugstore Cowboys* [1989], *Harold and Kumar Go to White Castle* [2004], and *A Scanner Darkly* [2006]). Given that filmmakers in the United States are provided with script-to-screen advice on how to represent drug use, addiction, and treatment in films, and financial incentives if they do so, it may not be so surprising that drug prohibition is not problematized in any significant way.

Since 1989, the U.S. Office for Substance Abuse Prevention (OSAP) developed guideline materials about drugs for film and television writers and health professionals.[47] They claim that their guidelines are based on scientific criteria. They recommend in their guidelines that writers should appropriately communicate that all illegal-drug use is "unhealthy and harmful for all persons" and that addiction should be presented as a disease and "abstinence" is the "viable choice for everyone." They also note that there is no such thing as "responsible" use, since all drug use is associated with risk, nor should there be references to "recreational use of drugs" since no "drug use is recreational."[48]

Spotlight on Depiction of Health and Social Issues, authored by the U.S. National Institute on Drug Abuse (NIDA), the Entertainment Industries

Council, and the Robert Wood Johnson Foundation, also outlines "accurate" depictions of drugs and drug users. Screenwriters are instructed to show that illegal drugs are very addictive. *Spotlight* describes addiction as biological, progressive, and permanent; thus, total abstinence is required. They go on to state that drug addiction is a compulsion, and "addicts" have lost their free will. Primarily, they tell scriptwriters to include dialogue of people reacting negatively to characters' illegal-drug use in order to "cast a shadow."[49] There is no discussion of harm reduction, cross-cultural, or social explanations of drug use in *Spotlight*, nor is drug prohibition mentioned.[50]

The disease model of addiction portrays drugs as dangerous and the drug user as immoral, pathological, and out of control. The authors of *Spotlight* claim that their views on drugs are based on scientific data; however, there is no scientific evidence to support biological or genetic explanations of addiction.[51] Critical researchers challenge addiction-as-disease discourse. Craig Reinarman explains that the "disease concept of addiction obscures the fact that it did not emerge from the accretion of scientific discoveries. Addiction-as-disease has been continuously redefined, mostly in the direction of conceptual elasticity, such that it now yields an embarrassment of riches. . . ."[52] Myths and ideologies about illegal drugs, drug users, and addiction as disease take on the authority and language of science and inform policy, treatment, and certainly the scripts of many TV and film writers. Furthermore, myths and ideologies about illegal drugs, users, and addiction shape how we think about "addicted" and "nonaddicted" bodies, as if there are categorical differences and responses to them.[53] In illegal-drug films, addicted bodies, especially poor and racialized bodies, are devalued over nonaddicted and White middle-class bodies.

In illegal-drug films, sympathy for "addicted" illegal-drug users is limited. White middle- and upper-class users garner the most sympathy in films (as do famous Black and White working-class people depicted in biopics such as *Ray* [2004] and *Walk the Line* [2005], respectively), and often they are depicted as "hitting rock bottom" but later entering residential treatment and attending NA or a twelve-step program where they successfully maintain their abstinence and successfully reenter mainstream society. There has been little effort by most scriptwriters and producers to problematize addiction-as-disease ideology.

Addiction-as-disease narratives are limiting because drug use is best understood as being shaped by social, political, economic, cultural, sociological, psychological, and biological factors. Paul Manning proposes that drug consumption should be understood as a cultural practice, because drugs are "inscribed with meanings and understood within symbolic frameworks" that are not divorced from class, gender, or race constraints.[54] In Britain, Canada, and the United States, normalized recreational use of drugs such as marijuana and ecstasy prevails. Yet outside of 60s and stoner films, representations of negative addiction, lack of control, addiction as disease, and abstinence prevail. Furthermore, fictional-film makers fail to more fully explore cultural uses of illegal drugs that are positive; for example, peyote ceremonies outside of the White appropriation of the ceremony in *Chappaqua*, spiritual and medicinal uses of marijuana, or an occasional opium smoker or heroin user. Outside of films produced in the 1960s, positive, therapeutic, and transcendental uses of psychedelic drugs are mostly absent from film narratives.

Illegal-drug films that focus on treatment rarely scrutinize drug prohibition and how it impacts on how drug treatment is shaped and funded (Only five films in the sample scrutinized prohibition in relation to its impact on treatment.). For example, in Canada, 73 percent of federal drug-strategy expenditures for 2004–2005 went to enforcement initiatives; the remaining 26 percent was allocated to research and policy development, education, prevention, treatment, and harm-reduction initiatives.[55] In the United States, 70 percent of federal drug funding goes towards criminal justice, prisons, and the military; the remaining is earmarked for treatment and education.[56] In Britain, criminal-justice enforcement rather than social and public-health initiatives and treatment remain a priority for federal funding. What this means is that in all three nations, drug services, in their many varied forms, including harm-reduction initiatives, day programs, counselling, residential programs, detox, and needle exchange, are underfunded and lacking. Similarly, so too is funding for social initiatives like stable and affordable housing. These issues are not addressed in illegal-drug-film narratives.

It would be a mistake to see illegal-drug films as a "mirror" image of society in all its diversity. Where films do chronicle some shifts and changes in narratives representing certain drugs, routes of administration, drug users, addiction, drug treatment, and regulation, they also serve to tell more enduring stories about morality, the nation, Whiteness, regulation and punishment, gender relations, law, law and order, threat, criminalized and racialized bodies, and containment. Regardless of the type of drug depicted in the film, these stories perpetuate fictions about people who use illegal drugs, the family, the nation, and the threat to them. The majority of illegal-drug films can be viewed as "accomplice" to law-and-order regimes and most often support criminalization. Is it any wonder that movie viewers themselves may not be able to conceive of drug use, addiction, and drug services in any other way but negative? Positive and healing aspects of altered states of consciousness and illegal-drug use are hidden from sight.

4 Ruptures in Addiction Narratives

Pleasure, Harm Reduction,
Consumer Culture, and Regulation

TRAINSPOTTING: PLEASURE, ADDICTION, WITHDRAWAL, AND CONSUMER CULTURE

In this chapter, a number of alternative films that challenge conventional addiction and treatment stories are discussed, as well as methadone maintenance, harm reduction, and drug-treatment-industry narratives. Except for the film *My Name is Joe* (1998), which is nuanced, British films have not been as wedded to twelve-step and AA narratives as U.S. films. Yet addiction and withdrawal scenes are quite similar to representations in U.S. films. The British film *Trainspotting* (1996) ignited a lot of controversy in the United States when it was released over whether or not the film glamorized illegal-drug use. Many reviewers saw the film as realistically and humourously capturing the lives of white working-class heroin users in Scotland during Margaret Thatcher's regime of privatization and free-market ideology. It is a fast-paced film based on the novel of the same title by Irvine Walsh and accompanied by a great sound track. Although the film is heralded as rupturing representations of illegal-drug users, it can be equally noted that it conforms to familiar addiction- and heroin-withdrawal narratives.

Renton, a White young working-class man from Edinburgh, is the main character and the voice-over narrator of the film (played by Ewan McGregor). We are introduced to his White working-class buddies and fellow heroin users, Sick Boy and Spud; Begbie, a violent alcohol user; Tommy, a "good boy" who suffers a tragic fall into heroin addiction, AIDS, and death; and Mother Superior, the likable dealer. The women represented in the film include Dianne, a young schoolgirl who only uses "soft dugs," and Allison, constructed as the bad mother heroin user. In the film, Edinburgh is depicted as bleak, grey, and run-down (most of the scenes were actually filmed in Glasgow); London, bright and clean, is depicted through a montage of tourist landmarks and colourful costumes. When Renton and his buddies take the train out to rural Scotland, we are informed by Renton that being Scottish "is shite." He explains, "We are colonized by wankers. . . . All the fresh air in the world won't make any fucking difference."

The film begins with a scene of Renton and Spud running away from the police on a city street because they have been shoplifting. Renton's voice-over states: "Choose life, choose a job, choose a career, choose a family, choose a fucking big television. . . ." In the next scene, we see Renton falling to the floor, flat on his back, nodding out, with a cigarette in his mouth and a belt wrapped around his upper arm. He narrates: "I choose not to choose life; I choose something else, and the reasons? There are no reasons. Who needs reasons when you got heroin?" He goes on to say, "People think it is all about misery and desperation, and all that is shite. Which is not to be ignored. What they forget is the pleasure of it." The film romanticizes the heroin "high," informing viewers, "Take the best orgasm you've ever had, multiply it by a thousand and you're still nowhere near it." Although *Trainspotting* is notable for depicting the pleasure of heroin use, as well as the juxtaposition of violence associated with Bigbie's alcohol use and social acceptance of Renton's mother's Valium use, pleasure comes at a high cost in the film via representations of addiction, painful withdrawal, immorality, risk of HIV transmission, arrest, prison, overdose, and death.

During the film, being clean and being addicted are both seen as transitory states, with two vivid narcotic withdrawal scenes. The first time Renton decides to get clean, we follow his "cleaning-up" process as he locks himself up in his room by nailing two large boards across the door (providing an iconic modern twist to the locked-room phenomenon, which relies on our understanding of drug discourse). He is shown unpacking everything he needs: food, waste-buckets, television, pornography, music, and Valium. The viewer never does get to see Renton actually withdraw from heroin because he decides that he should have "one more shot" while waiting for the Valium to kick in. He is successful though (without professional help). Later, Renton meets up with Sick Boy in a park. Sick Boy has also stopped using heroin, and Renton informs us that Sick Boy only came off heroin to annoy him, to show him how easy it is, "thereby downgrading" his "own struggle."

The next time Renton cleans up, the withdrawal process is portrayed more graphically. Following Renton and Spud's arrest for shoplifting, Spud is depicted receiving six months' prison time and Renton a conditional sentence at their trial. The judge explains that Renton is receiving a less punitive sentence because he is attempting to "help" himself by being on methadone maintenance. Renton celebrates at the local pub with his family and friends. Everyone is drinking heavily. Renton spots Spud's mother and he tells her that he is sorry that Spud got prison time and he didn't. He informs the viewer that he feels alone in the midst of his family and friends and that methadone is "state-sponsored addiction. Three sickly sweet doses of methadone a day instead of smack. But it's never enough. And at the moment it's nowhere near enough."

Renton leaves the pub and goes to Mother Superior's, their local heroin dealer. Following a very graphic and surreal shooting-up scene there, Renton

Trainspotting. Source: Polygram Filmed Entertainment/Photofest. © Polygram Filmed Entertainment.

overdoses on heroin and Mother Superior calls a taxi to take him to the emergency ward. This scene is accompanied by the Lou Reed lyrics, "lovely day." Renton's parents come to the hospital and bring him home. His father is depicted carrying him into his bedroom and placing him gently on the bed. This scene is startling in its contrast to the barren, trashed appearance of Mother Superior's apartment and the other dilapidated rooms we have seen Renton occupy with his buddies. Renton's bedroom in his parent's home is neat and tidy and viewers now see him as more than just a "heroin addict." Similar to the previous scene in the pub, he is depicted as a son from a caring working-class home. His concerned parents are represented as enacting "tough love" by taking control and locking Renton into his bedroom, forcing him to stop using heroin by going cold turkey. An outside bolt on his bedroom door is shown being locked so he cannot escape (reminiscent of the withdrawal scene in *The Man with the Golden Arm*). Renton lies in bed wearing striped pyjamas, tossing and turning, sweating, having nausea and chills, craving drugs, in pain, and hallucinating. He tosses and turns and screams in anguish as a montage of vivid hallucinations appear on the screen. Later, we see him being tested for HIV and he is negative, although Tommy, his buddy is not. Renton is off heroin now but he complains that boredom and depression have set in.

In the film, there is no "normal use" of heroin other than addiction. Renton and his buddies are either clean or depicted as "junkies." When they are addicted they live and hang out in shooting galleries and Tommy's filthy apartment after he becomes addicted. Heroin addiction is accompanied by degradation and death, and, although Tommy's death and Allison's baby Dawn's death are not directly due to heroin use, they are related to it through disease and neglect.

In order to leave heroin addiction and life in Edinburgh behind him, Renton is shown moving to London to work. Renton attempts reconstructing his identity, from "junkie" to "respectable" real estate agent, and aspiring member of the "normal" working class. Yet even here, the film critiques White middle-class life and working-class status. Later, his buddies follow him and convince him to help them buy some heroin that they can sell for a large profit. They are successful, but Renton rips off their profits (before Begbie or Sick Boy have a chance). The film ends with Renton walking down a London street with the cash he has ripped off from his buddies. He asks, "Why did I do it? . . . The truth is that I'm a bad person. But that's gonna change. I'm gonna change. . . . I'm cleaning up and I'm moving on. Going straight and choosing life. . . . I'm gonna be just like you. [And he smiles broadly.] The job, the family, the fucking big television, the washing machine, the car . . . mortgage, starter home . . . junk food, children . . . nine to five. . . ." In the film, heroin use and addiction are represented as an identity, in opposition to British White middle-class consumer culture. However, neither class location nor being straight or addicted is afforded much moral centre; and Renton could be viewed at the end of the film as embodying Thatcherism and conservative ideology: individualism, sobriety, entrepreneurship, profit, and embracing the free-market economy and middle- and upper-class consumer values.

The film makes clear that Renton and his buddies "respect and adore" the National Health Service, which provides them with clean "gear" and keep all of them safe from getting HIV, except for Tommy. Yet Tommy is depicted living in a hovel now in comparison to his neat apartment shown prior to his fall into addiction. The stigma of HIV/AIDS is represented by the word *PLAGUE* painted in large red letters over Tommy's doorway at his apartment. He has sores on his face and he asks Renton for money to buy drugs. The scene is problematic because of its linking HIV and addiction with physical and moral degradation.

In *Trainspotting* (1996), harm-reduction services are depicted as positive in the sense that the National Health Service provides needle exchange, thereby lowering the risk of infection. As well, Renton is depicted having safe sex by using a condom. The film also juxtaposes legal-drug use with illegal use. Renton's mother's legal Valium use is referred to and he later lists all of the legal drugs he and his buddies have taken. It is a long list. He notes that "the streets are awash with drugs you can have for unhappiness and pain; we took them all." And though *Trainspotting* is a sympathetic view of heroin users and clearly an unsympathetic view of alcohol users, it fetishizes shooting-up scenes throughout the movie. Heroin addiction is represented as all-encompassing, to such an extent that a baby dies of neglect in its crib because everyone is nodding out. Methadone maintenance is not depicted in a positive light in the film, but addiction to heroin is not presented as permanent, thus challenging addiction-as-disease ideology and Beat writer William Burrough's adage "Once an addict always an addict."

Scriptwriters and film producers have been wedded to the dramatic appeal of characters descending into addiction, moral and sexual corruption, criminality and deviance, death, and horrific withdrawal. If the illegal-drug user survives, what follows after withdrawal is most often left to the last few seconds of the film. By contrast, *Trainspotting* captures the boredom and depression that often follows withdrawal and characterizes life for working-class White youth in Scotland under Thatcherism.

REQUIEM FOR A DREAM: A NIGHTMARE OF ADDICTION

Requiem for a Dream (2000), a story about four drug users, has also been praised, like *Trainspotting*, for juxtaposing illegal-drug use with legal-drug use. *Trainspotting* is a comedy punctuated by dramatic moments, and heroin use is depicted as oppositional to consumer society and to legal-drug use such as alcohol; most importantly, addiction is not represented as permanent. In contrast to *Trainspotting*, the U.S.-produced *Requiem for a Dream* is represented as a vivid, full-on sensory assault, a "nightmare" of addiction in which heroin, TV, legally prescribed pills—amphetamines (diet pills) and sedatives—and food are portrayed as addictive and destructive;

further, addiction to any substance or activity is depicted as a normalized response to a psychologically dysfunctional society. On the director's commentary, Aronofsky says that he wanted to depict the "lengths people will go to escape their reality—coffee, TV, heroin." He continues, "When you feed the hole [in your life], it'll grow . . . and it'll devour you." *Requiem for a Dream* is set in Coney Island, Brooklyn, in a working-class urban area. It is a cautionary morality tale about the spectrum of addictions, degradation, delusion, and desire (the desire to be rich, thinner, loved).

The films' two main male characters are Harry, a young White man, and Tyrone, a young Black man. Both are working class and they are initially depicted as recreational illegal-drug users who attempt to "work" in the drug trade to make enough money to open a clothing shop for Marion, Harry's girlfriend. Their early drug use is depicted as "undeserved pleasure" that soon transforms into horror. They are street dealers whose dream of "one big score," quick profit, and wealth is thwarted when they become horribly addicted to heroin. Heroin is portrayed as highly addictive and associated with sexual, moral, and physical degradation. Drug paraphernalia is fetishized throughout the film, and several close-up shots of injecting-drug use occur throughout, accompanied by amplified sound effects. In the film, Harry is depicted as being so addicted that he ignores an abscess on his arm. It becomes a huge bloody hole that grows throughout the film, a horrific visual symbol of his degradation. When he finally sees a doctor at a southern hospital, the doctor, breaching confidentiality, calls the police and reports on him and Tyrone. They are arrested and sent to prison. Harry's arm is amputated at a prison hospital, a dehumanizing, cold place and Tyrone is brutalized by a racist White prison guard.

Marion, Harry's girlfriend, is a young White woman from a dysfunctional, wealthy family. When their drug money disappears, Marion is pressured by Harry to have sex with her former therapist to obtain money to feed their growing heroin habit. Thus, she begins to work in the sex trade for her drugs. Marion's further sexual degradation parallel's Tyrone's loss of his arm and imprisonment; she is preyed upon, sexually and physically victimized by an "evil" Black male drug dealer/pimp, and coerced to take part in a "sex party."

Sarah, Harry's mother, is represented as an older Jewish widow who is lonely in the absence of her son and the death of her husband and who longs for Harry to settle down and marry. She is a television-obsessed woman who is preapproved to become a contestant on her favourite game show. We watch her spiral into delusion and she starts hallucinating. She is shown using legal drugs to diet, in order to wear a favourite red dress on the show, and sedatives to sleep. Her legal addictions are linked to loneliness, desire, and insanity, and she is depicted as self-destructive. At the end of the film, Sarah is in a psychiatric ward receiving electroshock therapy at the same time that Harry's arm is amputated. She too is dehumanized by the health care system.

Requiem for a Dream ends in despair and all of the characters suffer greatly; they all fall from grace and there is no hope for recovery. In fact, drug-treatment services are rendered invisible. One film critic states that the director of *Requiem for a Dream* is intent on lovingly arranging his characters and then cruelly and gleefully destroying them. He says the director turns "drunk on his own rush for destruction."[1]

We now recognize film narratives that link illegal-drug use with moral, sexual, and physical degradation. In many films, treatment and specific addiction ideologies are explicit. Contemporary films often include drug-treatment, twelve-step, and AA/NA narratives. Some films, like *Requiem for a Dream,* are significant for examining both legal and illegal drugs; however, they reaffirm conventional addiction narratives even though drug treatment is absent from the script.

ALTERNATIVE REPRESENTATIONS: *GRIDLOCK'D* AND *CURTIS'S CHARM*

One film that is noteworthy for challenging conventional addiction and treatment narratives is *Gridlock'd* (1997). *Gridlock'd* stands out for depicting some of the obstacles to obtaining welfare, medical care, and drug treatment for poor and working-class people in the United States by problematizing what it might be like living in the richest nation in the world, one that does not provide universal health care and where federal, state, and city cutbacks, informed by neoliberal ideology since the 1980s, have gutted social and economic supports and increased funding for the war on drugs. In 1992, former President William Clinton proclaimed that he would "end welfare as we know it." He set about dismantling the welfare state, advocating workfare instead of cash support, and initiated further cutbacks to federal funding for social supports.[2] At the same time, public housing decreased and prison rates increased.[3] Writer and director Vondie Curtis-Hall states in the DVD notes that he "drew on his own experiences growing up in Detroit. . . . I wanted it to be something that was real, so *Gridlock'd* is about a day in my life." The film is a "male buddy film" that follows the quest of Stretch and Spoon, a White man (Tim Roth) and a Black man (Tupac Shakur) in their early 30s. They are both using heroin, and the film is notable for depicting a multiethnic cast and race as a political construct is explored in the film. Stretch and Spoon are musicians and close friends who play in a jazz band with their lead singer, a Black woman named Cookie who is Spoon's girlfriend. They all share an apartment together. Spoon is depicted as the "levelheaded" one in contrast to Stretch's "unpredictability," and the three main characters have created a loving family for themselves.

Gridlock'd centres on Stretch and Spoon's decision to stop using heroin after Cookie overdoses. Their quest to change their life and to achieve sobriety is thwarted at every turn; events represented with both humour and drama. The gridlock of medical, drug-treatment, and social-service red tape is illuminated as Stretch and Spoon attempt to negotiate these bureaucratic systems, which are interlocked. The resistance they encounter and the things they end up doing in order to get into detox and residential treatment reveals just how difficult it is to obtain medical care and drug treatment in the United States. The reality of HIV/AIDS is also explored in the film. And though the film emphasizes the violence of the drug trade and fetishizes heroin paraphernalia (repeatedly we see shots of lit wooden matchsticks, match flames heating spoons and bottle caps, needle and tourniquet, and the rolled dollar bill for snorting), drug use is increasingly depicted as a "job" in the film and one that is providing little pleasure anymore.

As the film begins, Stretch, Spoon, and Cookie are gathered around the TV at home. It is a few minutes before New Year's. It soon becomes apparent that Cookie has overdosed. The men grab her and drag her to the bathtub. The camera shows Cookie immersed in cold water, but she still does not respond. Spoon cries out, "We got to get her to the hospital." Next we see them with their arms around Cookie, one on each side, holding her up as they drag her unconscious body onto the street. They attempt to hail a cab but none will stop. The street is empty. Spoon directs them to a phone booth and calls emergency. He connects and then shouts to Stretch, "They put me on hold! I can't fucking believe it! Cookie is fucking dying and they put me on hold!" When emergency comes back on the phone line he says, "A woman been shot, a white woman. . . . There's a whole bunch of Black people out here shooting and burning cars, talking about revolutions. You better send some motherfuckers out here." He slams down the phone receiver and says to Stretch, "They're on their way." The audience understands that in White-supremacist America, only White bodies matter.

Yet the expected ambulance does not arrive. The next shot is of Spoon, Stretch, and Cookie still waiting in the lit telephone booth. They finally take off with Cookie between them and run to the emergency room, dragging Cookie all the way there. When they get to the hospital, it is packed full of people sitting on plastic chairs waiting to be seen. They walk up to the counter to speak to a female receptionist. She asks if Cookie has insurance. She hands Spoon a clipboard and tells him to fill out the form. Spoon fills it out and hands it back to the receptionist, asking: "Can I see a doctor now please? She responds, "Just a minute, sir. You have a Social Security number? Medical, Medicaid number? . . . A photo ID? And the address of her next of kin?" Spoon replies by shouting, "You ask me about some fucking numbers. . . . I need a fucking doctor!"

Later, we see Cookie lying on a hospital bed and Spoon and Stretch are sitting next to her. Spoon wonders if Cookie will die, whether their luck is running out. He wonders if Cookie's overdose is a sign that he should stop using heroin. He says, "We don't even get high on the shit no more.

Gridlock'd. Source: Gramercy Pictures/Photofest. © Gramercy Pictures.

We just do it to keep from getting sick. That shit ain't fun no more." That same night and the following day, Spoon and Stretch get into trouble with a big-time dope dealer, and they are also blamed by the police for the murder of their local dealer. They are innocent, but these events make their quest to get off the street and into treatment even more urgent. Stretch agrees to "kick" with Spoon, and in the morning we see them walking quickly down the street. The urban landscape is bleak and there is trash everywhere. They walk up to a rehab centre. Outside there are a lot of men hanging around. Stretch sees a mutual friend who asks them, "This your first time getting into rehab?" Spoon says yes and the man tells them that they have to get a Medicaid card, and it will take up to 6 weeks, unless they get tested for HIV. Spoon says there is no way he is taking an HIV test. The next scene shows a nurse taking a blood sample from Spoon's arm and she tells him his name will be put on a HIV/AIDS waiting list. She also tells him it will take over a week for the results and he will still need his Medicaid card. Later, Stretch quietly tells Spoon, "I'm HIV positive. . . . I woulda mentioned it before; I didn't know how you'd take it. I'm always using my own works and everything. You're the first person I ever told." In a number of scenes, we see Spoon and Stretch entering an outpatient office and then a welfare and Medicaid office. They are denied access to treatment by every agency. All of the government buildings in the film are depicted as stark and rundown with many people waiting to be seen, watched by security guards who use metal detectors, and tired and harassed government workers.

Spoon and Stretch bump into the dealers who are looking for them and Stretch gets shot by one of them. He's shown bleeding heavily and cannot go on, so they hide behind a garbage bin in an alley until nightfall. Stretch worries that he is going to die. He is assured by Spoon that he only has a flesh wound. Then Spoon comes up with a new idea to get both of them off the street and into detox. Spoon says, "Here's what we're gonna do. I want you to stab me" (he gets out a small pocket knife from his pocket). Stretch makes clear that he will have nothing to do with this new plan. Spoon argues, "If we're in an emergency room we're off the streets. Once we're in the hospital we can kick, Stretch! What the hell are you tripping off, I'm the one gonna be cut. Besides, it's a pocket knife." Stretch finally relents and he asks where he should stab Spoon. Spoon replies, "What do you think is best?"

Stretch: "Well, if I stab you in the stomach I might hit some organs and shit."

Spoon: "Yeah, right. Not in the stomach."

Stretch: "What about the arm?"

Spoon: "Nah, too wimpy."

Stretch: "Well, you could turn around and I'll stab you in the back?"

Spoon: "Nah. You'll fucking paralyze me. Not the back [he holds up his shirt and looks at his stomach and then gestures with his hands]. Okay. My liver's on the left, stomach's on the. . . . No!" Finally Stretch says, "What if I stab you between the organs?" Spoon agrees that this is a good idea. Stretch stabs him and Spoon yells, doubling over in pain. He then realizes the knife blade didn't even break the skin because it is so dull. So he says, "Do it again!" Stretch complies and then looks at the damage done and says, "Looks good though." And Spoon asks, "You think so?" "Yeah, It looks good." Spoon puts his arm around Stretch's shoulder and they walk down the alleyway. Stretch asks Spoon, "You all right?" and he says, "Yeah, shit, that hurts."

The camera shifts to Cookie, who is waking up to find herself in the hospital. She gets up and dresses, walks out to the hall and calls home from a pay phone. She leaves a message for Spoon and Stretch saying that the record agent will be coming by soon to hear them play, "Thinking maybe you guys should start thinking about kicking. This could be a really big break for us. You know."

The movie ends with a scene of all of them playing at a club. It is assumed that Spoon and Stretch have kicked their habit. Through comedy and drama, *Gridlock'd* provides critiques of medical and drug-treatment bureaucracies and the welfare system in the United States. It also depicts drug-related harms, including overdose, HIV/AIDS, drug-trade violence, and police corruption. At the same time, *Gridlock'd* also fetishizes heroin use and employs a number of scenes and stills that we have come to recognize, especially shooting-up scenes, and Cookie is sexualized to a certain degree in the film. She is scantily dressed a number of times, in contrast to the fully dressed males, and in one scene we see her sitting on Stretch's lap and kissing him even though she is Spoon's girlfriend. Stretch is represented as unable to respond to her advances because of his heroin use, a common representation of male users in films. *Gridlock'd* ruptures conventional representations at the same time that it conforms to them. Significantly, Spoon and Stretch cease using illegal drugs (off camera) and Cookie does not die after overdosing. As well, unlike many illegal-drug-film depictions, friendship between racialized and White subjects is realized.

The Canadian film *Curtis's Charm* (1995) also tells the story from the illegal-drug user's perspective, based on a book of the same name by Jim Carroll. The film is surreal and crack is the main drug in the film. The characters in the film are multicultural, and crack, paranoia, and voodoo are central to the story. The film director, John L'Ecuyer, who drew from his own experience as an ex-heroin user, states, "It was important to me that the story was so authentic. Jim the recovering addict, and Curtis, who is at the height of crack paranoia, are polar opposites, but they're from the same world. . . . I wanted the audience to buy into that experience, to show that for a crackhead, that paranoid delusion is reality."[4]

Curtis's Charm also depicts a sense of ambiguity about addiction and recovery. Again we follow two young urban working-class men, one White, one Black, who have a warm relationship. Jim is a young White ex-user, and he is portrayed as a "big brother" to Curtis, who is still using crack. Jim feels that he has a fraternal obligation to Curtis after spending time together in drug treatment. In the film, Jim reveals how Curtis and he met at a "skanky treatment centre on the West Side, with an 'Ivy League–campus' " look, "before the twelve-step shit." When Curtis asks Jim about his sobriety, Jim says, "I don't count the days." He then says being clean "is weird. I'm happier, I think. Things aren't as crazy. . . ." Jim does not condemn Curtis's drug use, but he is concerned about whether he is using too much.

Jim agrees to help Curtis, but on Curtis's own terms. At one point, Jim creates a "magic charm" to ward off the voodoo that is terrifying Curtis, and he introduces the notion of purification. Curtis responds, "How am I supposed to purify myself at this point? We're like two fucking germs talking to each other." Jim notes that when he was in treatment, "[he] was like a drug-infested microbe." Jim talks a bit cynically about Curtis doing the "twelve-step shuffle. . . . Hi, my name is Curtis." In the film, the characters use a language of sickness/disease and cleanliness/purification that has a double meaning, addressing drug use and voodoo. Purification is presented as a way to move forward out of crack use and the spell of black magic. And though Jim calls Curtis a "fucked-up, coke-addicted child," he seems to be genuinely caring for him, and the audience is sympathetic to him too. Curtis is depicted as delusional, his crack use and fear of "magic and voodoo" come into question as the film unfolds, and viewers might begin to question whether Curtis's delusional and paranoid world stems from his crack use or not. At the end of the film, Curtis is killed by tough White guys who hate "crackheads," and we come face to face with societal prejudices about crack users, focusing on Black youth, White vigilante murder, violence, and social marginalization. *Curtis's Charm* shows empathy for both Jim and Curtis. The drug narrative is ambiguous, and the film critiques twelve-step programs and acknowledges the possibility of "managed use." Yet representations of being "clean," polluted and diseased bodies, and epidemic also inform the film. *Curtis's Charm*, though sympathetic and critical, also embodies conventional narratives about addiction and recovery.

HALF NELSON: LOSING AND GAINING CONTROL

Half Nelson (2006), set in Brooklyn, follows the life of Dan (played by Ryan Gosling), a young White teacher from a working-class background. He periodically uses crack cocaine, and it interferes with his work and personal relationships. However, unlike the crack users portrayed in *New Jack City*, *Losing Isaiah*, and *Traffic*, Dan never falls completely from grace, and by the end of the film it looks as though he may be moving away from problematic use. Dan, like the White female crack user in *Traffic,* is afforded more sympathy than portrayals of Black crack users in film. Drug treatment is absent from the narrative, and crack use is not understood from an addiction-as-disease lens. His crack use is not static and it is tied to unresolved personal problems. Significantly, he is not ridiculed or demonized in the film, as are crack users in *Clockers*, *New Jack City*, and *Losing Isaiah*. Nor is he murdered, as were Curtis in *Curtis's Charm* and Pookie in *New Jack City*. *Half Nelson* provides an alternative template to understand periodic, problematic use of illegal drugs, even those originally thought to be "instantly" addictive.

METHADONE AND HARM-REDUCTION NARRATIVES

Since the late 1950s and early 1960s, critical sociological explanations of drug use countered both medical and criminal models.[5] Howard Becker examined how what we experience after we take a drug and even signs of withdrawal are a learned affair. He and other critical researchers propose that cultural, social, psychological, and biological factors shape drug use, not just pharmacology. Drug researcher Norman Zinberg made clear how "set and setting" shape people's drug use. Set refers to people's experiences, attitudes, and expectations about a specific drug. Setting refers to the social, cultural, and physical setting in which the drug is consumed. Set and setting shape people's long-term relationships with specific drugs. We can have good or bad relationships with specific drugs, although this is not predetermined or necessarily static.[6]

In the 1980s, harm reduction emerged in the Netherlands and Britain, and in many ways it draws from critical sociological and cultural explanations of drug use and challenges medical and criminal models of addiction. It emerged in response to the growing HIV/AIDS epidemic in the 1980s and the failure of the state to address it. Early on, harm reduction was advocated and put into practice by drug users (through drug-user organizations, unions, and community groups). In Britain, harm reduction was adopted and policy and practice shifted. The role of the clinics and psychiatrists lessened as new programs emerged with a wider base of professionals such as social workers and addiction workers.[7] Originally, harm-reduction initiatives attempted to provide practical, nonjudgmental services to reduce drug-related harm to the individual and society. Abstinence is not necessarily required; rather, it is viewed as one option amongst many others. Needle exchange was one of the first harm-reduction programs to emerge to counter rising HIV/AIDS rates of infection. Today, a range of harm-reduction services exists in Britain and Canada, including safer crack kits, controlled drinking programs, maternity programs, and heroin maintenance.

However, harm reduction is not without its critics. Drawing from the writings of Michel Foucault on biopower, governmentality, and normalization, critics argue that harm-reduction policy and practice emphasize self-governance and risk management.[8] It might also be argued that harm reduction at its worst draws from Thatcherism. At its best, it supports grassroots initiatives by drug users themselves, and it paves a path, if one chooses to follow it, away from the medical/criminal models of addiction by emphasizing the social, and the effects of prohibition. Health, human rights, and the inclusion of drug users themselves should be central to harm-reduction practices.

It is somewhat rare to see depictions of harm-reduction services in illegal-drug films. Today, methadone maintenance is also considered a harm-reduction practice (a replacement therapy for heroin and narcotics addiction). During the late 1960s and early 1970s, U.S. soldiers and veterans of the Vietnam War spurred on shifts in drug treatment. During the Vietnam War, U.S. soldiers were exposed to heroin in smoking form and some became addicted to the drug. Marijuana was also made available by the locals once they realized that it was in demand.[9] By the 1960 and 1970s, responding to rising drug use by White middle-class youth and returning Vietnam vets, drug treatment centres and twelve-step programs sprung up around the United States and elsewhere; prescribing methadone as a narcotic-maintenance drug also contributed to significant shifts in addiction treatment and drug policy. Drs. Dole and Nyswander are credited as the doctors who first publicized the use of methadone for narcotic maintenance. Methadone was credited with "reducing crime" and treating narcotic "addicts" who had a "disease," believing that methadone blocked the heroin "high." Dole and Nyswander set up the first methadone clinic in the United States, recommending high daily doses of methadone to effectively block the "euphoric" effects of heroin.[10] In the early 1970s, methadone maintenance was recommended by Edward Brecher and the editors of *Consumer Reports*' 1972 report *Licit and Illicit Drugs*, and the Canadian *Le Dain Commission* (1972), as the hope of the future. In 1972, four methadone units were established in Canada.[11] The emergence of methadone maintenance helped to establish addiction as disease firmly in the national consciousness in Canada and the United States.

In Britain, the second Brian Report, published in 1967, reflected concerns about changing drug use. In the eighteenth and early nineteenth centuries, people were introduced to narcotics through therapeutic use; now a new population of users was emerging. Like their predecessors, they were White; however, it appeared that "recreational" use preceded their addiction. Similar to users in the United States, they were also younger. New questions were asked about the ethics of prescribing narcotics to these new users, and concern arose about containing what was perceived as a growing problem and excessive prescribing practices by a small handful of doctors.[12] The second Brian Report recommended that only "specialist psychiatrists," rather than private general practitioners, be allowed to prescribe narcotics for maintenance in special-treatment centres or clinics.[13] Lart argues that "it was from the medical profession's new construction of the disease as addiction that the public-health measures of specialist clinics, notification, and controlled prescribing emerged."[14] Although illegal-drug users can consult their physician in Britain, doctors are no longer able to prescribe heroin or cocaine for maintenance or detox purposes unless licensed to do so. Even though heroin is still prescribed in Britain, by the late 1970s, methadone rather than heroin was the favoured maintenance drug. However, as noted earlier, harm-reduction discourse emerged in the 1980s, disrupting addiction-as-disease ideology. Reduction of harm, self-regulation, and education were promoted, and methadone maintenance was adopted as one strategy to stabilize and reduce harm to people addicted to heroin and other narcotics.

A few early films depict methadone maintenance, reflecting the fact it was advocated by doctors for addiction by the late 1960s and early 1970s. Two early films depict heroin users trying to get on methadone maintenance: *Trash* (1970) and *Sid and Nancy* (1986). *Trash* (1970) is a gritty film, produced by Andy Warhol. Its main focus is on heroin use. In the film, we are introduced to Joe, a young White working-class man, who is addicted to heroin (as he is apparently in real life). Getting "high" is constructed as the most important thing in Joe's life. He and his girlfriend are shown attempting to get on at one of the new methadone clinics, but the clinic is full and it has a long waiting list. Ironically, Joe cannot register because he does not have housing. The film begins and ends with Joe addicted to heroin. In the British/U.S. production *Sid and Nancy* (1986), set in the 1970s (a portrayal of Sid Vicious of the Sex Pistols and his girl-friend), the two main characters are more successful than Joe in *Trash*, and they obtain treatment through a methadone clinic in London. However, Sid and Nancy fail to stay "clean" and there is a certain fatalism to their drug addiction. Nancy tells Sid, "You'll never get straight. You'll never get straight, Sid." Neither Sid nor Nancy stays straight, and both are dead by the end of the movie through overdose death and murder. Their drug use is depicted as facilitating their self-destruction.

A few films produced from the late 1980s to the 2000s also depict meth-adone as an option. In *Drugstore Cowboy* (1989), the main character Bob goes on a 21-day methadone detox program. He does not complete the pro-gram because he is shot and wounded; however, the methadone counsel-lor is represented as sympathetic and welcoming. In *Permanent Midnight* (1998), the main character goes to a methadone clinic and the worker there is sceptical that he can succeed, and he decides not to try it. A number of British films, including *Trainspotting* (1996), *My Name is Joe* (1998), and *Clean* (2004), refer to methadone maintenance, although none of them are great endorsements. The Canadian films *Protection* (2001), *Barbar-ian Invasions* (2003), *On the Corner* (2003), and *Mount Pleasant* (2006) also depict scenes in which characters take methadone or refer to metha-done when they stop using illegal drugs like heroin. In *Protection* (2001), methadone is represented as failing to help a young woman stay off heroin (along with counselling, parenting skill, and drug counselling). *Barbarian Invasions* and *On the Corner* represent methadone as problematic, and then accepted by the characters, who stabilize, stop using heroin, and move forward in their lives. The young girl in *Mount Pleasant* hopes to go on methadone, but because her older sister refuses to allow her to stay with her to stabilize, she never does get on the program.

Ambivalence about methadone maintenance and policy has not been well expressed in film. Philippe Bourgois points out that in the United States, methadone maintenance is the "largest biomedically-organized and federally controlled drug treatment modality."[15] He explains that it "represents the state's attempt to inculcate moral discipline into the hearts, minds, and bodies of deviants who reject sobriety and economic produc-tivity."[16] Methadone policy often fluctuates and it can be quite punitive. Methadone maintenance is rejected by many heroin users because of its side effects, its harsher withdrawal symptoms, and rigid and oftentimes bizarre and ever-shifting policy.[17] Furthermore, drug users and research-ers alike question why heroin is "assumed to inevitably lead to addiction and destructive patterns of use,"[18] and why it is not provided instead of methadone in a less rigid environment since it has fewer side effects and appears to have better social, economic, and health outcomes for users.[19] Legal heroin is still available for maintenance purposes in Britain, and the North America Opiate Medication Initiative (NAOMI) project in Canada also provides heroin maintenance to a small number of users in urban cities; however, the United States does not allow heroin maintenance, and methadone maintenance continues to be the preferred treatment modality, outside of abstinence, for narcotic addiction in all three nations.[20]

In the French-Canadian film *Barbarian Invasions* (2003), methadone maintenance is briefly shown in a slightly positive light. In the film, the main character, Remy, is dying of cancer. Remy is a man with left-leaning politics who lived life to its fullest. He is portrayed as an intellectual, a "sensual socialist." Remy taught at a university before he became ill, and he has a warm relationship with his ex-wife and a close-knit group of friends. The film highlights the importance of ideas and art and the decline of the "American Empire." All of the main characters in the film are represented as French Canadian, White, and upper-middle class.

At the beginning of the film, we see Remy in a hospital bed in a Montreal hospital. Due to cutbacks, the hospital is overcrowded. Remy is in terrible pain, and the morphine he is being given no longer helps to relieve his suffering. His son Sebastien finds out from a friend who is a doctor that heroin is thought to be "800 times more effective than morphine" as a pain medication, so Sebastien sets out to obtain heroin for his father. He is unable to buy it through legal means, so he tracks down a family friend, Nathalie, who is said to be addicted to the drug. Unlike most female characters represented as addicted to heroin in film, Nathalie's heroin use is not sexualized, nor is she depicted as deviant, criminal, or physically degraded. Nathalie is depicted as a young White woman who works full time as a proofreader for a book-publishing company. She has her own apartment, which is clean and comfortable. She is well groomed and intelligent. There is nothing about her appearance that would signify heroin use, except possibly her pale complexion. Sebastien offers to pay for her heroin supplies as well as his father's, plus a fee for her time, and she agrees to his proposal. Here the script conforms to tired narratives about heroin users when she warns Sebastien that he should not trust "a junky, they make a habit of lying." Yet throughout the film, Nathalie doe not lie; in fact, Remy ends up calling her his "guardian angel."

Nathalie visits Remy in the hospital and she introduces him to heroin. She explains that heroin is "morphine mixed with chemicals." She teaches Remy to inhale the heroin, riding the dragon, and his heroin use is represented as therapeutic and positive. His pain is lessened and he is better able to be present with his family and friends, including Nathalie, during his last days, when they take him out of the hospital and gather together at a lakeside cottage. In an earlier scene, Nathalie is depicted at a pharmacy where she is instructed on how to take prescribed oral methadone. The pharmacist warns her that she will be kicked off the program if she breaks the rules.

At the cottage, Remy can no longer eat, and rather than smoke, Remy's heroin for pain management is injected. At the end of the film, Nathalie's care and friendship with Remy helps her turn a corner in her own life. Remy has little time left in this world and he decides to end his life. A friendly nurse sets up an IV drip for Remy and Nathalie prepares a tray of heroin injections. These are injected into the IV drip, and Remy dies quickly and peacefully surrounded by family and friends.

The *Barbarian Invasions* never condemns Nathalie's heroin use, and her shift to methadone is represented as an emotional shift. It is made clear in the film that risk of overdose and death is always present when buying on the illegal market, and Nathalie's shift to methadone use represents her embrace of life and a future. In the film, it is not clear whether Nathalie's methadone use is for detox or maintenance purposes. As well, the film does not make clear that heroin use for palliative care in Canada has been legal since 1984. Few Canadians are aware of this, including law-enforcement agents, because of the strict protocols surrounding the drug's use. Most provinces have not made the drug available due to the strict security measures surrounding transporting, storing, and prescribing it. Thus, for all intents and purposes, it remains unavailable to Canadians for pain management.[21] Interestingly, another French-Canadian film, *Night Zoo*, produced in 1987, depicts a young man giving his working-class father illegal drugs near the end of his life in a Montreal hospital. The better management of his pain allows him to go on one last night trip with his son to the local zoo. It is a moving scene. Both *Barbarian Invasions* and *Night Zoo* critique the legal/illegal divide, neoliberal ideology, privatization, and cutbacks in health care in Canada.

U.S., British, and Canadian films rarely depict scenes such as Remy's positive heroin use in *Barbarian Invasions* (2003), nor do they include actual scenes where characters employ harm-reduction practices, such as going to a needle exchange or reaching for a condom. Neither do they have scenes of characters taking their methadone at a clinic: being subjected to urine tests or having conflict over dosages or punitive pickup and dispensary times and/or lowered doses. Nor do contemporary illegal-drug films include narratives about hepatitis C, which is surprising, given high infection rates for injecting-drug users in all three nations. Narratives about HIV/AIDS are also surprisingly absent. Given the political environment surrounding drug policy, it is not surprising that so few Hollywood films are depicting harm-reduction initiatives. The U.S. government (especially under Bush Jr.'s administration) has actively rejected harm reduction as a viable option and all illegal-drug use is considered abuse; in 2007, Canadian Prime Minister Stephan Harper's Conservative government eliminated harm reduction from its new National "Anti-Drug" strategy.

NEW DIRECTIONS

Whereas the films discussed in this chapter illuminate representations of illegal-drug users, addiction, and drug treatment, more recent films are questioning the intersection of illegal drugs, addiction, and what is referred to as the drug-treatment industry. The animated film *A Scanner Darkly* (2006) exemplifies this genre, based on Philip K. Dick's novel of the same title and set in Orange County, California, a few years into the future. It is made clear in the film that 20 percent of the population is addicted to an illegal substance called Substance D. Where the film *Requiem for a Dream* (2000) depicts an addicted society trying to fill the psychological and spiritual void with junk culture and substances, both legal and illegal, the focus of *A Scanner Darkly* is on regulation and surveillance, drug treatment, corporate, and law-enforcement complicity.

In the film *A Scanner Darkly*, Substance D is portrayed as a red capsule that people ingest, made from the compounds of a small blue-petalled flower. The effects of the drug seem similar to depictions of methamphetamine, in the sense that people who take too much seem to experience anxiety, twitch, and get paranoid. The film also plays on fears related to permanent brain damage due to excessive use. The film depicts a society under constant surveillance, without their knowledge, and the life of Fred (played by Keanu Reaves), an undercover narcotics agent who becomes addicted to Substance D in the line of duty.

The movie begins with a White man in a suit speaking at a podium, a Brown Bear Lodge member, introducing a guest speaker to an audience consisting largely of White men in suits. The Brown Bear Lodge moderator introduces Fred as an "undercover narcotic agent from the sheriff's office who's out there on our behalf fighting this awful Substance D epidemic." The moderator elaborates, "It's no secret we're living in a culture of addiction. Nearly 20 percent of the population can now be classified as addicts. And as far as anyone can tell, there is but one company that is working and helping the situation. That company is our sponsor—New-Path." Behind the podium we can see a banner with the New-Path logo on it. Fred comes up to the podium and says:

> I'm going to tell you what I'm afraid of. What I fear night and day is that our children, your children and my children . . . [will become] addicted to Substance D for profit by drug terrorists. . . . Each day this disease takes its toll on us. . . . Substance D. D is for dumbness and despair and desertion. The desertion of your friends from you. You from your friends. Everyone from everyone. Isolation, loneliness and hating, and suspecting each other. D is finally for death. Slow death.

The film portrays Fred straying during his speech, wondering out loud why people addicted to Substance D are arrested and punished rather than given the drug legally, but he quickly gets back on track through the urging of his boss, who is electronically monitoring the talk and can speak to Fred without the audience's being aware. We come to realize that New-Path has a profitable contract with the government and it is running "recovery centres" throughout the nation, yet it is made clear that "recovery" is unattainable for most people because Substance D causes permanent brain damage. When Fred becomes addicted to Substance D, he is taken to a New-Path recovery centre and he is eventually sent to one of their rural recovery farms. At the farm, he is brought to a small barrackslike cell with bars on the windows and he is told that this will be his new residence. He does not resist and it appears that he has "lost his mind." He is sent to work in the cornfields and we see that, in between the rows of corn, a small blue-petalled flower also grows.

It is made clear that Fred's sanity and health were sacrificed in order to infiltrate New-Path, against whom his former boss is hoping he will provide evidence. At the end of the film, we see Fred working in the field as a New-Path executive approaches him and says, "Flower of the future. Not for you. . . . This isn't your god anymore. Although it once was."

The film ends with the postscript: "This has been a story about people who were punished entirely too much for what they did. I loved them all. Here is a list, to whom I dedicate my love." *A Scanner Darkly* is one of a small group of films that critique addiction rates in relation to the drug-treatment industry and the construction of legal and illegal drugs.[22] The film also critiques law enforcement and surveillance and global politics. In the film, these activities are represented as intersecting with the drug-treatment industry, highlighting how the regulation of illegal-drug users is linked to capitalism, governments, corporations and profit, drug treatment, criminal justice, and militarism.

CONCLUSION

The 1990s and 2000s bring a few references to harm reduction in illegal-drug films, and very occasionally HIV/AIDS is represented (as in *Trainspotting* and *Gridlock'd*), but there is still ambivalence in film representations in regard to illegal-drug use, addiction, roots of addiction, and treatment. Representations of methadone maintenance are few, and often they are negative. *Gridlock'd* is one of the only films in the sample to explore how difficult it is for poor and working-class people to access drug treatment in the United States. The *Barbarian Invasions* highlights the positive therapeutic use of heroin, and *A Scanner Darkly* illuminates the intersection of the drug-treatment industry, law enforcement and surveillance, and global politics. These films counter conventional film narratives about addiction and degradation and provide alternative stories about illegal drugs, treatment, and regulation.

5 Drug Dealers
A Nation Under Siege

In this chapter, I examine a number of U.S.-produced films that represent illegal drugs, drug traffickers, and the nation. A host of illegal-drug films portray drugs and dealers as the number one menace that confronts the United States today. Criminalized space, where opium dens and urban streets are havens for drug dealers, drug epidemics, disease, and crime, is clearly laid out in illegal-drug films.[1] Illegal-drug users, dealers, and producers are constructed as "exiled and spatially separated"[2] bodies, bodies that are criminalized and pathologized. In these illegal-drug films, dealers and traffickers are represented as preying on innocent people and contributing to the breakdown of families and communities. White moral women are represented as the moral barometer of Western nations; therefore, women's drug use is often represented as a failure of nation building.

Defending the border and the nation from dangerous drugs, foreign cartels, and local drug dealers remains a central theme in illegal-drug films; so too are representations of criminalized space that threaten communities. Illegal-drug films embody these fears, as do politicians and health officials. For example, in 1998, the chief medical health officer for Vancouver responded to the HIV/AIDS problem in the Downtown Eastside of Vancouver, BC, by stating that "the drug scene is not just in the Downtown Eastside; it's *coming* to a neighbourhood near you."[3] Space, then, takes on moral boundaries, and it is the drug dealer who is represented as taking on almost mythical proportions both in the print media and in Western film representations.[4] Although there are exceptions, the media's most hateful depictions are reserved for the drug dealer/trafficker. With some exceptions, drug traffickers are depicted as violent, evil, sadistic, immoral, greedy, and corrupt men who lure innocent youth and draw moral women into drug addiction and crime. They are represented as a threat to the family, the community, and the nation. They are also constructed as guilty in the eyes of law enforcement and society, and, therefore, deserving of the brutal treatment handed out to them by criminal-justice vigilantes, family members of the victim, and justice-seeking police officers. Drug sellers are routinely shot and killed in movies and TV shows before they can be arrested or brought to court. Greed, power, and violence characterize representations of drug traffickers. However, these representations are not static. A number of illegal-drug films produced in and outside of Hollywood are sympathetic to the "lone trafficker," who is portrayed as moral in a violent world.

EARLY REPRESENTATIONS OF DRUG TRAFFICKERS AND THE NATION IN U.S. FILMS

Early film producers were fond of depicting opium use in short films; others focussed on the opium trade. The U.S. short silent film *The Opium Smugglers*, produced in 1913, kicked off a host of films in which opium smuggling is the main theme. As discussed in chapter 2, these early films were often parodies, and drug use and smuggling were depicted as absurd. The heads of drug-smuggling rings were often White men, even though their underlings might be depicted as foreign.[5] *The Mystery of the Leaping Fish* (1916), a parody of the Sherlock Holmes genre, provides the framework for future illegal-drugs films that focus on trafficking; the film features Coke Ennyday, a cocaine and laudanum user, who is asked by the police to break up an opium-smuggling ring.

In the film, Chinese and Japanese men are running an opium-smuggling operation out of a waterfront bathhouse named the "Leaping Fish" and a Chinese laundry named Sum Hop, run by a Chinese man named Fishy Joe. At the top of the opium-smuggling operation is the boss, named Man of Mystery, who is wealthy and White. He has an "Asian" servant and henchmen, bundles of cash, and he wears expensive clothing.

In the film, Bessie, a young moral White woman, works at the Leaping Fish. Unaware of the opium-smuggling operation, she gets caught up in their affairs when the Man of Mystery is threatened by Fishy Joe, who says, "Give me that girl in marriage within the week or I will spill the beans." The Man of Mystery tells her that she has one week to marry Fishy Joe. Bessie tells Coke Ennyday about her situation, and he says that he will protect her, but she is later kidnapped by a gang of Asian men working for Fishy Joe. She is stuffed into a laundry bag and put into the Sum Hop's laundry carriage. As the carriage drives away, she struggles to get out of the bag and discovers that it also contains packages of opium. She opens a package and uses the opium to write "Help" on a laundry bag—throwing it out of the back of the carriage in order to leave a trail.

Bessie is eventually brought to the Sum Hop laundry, identified by a caption that reads "In Chinatown, the laundry where the gang does its dirty work." At the laundry, Fishy Joe leers at Bessie and he curls his hands into the shape of claws as he grabs her arm, with the caption "Girl, you are in my power!" She resists and brutally hits him in the face, kicks him, and throws laundry at him. It is one of the most violent scenes in the movie even though it is presented as comedy. Bessie is eventually "rescued" by Coke, but in many ways the scene of her pummeling Fishy Joe is a parody of defenseless White womanhood because she can clearly take care of herself. When Coke arrives to save Bessie, he is depicted battling with a number of "Asian" men and injecting cocaine into his opponents, who then dance and run out of the room. He then battles with the Man of Mystery; he slaps him in the face and says, "That means fight in my country," establishing that the Man of Mystery is a foreigner to the United States. Coke wins the fight, the camera cuts to the Man of Mystery, his expensive clothes are ripped to shreds, and he falls to the ground. Coke races out of the room and blows clouds of cocaine into a group of thugs, which renders them unconscious. Meanwhile, the police are lost, driving in a van, going around in circles. They finally arrive at the laundry and knock on the door, but when no one answers, the caption reads "Nobody home," and they leave. The film ends as the camera zooms in on Coke and Bessie hugging after having defeated all of their foreign opium-smuggling opponents.

Although mild compared to contemporary films, violence against criminals is normalized in the film, especially against racialized criminals and gangs, evoking a discourse of a general "Asian menace." In the United States and Canada, local and national newspapers also targeted Chinese men. In the early 1900s, newspaper articles in Canada, such as "What Opium Does: Young British Columbia Girl Found Among Chinese," fueled anti-Chinese discourse and exclusionary immigration law and drug policy.[6] Western law and film representations privilege the White imperial subject. In the "national imaginary," aboriginals, immigrants, and racialized Others are most often demonized and blamed for creating and bringing with them social problems, criminality, and backward cultural practices.[7] In the *Mystery of the Leaping Fish*, opium smoking and drug trafficking by foreigners, and Asian sexuality, are depicted as a threat to the White imperial subject. Japanese and Chinese people are vilified, and there is little distinction between diverse Asian cultures in the film. The film supports and perpetuates the ideological framework for future media representations that privilege Whiteness in depictions of women, drug sellers, and foreign Others.[8] It also provides a framework for discourse related to illegal drugs, criminal justice, and punishment. In contrast to later films, the police in the film are depicted as older White men, and they are honest but incompetent and at times absurd.

Early films produced in the 1920s and 1930s, especially those produced with the help of the police, Anti-Narcotics League, and H. J. Anslinger, the U.S. commissioner of narcotics, such as *Human Wreckage* (1923), *The Cocaine Fiends* (1935), *Assassin of Youth* (1935), *Marihuana, the Weed with Roots in Hell* (1936), and *Reefer Madness* (1936), make clear that "Dope is the gravest menace which today confronts the United States" and "Marijuana is that drug—a violent narcotic—and unspeakable scourge— *The Real Public Enemy Number One!*"[9] In these films, White middle-class youth are preyed on by ruthless dealers, and women are portrayed as vulnerable to the lures of deviant men, the city, addiction, and sexual immorality. The Federal Bureau of Narcotics continued to support the production of antidrug films in the 1940s, including *To the Ends of the Earth* in 1948 and *Johnny Stool Pigeon* in 1949. Similar to *Cocaine Fiends* (1935), *Assassin of Youth* (1935), and *Reefer Madness* (1936), these propagandist films were meant to educate innocent viewers about the dangers of specific drugs, users, and traffickers. U.S. Commissioner of Narcotics H. J. Anslinger also appeared in *To the Ends of the Earth*.[10]

To the Ends of the Earth (1948) dramatized the Federal Bureau of Narcotics' role in stopping drug smuggling into the United States.[11] These films clearly lay out the threat to U.S. law-enforcement's valiant efforts to contain illegal-drug smuggling and dealing. The absence of Black, Latino, and other racialized peoples in these films reaffirms Whiteness. However, the mythical racialized trafficker did not vanish from the public imagination because images of racialized drug smugglers and traffickers were abundant in print media and law-enforcement discourse about drugs.[12]

Illegal-drug films produced in the 1950s were also cautionary tales highlighting the dangers of drugs and drug traffickers for White citizens. These films also represent White flight from the cities and fears about the encroachment of illegal drugs and the people who sell them in White suburbia. Films such as *Teenage Devil Dolls* (1950), *The Cool and the Crazy* (1958), and *High School Confidential* (1958) exemplify the genre. In these films, White middle-class high-school students are depicted as at risk and vulnerable to drug traffickers. Whereas marijuana is the demon drug in *The Cool and the Crazy*, *High School Confidential* links marijuana with heroin use. H. J. Anslinger (then still the U.S. commissioner of narcotics) and several narcotics agents were active in shaping *High School Confidential*, in which illegal drugs are linked to youth deviance, jazz, rock 'n' roll, Beat poetry, car racing, and sexual promiscuity. A police officer speaks to a high-school principal and teachers about marijuana:

> There's a high school in Indiana. . . . They had no problem three years ago. But out of a total enrollment of 1200 students, 285 were found to be using marijuana or heroin. And this dreadful condition was only uncovered through a horrible accident. One student, desperate for money to pay for his habit, sold bennies for quarters and dimes to kids in elementary school. It was the death of a thirteen-year-old, who had been addicted to marijuana and heroin, that exposed the ugly facts. But by that time, it was too late for forty-one teenagers who were addicted. It could happen here.

The officer in the film recklessly conflates marijuana with heroin use and appeals to audiences' fears about risks to youth. Anslinger's films consistently ignored factual knowledge of drugs to generate public fear and harsher laws.[13] In these 1950s films, the elementary and high-school schoolyard is a site of corruption and risk where devious drug dealers lure innocent White youth into addiction. The White police are represented in the film as the authority on drug dealing and solution to the epidemic. One police officer reprimands the principal and teachers for being naive in supporting "progressive education," for by doing so they have been blind to the fact that the high school is a site for drug dealing and addiction. In *High School Confidential*, Mr. A. is depicted as a violent drug dealer who owns a jazz club, with a henchman who supplies a number of male high-school students with drugs to sell. Illegal-drug films often depict drug dealers ratting each other out and one of his youthful dealers turns on him. Through their actions depicted in film and police narratives, the message is clear that drug dealers are morally bankrupt, willing to cheat and inform on each other, and can never be trusted.

Antidrug laws in the United States became increasingly harsh between the 1930s and 1950s. In 1956, the "death penalty was applied to the sale of heroin to minors."[14] In the late 1950s, films like the *The Pusher* (1959) introduced viewers to violent Puerto Rican and Mexican drug dealers and gangs who threaten White citizens, luring them into addiction. From the 1950s on, Hispanic, Irish, Italian, Asian, and Black men have all been demonized as illegal-drug dealers. Gang culture is portrayed in film as homogeneous and static, and racialized men are depicted as violent predators.[15]

Despite harsh penalties and antidrug propaganda, including fear-driven "educational" films made with the help of police officers and the federal drug czar, H. J. Anslinger, illegal-drug use and trafficking were not curtailed. In fact, by the late 1950s and early 1960s, drug use had increased substantially and became associated with White middle-class youth culture. Anslinger had been convinced that his antidrug campaign would deter illegal-drug use and trafficking in the United States.[16] However, it had the opposite effect, and youth in the 1960s found his films and antidrug propaganda to be unbelievable and funny.[17]

THE 1960S: THE "AMERICAN DREAM" AND DRUG TRAFFICKERS

As noted in chapter 3, counterculture sentiments were expressed in films produced in the 1960s. Then, moviegoers were provided with alternative depictions of drug dealers and illegal drugs. This section examines themes related to drug trafficking that were not addressed in the previous chapters. The film *Easy Rider* (1969) served to disrupt conventional discourse about the drug dealer and the American Dream. In the film, two White youths, Wyatt (played by Peter Fonda) and Billy (played by Dennis Hopper), are illegal-drug users and dealers who are transporting cocaine from a small Mexican border town to Los Angeles. Both Wyatt and Billy are depicted in the film as counterculture characters (evidenced by their clothing, hair styles, and behaviour).The drug trade is their means to drop out of the system. Wyatt's bike, a California chopper, has an American flag painted on the gas tank, and he also has the flag on his helmet and on the back of his leather jacket. Both the American flag and their motorcycles are powerful iconic presences in the film. They represent freedom and the American Dream. The song "Born to be Wild" accompanies one of the first scenes of Wyatt and Billy riding their bikes down the highway. The money they eventually gain from their drug deal is stashed in the gas tank. In the feature notes, Peter Fonda says of this scene, "Fucking the flag with money," destroying ourselves through materialism. The film depicts their travels to secure the one big score of cocaine that will provide them with the means to retire to Florida. The film depicts Wyatt and Billy sympathetically, reflecting societal and political shifts in the 1960s. The drug trade is represented as a form of capitalist entrepreneurship that can provide the means to drop out of the system.

Following their successful drug deal, Wyatt and Billy are sitting around a campfire when Billy comments, "We've done it, we're rich. We did it, man." Rather than agreeing, Wyatt says, "We blew it." Billy disagrees, "Go for big money, you're free." Wyatt reiterates, "We blew it." Dennis Hopper notes in the film commentary that their pursuit (even temporarily) of the American Dream, of getting rich through one big score, leads the men to lose sight of their freedom. The film is then not about getting rich; rather, it is about "freedom," and it critiques the notion of the American Dream by juxtaposing getting rich as a form of slavery to the system. The next day we see them riding their motorcycles on the highway; a river runs by it. Two men depicted as White rednecks, civil vigilantes in a pickup truck, drive by them. They point a rifle at them through the window and shoot, killing Billy and then Wyatt. Wyatt's motorcycle is seen from the air burning, flames engulfing it. Billy and Wyatt are murdered and their drug deal and their quest to "drop out" is not realized. Unlike conventional illegal-drug films, Billy and Wyatt are represented as caring and moral characters. Drug dealing is not represented as associated with violence; rather, White conventional society is the site of violence. In the film, White mainstream America itself is represented as a threat to freedom and to them personally.

Superfly: an alternative black hero

In the early 1970s, a number of "ghetto films," or blaxploitation films, emerged in the United States, including *Sweet Sweetback's Baad Asssss Song* (1971) and *Shaft* (1971); although not illegal-drug films, they ably represent the genre. These films clearly represent the emergence of gifted Black directors and actors produced by political and social shifts in the United States. The civil-rights and the Black Panther movements, alongside countercultural shifts in the 1960s, paved the way for a number of counterhegemonic films by Black directors. *Superfly* (1972) is one such film. *Superfly's* main character, Priest, is a drug dealer (played by Ron O'Neal). However, where *Easy Rider* depicts White America, *Superfly's* Priest is a Black drug dealer. He uses cocaine throughout the film, although it does not impair him in any way. He also sells cocaine, and his involvement in the drug trade is depicted as the only job in town for a Black man in racist and class-biased America. The film locates the drug trade in a racialized political economy of crime framework, calls into question the "American Dream," and features a Black man as the hero at a time when there was a dearth of Black heroes in Hollywood films. Just as significantly, Priest is truly heroic and ethical, even though he is a drug dealer, in contrast with the brutal, greedy, violent dealer we have come to recognize in contemporary film representations. *Superfly* is also an existentialist movie, and Priest is depicted as searching for the truth.

The film opens in New York City as two Black men walk down the street. The song, "Ghetto Child" by Curtis Mayfield, plays in the background. Priest is depicted as a light-skinned Black man with straight hair reaching down to his shoulders. We see him dressed in a stylish long maxi-coat and white hat, and he drives through the city in a large black Eldorado convertible. We sympathize with Priest because it is made obvious that he wants more than material wealth. He has some of the trappings of the rich dealer, symbolized by the gold coke spoon around his neck, gold rings, a White girlfriend, a superfly car, cool clothes, and a nice apartment which houses a colour TV and eight-track stereo. We understand that the drug trade has provided a level of wealth to Priest that is unavailable through legal or "jive jobs" available to inner-city Black men. Yet Priest is depicted as being dissatisfied with the materialistic rewards of the drug trade. His apartment is filled with art, including African sculpture, shelves of books, and a chessboard representing the tension between materialism and the "higher purpose" that Priest desires for his life. Priest states that he wants to leave the drug trade "before I have to kill somebody, or somebody ices me."

In his quest to leave the drug trade, Priest turns to Scatter for help, an older Black man, a mentor figure, and father substitute for Priest. Their relationship is based on affection, trust, and mutual aid. Scatter was originally responsible for helping set Priest up in the cocaine trade, but now he is out of the trade and runs a restaurant/bar. Priest asks Scatter to help him make his last "big deal," thus inadvertently drawing him back into the drug trade he had escaped. The White police in the film, who control the higher levels of the drug trade, are depicted as evil, ultraviolent symbols of corruption and immorality in White-supremacist U.S. society. They control the racialized inner-city communities, and they prevent people from getting out of drug dealing.

Priest sees his participation in the drug trade as a means to "buy me some time" before he can escape. Yet Priest's quest to be free of the ghetto and the drug trade is challenged by the crooked Police Commissioner Reardon, a White drug kingpin, and his corrupt police officers. Commissioner Reardon says to Priest, "Thought you were gonna be the best dealer I ever had. What the hell do you want to quit for? What else can you do? You're making more goddamn money than you ever made in your life. You just wanna be another two-bit Black junkie?"

Eddie, Priest's partner, is not really interested in leaving the drug trade, and he says to Priest, "Eight-track stereo, colour TV in every room, and can snort half a piece of dope a day. That's the American dream, nigger; well, ain't it? . . . I know it is a rotten game; it is the only one the man left us to play and that's the stone cold truth." Later Eddie says, "Fantasy about getting out of the life . . . What the fuck are you gonna do besides hustle? . . . Maybe this is what you suppose to do . . . think about it." But Priest disagrees with Eddie. He walks in Central Park with his longtime girlfriend, a Black woman, who seeks to help him. The park represents a contrast to Priest's urban reality, and he tells his girlfriend that he wants to "just to be free . . . Just can't be happy the way it is now. I never was." Priest wants more of life and he takes steps to exit the trade.

Eddie eventually snitches on Priest, and the police murder Scatter by injecting him with a hypodermic needle full of heroin. In the final scene, Priest goes to his apartment and picks up a briefcase full of drug money. In the elevator, he is joined by his girlfriend disguised as a bag lady. They switch briefcases and both walk out on to the street. Because she is a poor Black woman, she is unnoticed by the White police officers watching the apartment. A bunch of White policemen confront Priest, take the (empty) briefcase, shove him into a car, and drive him down to a wharf where the top trafficker, the corrupt commissioner, is waiting for him. Always cool, Priest snorts cocaine in front of the commissioner and challenges him. They fight and Priest gets to once again demonstrate his martial-arts moves. Priest shouts, "Kill me and all your family dies. I took out a $100,000 contract on your family. I hired the best killers there are: 'White killers.' Nothing better happen to me." He walks away, still looking cool, and gets into his superfly car and drives away.

Unlike Billy and Captain America in *Easy Rider,* who are murdered after their big deal, Priest goes unpunished for his deeds, and in fact we applaud him as he rides off into the sunset in his superfly car. He gets to keep the drug money, his girlfriend, his pride, and he has humiliated the crooked commissioner and the police. Priest "stuck it to the man" and lived to tell the tale. The film commentary notes that the character of Priest is a symbol of Black independence, while recognizing that independence requires a material base. Unlike many contemporary illegal-drug films, Priest is depicted as a drug dealer who represents an antiestablishment and Black aesthetic. Drug dealing is represented as an economic necessity in order to escape the poor ghetto neighbourhood. For Priest and his partner Eddie, the drug trade is the only avenue open to them to achieve the American

Dream, and as viewers we are sympathetic to Priest's plight. Unlike other characters represented in blaxploitation illegal-drug films, Priest wants more than material wealth and status. Although he dresses cool and has a superfly car, he is not shown wearing a lot of "bling," visual symbols we have come to associate with later representations of illegal-drug dealers (and rappers) in the inner city. We see him training in marshal arts and self-defense, but he is not depicted as overtly violent, sadistic, or greedy. Nor does the film focus on Black-on-Black violence or the corruption of youth by Black dealers.

In the film, there is no distinction between legal and illegal drugs, and alcohol, tobacco, cocaine, and marijuana use are normalized. Deviance is not punished in *Superfly*; rather, it is presented as an omnipresent part of the social world in which Priest lives. And crime is portrayed as being successfully used by Priest as an avenue for escape. When the film was released in the United States, inner-cities viewers were ecstatic. The special features and film commentary on the DVD release notes that Priest's victory over the "man" was applauded by movie viewers. In fact, the commentator states that he watched *Superfly* when it was released in a Missouri theatre, and there the whole audience leapt to their feet and applauded when Priest called Commissioner Reardon down.

Gordon Parks, Jr., the director of *Superfly*, died before he could make any more films. Whereas *Shaft* (1971) is most often cited as the first blaxploitation film, the commentator on the DVD edition argues that *Superfly* is better because it is not just about gangsters and hustlers in the inner city or the glamorization of gangsterism; rather, Priest is not viewed as a criminal by viewers. Instead, viewers see him as an entrepreneur and a man who can laugh and be affectionate and strong. Ultimately, he is a Black man who escapes the ghetto and his White oppressors. In *Superfly*, the top drug dealers are shown as White and officers of the law. They are constructed as ultraviolent men and a menace to the community, a representation that endures in contemporary illegal-drug films.

Both *Easy Rider* and *Superfly* rupture conventional illegal-drug discourse about trafficking. Furthermore, both films provide the viewer with a promise of a world not shaped by consumerism, and they represent conventional society, rather than lone drug dealers, as a threat to freedom.

Superfly is an anomaly, and later illegal-drug films, including blaxploitation films like *Cleopatra Jones* and *Coffy*, both produced in 1973, and later movies labeled "ghetto films" like *New Jack City* (1991), can be viewed as mirror opposites of *Superfly*. Whereas *Superfly* is a counterhegemonic drug film, in films like *Cleopatra Jones*, *Coffy*, and *New Jack City* all drug dealers are ultimately greedy and ultraviolent. In these films, the ghetto is constructed as "inescapable" and Black-on-Black violence is represented as the norm. The heroic figure is depicted as the Black justice agent rather than the Black drug dealer. In *Cleopatra Jones*, *Coffy*, and *New Jack City*, drug dealers are depicted as a menace to the community. *Cleopatra Jones*

Cleopatra Jones. Source: Warner Bros./Photofest.
© Warner Bros.

does depict the law agent as a powerful and beautiful Black woman, and, in the spirit of *Superfly*, the drug-smuggling and dealing family is White. It is headed by a vicious and violent woman, named "Mommy," who is portrayed as more deviant than her ineffective sons. *Coffy* introduces viewers to a young Black nurse of the same name who sets out to murder drug dealers after her young sister becomes addicted. The failure of White law enforcement to deal with the "drug problem" is a theme in the film; working outside the law—police and civil vigilantism—is portrayed as the only way to successfully bring down dealers. U.S.-produced "ghetto films" such as *New Jack City* (1991), *Boyz n the Hood* (1991), and *Clockers* (1995) incorporate similar law-and-order themes, as do drug films outside the ghetto film genre, such as *Gridlock'd* (1997) and *Traffic* (2000). In all these films, top drug dealers are represented as dehumanized, greedy, immoral, violent, and unsympathetic characters.

Following the production of films like *Easy Rider* and *Superfly*, the backlash to normalized illegal-drug use and drug dealing was almost immediate on screen and off. In 1969, President Nixon, reminiscent of the film narrative in *Reefer Madness* (1936), declared that illegal drugs were America's number one enemy. He introduced a new set of drug-prohibition initiatives contained in the Controlled Substance Act in 1970. President Nixon is responsible for creating the term "war on drugs" to describe his new domestic and international prohibition initiatives. Responsibility was given to the Bureau of Narcotics and Dangerous Drugs and then to the newly established prohibition agency, the Drug Enforcement Administration (DEA), created in 1973. A host of films produced in the 1970s reinforced antidrug discourse, including *Joe* (1970) and *The French Connection* (1971). The narrative of these films links illegal drugs with criminality and violence, and the dominant discourse that emerges in *Joe* is that of the drug dealer as evil. *Joe*, a working-class man, and Frank come together in the film to "cleanse" the streets of drug dealers whose deaths at the hands of "concerned citizens" is justified. White vigilante justice is constructed as noble and as a civic assistance to the police, and violent masculinity is normalized.

The French Connection: a weak and flawed criminal justice system

Whereas *Joe* (1970) is a film with little cultural weight, *The French Connection* (1971) received international acclaim and a number of film awards, including best director, film, and actor (for Gene Hackman's portrayal of Popeye). The film is a suspense story, loosely based on Robin Moore's nonfiction book of the same title, and a number of New York police detectives worked as technical advisors on the film. One of them, Eddie Egan, plays a small part in the film, and he and his partner Sonny Cloudy Grosse, who also worked on the film, serve as the prototypes for the film's two main characters.

The film involves heroin smuggling (the French Connection), two white police officers in the narcotics division, and violent drug dealers in New York City and France, and a large shipment of heroin serves as the focus. The film is mostly set in New York City right before Christmas. The city looks cold, gritty, and uninviting, and the New York waterfront is grey and dreary. In contrast, the opening visuals of the film depict Marseilles as warm, sunny, and habitable and the deep blue Mediterranean looks crystal clear and inviting. The *French Connection* is interesting in its interpretation of the "border narrative," usually reserved for Mexico, South American countries, and Afghanistan as the drug-source nations of the illegal trade. Here, heroin moves through France before being shipped off to New York. Yet the film does not stray too far from prevailing "border narratives," as the French people in the film are portrayed as murderous, brutal, and willing to kill innocent bystanders in their quest for profit. Popeye derogatorily refers to French people as "frogs" throughout the film,[18] an inadvertent reminder that such stereotyping is not new and can resurface quickly given the right social and political setting. The drug trade and law enforcement are represented as male domains and women are largely absent from the film narrative.

In *The French Connection*, all of the New York police are portrayed as White men. The film focuses on two officers in the narcotics division: Popeye, racist and violent, and his partner Cloudy, who is "good" and moral. After a long heroin drought, locals in the know begin to speculate that a huge heroin shipment is expected that will allow a "lot of sick people . . . to get well." In the film, a number of low-level street dealers are depicted as Black men, whereas the high-level and middle-level dealers are all White. Black street dealers represent the "Black underclass" and are recipients of Popeye's racism and brutality, as well as his link to larger drug deals in the making. For instance, in one early scene, in which Popeye and Cloudy are undercover; they apprehend their suspect, and he is brutally beaten by Popeye, who wants him to reveal his drug "connection." Later, we see Popeye in a bar where he savagely beats up his informer, a young Black man.

Charnier (or Frog One, as he is referred to in the film a number of times) is represented as an older White kingpin trafficker from France, a former longshoreman who has become successful in the drug trade. In the film, Charnier says that he has not done a day of legal or "real work" since he "left the crane" to enter the drug trade, thus informing viewers that drug trafficking is not "real work." Charnier is not physically violent, but he is so powerful that he can hire a henchman, Nicoli, to do his dirty work. Charnier is depicted as cultured and refined in the scene of a long multi-course dinner that Popeye views from the outside. Standing on the bleak cold street, Popeye eats pizza and drinks bad coffee that he spits out on the pavement. Charnier is decked out in warm, expensive, and classic clothes in contrast to Popeye's worn-out-looking trench coat that can hardly provide warmth from the winter cold. Charnier's henchman, Nicoli, is represented

The French Connection. Source: Twentieth Century Fox/Photofest. © Twentieth Century Fox.

as a cold-blooded murderer who kills a French detective at the beginning of the film. The film depicts a famous car and elevated-train chase scene, following Nicoli's attempt to murder Popeye. Quite a number of innocent people are killed by Nicoli during the chase scene and the ultimate train crash. Following the crash, Popeye shoots Nicoli in the back, killing him.

Illegal drugs are rarely shown in the film. The filmmakers correctly assume that viewers will identify tightly wrapped plastic bags as containing drugs, and depictions of white powder as heroin or cocaine. Throughout the film, the narrative relies on the hegemonic assumption that heroin is "bad" in order for the film to make sense. Coffee, alcohol, and tobacco are all normalized in the film. Popeye and Cloudy go to a bar to drink after work and other police drink on duty. Coffee and tobacco are also consumed throughout the film, reproducing the normality of the legal/illegal dichotomy.

Whereas the film depicts drug dealers as brutal and violent, Sal, who hopes to broker the drug deal in order to break into the big leagues, is depicted as a sympathetic character. The drug trade is seen as a form of capitalist entrepreneurship for this working-class man, just as it might have been for Charnier a long time ago. The themes of the violent dealer and the capitalist entrepreneur shape drug films today (to name just a few; see *Atlantic City* [1980], *Scarface* [1983], *Goodfellas* [1990], *Boyz n the Hood* [1991], *New Jack City* [1991], *Pulp Fiction* [1994], *Clockers* [1995], *Traffic* [2000], *Layer Cake* [2005], *Sweet Sixteen* [2002], and *25th Hour* [2002]). Sal's extravagant lifestyle, with fancy new cars and free spending, is key in bringing him and the other traffickers down, for Popeye and Cloudy notice early on that he is living beyond his means and tail him.

Suitcases full of money in *The French Connection* remind viewers how much is at stake. Yet for all of the traffickers' brutality, the White police are also depicted as ultraviolent; they are shown threatening and hitting drug users and street-level dealers, risking public safety in long car-chase scenes, and bending the rules. However, police are represented as hard working and their violence is depicted as justified, a necessary tactic in light of the restraints of the law. In the final climatic shoot-out at a warehouse, the police kill a number of the drug traffickers. The climatic shoot-out is problematized by a final scene in which Popeye accidentally shoots and kills the federal agent, Mulderig, while pursuing Charnier. Popeye is depicted as pumped up and unconcerned, and his lethal mistake is depicted as justified in the pursuit of justice. After killing Mulderig, Popeye moves on to look for Charnier. We hear a single gunshot. However, we are informed later that Charnair's body is not found, and it is unclear if the top kingpin remains free and unpunished.

The final scene illuminates the failure of the criminal-justice system, even though a number of drug traffickers are killed in the shoot-out. At the end of the film, the system's failure is reinforced by highlighting on the screen the sentences of some of the dealers involved. For example, Weinstock, the New York kingpin, has his case dismissed for lack of proper evidence, and another is found guilty of only a misdemeanor. The viewer is informed that both Popeye and Cloudy are transferred out of the narcotics division and reassigned. Popeye is never held accountable for killing Mulderig.

In films such as *Easy Rider* (1969), *Joe* (1970), *The French Connection* (1971), and *Superfly* (1971), new discourses about criminal justice and vigilante justice emerge. No longer are the White police represented as absurd or comical. Rather, the police are depicted as even more brutal than the dangerous drug traffickers they wish to stop. And it seems the more brutal the representation of the drug dealer, the more brutal the law-enforcement agents are. In *Easy Rider*, *Coffy*, and *Joe*, civil vigilantes are depicted as murdering drug dealers, and they are celebrated in *Coffy* and *Joe*. In *Superfly*, the white police are the top dealers, and they are represented as greedy, violent, and the most corrupt characters in the film. They, like the White police agents in *The French Connection*, are depicted employing illegal tactics, violence, and murder in order to catch the drug trafficker. In *Easy Rider*, *Coffy*, *Joe*, *Superfly*, and *The French Connection*, drug dealers are constructed as guilty and dispensable without the benefit of a trial. Both *Joe* and *The French Connection* perpetuate myths about justice, police powers, and the court system. These early 1970s films represent the criminal-justice system as weak and flawed, and both the public and the police are hindered in their fight against drug dealers. Thus, murder, excessive violence, and illegal strategies are viewed as normal and necessary tools in pursuit of vigilante justice.

The Panic in Needle Park: criminal addicts

The Panic in Needle Park (1973) offers a more sympathetic view of a poor White street hustler, Bobby, who is addicted to heroin and eventually secures a job working as a street dealer for Santo, a high-level heroin supplier. In the film, Bobby (played by Al Pacino) is depicted as a recidivist criminal addict. Needle Park in New York City is his home, an inescapable haven and trap for a multiethnic group of poor street hustlers and heroin addicts. The neighbourhood is under constant surveillance by the White police, who are shown actively pressuring users and dealers to rat on one another in order to avoid lengthy prison sentences. Bobby is finally able to change his fortunes when he begins to work with Santo. Santo is a Black male who has a limousine, nice clothing, and armed henchmen. However, unlike the henchman in *The French Connection*, or the violent dealers in *Cleopatra Jones* and *Coffy*, Santo and the street dealers in *The Panic in Needle Park* are not depicted as violent; instead, it is the "junkies" and street dealers who are portrayed as dishonest and immoral, always ready to rat on their friends when the police press them. At the end of the film, Bobby's girlfriend, portrayed as an innocent White middle-class woman who is now consumed by her escalating heroin habit, rats on him in order to avoid going to prison. Although it is impossible not to sympathize with Bobby and his girlfriend's plight, the film links small-time street dealing and heroin addiction with property crime, and it makes clear that people addicted to heroin will never go straight. No matter how much we sympathize with them, heroin users are represented as recidivist criminal addicts. As well, the film narrative repeats the tired refrain that moral young White women are vulnerable to and lured by dealers into a life of addiction and destitution.

In 1973, the Rockefeller Drug Law was enacted in New York to respond to the heroin epidemic depicted in *The Panic in Needle Park*. Harsh mandatory sentencing limited judges' discretion and the sentencing scheme was even harsher than federal drug laws. Early on, politicians and law officials proclaimed that these new laws were aimed at bringing down the drug kingpins. However, it became clear right away that it was low-level street dealers and users, especially poor people of colour, who were disproportionately targeted by the new laws, and the prison population exploded.[19] The Rockefeller laws are still on the books in 2007.

Scarface: Latino cartels

The 1983 production *Scarface* is a remake of the classic 1932 production of the same name. In the early film, violent criminal gangs and alcohol prohibition and the illegal trade are the focus of the film. The early film is loosely based on Al Capone's life, an Italian American. Tony has a thick accent and his mother is portrayed wearing an "ethnic" shawl, dangling earrings, and long skirt. In the 1983 production of *Scarface*, produced by Brian De Palma, ethnicity is also central to the narrative: Cuban men and Latino gangs are represented as central to drug trafficking.

Scarface (1983) begins with scrolling text that describes the mass migration from Cuba to the United States in 1980. We are told that boats were filled with the "dregs of his [Castro's] jails." The film cuts to images of boats leaving Cuba and tracks them until they arrive on the coast of Florida. The camera zooms in on an image of the U.S. flag and then to the main character, a young Cuban man named Tony (played by Al Pacino, in yet another criminal role) who is being interrogated by American immigration and law officials. Tony is shown earning a fortune through the cocaine drug trade that entices new refugees as a route to wealth. Tony kills for fun and throughout the film gang members are viciously beaten and murdered.

Tony's rapid rise to wealth and power is contrasted with the subsistence-level incomes of his hardworking mother and sister. Drug dealers are men of colour and most are depicted as refugees and immigrants. Drug trafficking is represented as the domain of "foreign others," and throughout the film Tony repeatedly condemns Cuban communism. In contrast, Tony comments about life in the United States. "In this country you have to make the money first. Then when you get the money you get the power. When you have the power then you get the women." The real money brokers in the film, the bankers and lawyers, are White, as are the police, who are corrupt and complicit in the drug trade.

In the film, Bolivia is portrayed as the main drug-source nation, and we see the movement of cocaine from it to the shores of Miami (similar to the representations of Cuban refugees in the film who arrive in Miami and become drug dealers). The U.S. border is represented as porous and vulnerable to racialized and criminal others. Tony is shown becoming more violent and greedy as the film progresses; however, his lawyer is skilled at keeping him out of prison. In *Scarface* and other illegal-drug films, defense lawyers are depicted as guilty by association. Tony's cocaine use increases as the film progresses. Cocaine use is accompanied by paranoia and agitation. Violence is omnipresent and gang fighting escalates until the final bloodbath at the end of the film, where Tony finally dies.

Jonathan White (1991) writes about the influence of *Scarface*. He notes that the film impressed upon the national consciousness that greedy and violent Latin-American immigrants/refugees were associated with the cocaine trade.[20] By the 1980s, representations of racialized gangs had become more violent. Similar to the syringe, the rolled dollar bill, and suitcases lined with U.S bills, the gun became an important symbol of drug-trade violence and hypermasculinity.

Boyz n the Hood and *New Jack City*: black ghetto gangs

The 1991 film *Boyz n the Hood*, written and produced by John Singleton, is unique because without ever explicitly showing drug dealing, the lure and the risk of drug-trade gang violence is an undercurrent in the film narrative. In the film, young Black men and the streets of South Central Los Angeles are under constant surveillance by the police. Black-on-Black gang violence, murder, dysfunctional families, and police violence intersect, making the neighbourhood inescapable. High-level traffickers are absent from the film narrative. The film critiques the invisibility of Black fathers. The character Furious is depicted as an authoritarian, patriarchal Black father who will be able to teach his young son Tre "to be a man." The film constructs a hegemonic family-values narrative in which gang violence stems from family dysfunction. Yet it also shows South Central Los Angeles as a community under siege by gang violence and police surveillance and violence. The police are represented as a racist "occupying army," and Black prison time is normalized as the character Doughboy moves in and out of prison. Ultimately, even "good" boys like Tre cannot escape the matrix of oppression and drug-related gang violence. Gang violence is associated with young Black men; it is spreading and barely contained.

New Jack City (1991) is set in New York City in 1986 during the Reagan era, and it offers a narrative about the emergence of crack cocaine use and trafficking in a predominantly Black neighbourhood in Harlem. The film, similar to *Scarface* (1983), focuses on the activities of the leaders of racialized and violent drug-dealing gangs; however, unlike the wealthy Latino cartel traffickers in *Scarface*, the drug dealers in *New Jack City* are small-time in comparison. Local Black drug dealers are represented as a violent threat to inner-city communities and the nation. The film opens with a wide aerial view of New York City. We see the Twin Towers, and in the background we hear the voice of a male radio announcer talking about unemployment and the gap between the rich and the poor. The announcer also reports the drug-related death of a child who the police said "just got in the way." We are introduced to Nino Brown, an entrepreneurial Black drug trafficker who is violent and misogynist and the leader of the Cash Money Boys, who have little value for human life. His friend and business partner Gee Money convinces him that crack is the drug of the future. He says, "Be going crazy over this, man. And the bitches! Oh lord! The bitches do anything for this, man." He then says, "Times like these, people want to get high." He shows Nino a small glass vial filled with crack. He opens it and the camera closes in as he pours it out on the table. They pull out a map of the Carter apartments and set out discussing how they will take over the area with crack and displace the Italian mob that usually works the area.

We are also introduced to Scotty Appleton, a righteous Black undercover police officer played by Ice-T. In sharp contrast to Priest, the heroic Black cocaine dealer in *Superfly* (1972), Scotty is represented as the "hero" in *New Jack City*, even though he is a rogue cop prone to vigilantism and excessive violence. When we first encounter him, he is running after a young Black crack user named Pookie who has stolen a shoulder bag full of money from him. Pookie eventually runs into a playground full of children and pulls out a gun. There is chaos in the playground as parents and children run away screaming. Pookie shoots at Scotty but he misses him. Scotty then shoots Pookie in the foot and he falls to the ground in the playground. He identifies himself as a police officer. Scotty eventually befriends Pookie and helps him stop using crack. In order to repay him for his life, Pookie later offers to go undercover to bring down Nino Brown.

Meanwhile, Scotty's direct police superior, a young Black man, is depicted arguing with the city's Black police commissioner, as he tells him that crack is an epidemic. "You're talking about a war out there that we're losing, but you're not going to give me what I need to win. I need some cops who know these streets. I need some New Jack cops to take down a New Jack gangster." The commissioner finally agrees to his plan. Then the camera cuts to a bloodbath of drug-trade turf violence as Nino and his gang take over control of the Carter apartments. We see a young Black woman murder another dealer at close range. Killings take place in front of small children in an apartment, as well as in drive-by shootings. Earlier, the camera zooms in on a group of mostly Black children in a schoolyard. Drawing on Nancy Reagan's "just say no" campaign, their teacher asks them, "If you just say no, what are you going to say yes to?" The children respond loudly, "We say yes to education . . . to make a positive impact on our nation."

Nino and his gang set up a crack-production lab and trafficking empire in the Carter apartments. It is a local affair and we see Nino and his associates becoming rich. In one scene, we see Nino surrounded by little children, and he is giving them money. An elderly Black man comes rushing in and yells at him and tells him that he is instrumental in killing his own people.

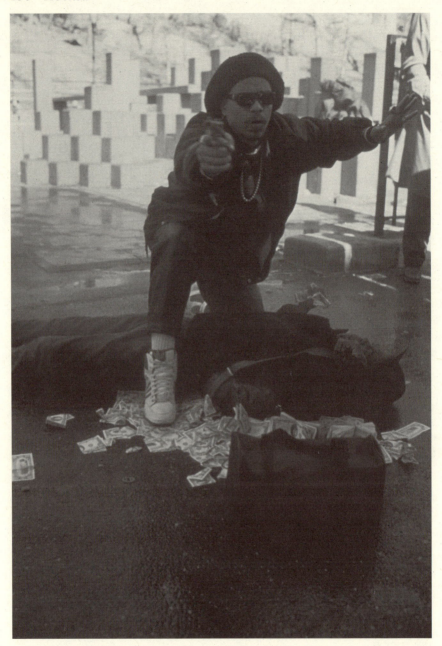

New Jack City. Source: Warner Bros./Photofest. © Warner Bros.

He says, "You're committing genocide on your own people. With the silk suits and fancy cars . . . You're an idol worshipper. You're killing your own people with them little white devils you're putting in that bottle." Nino's only female associate and girlfriend, depicted as always ready to kill, turns to Nino and says, "Let me smoke this old dude!" She does not get her way but instead she and her associates brutally beat the elderly man.

Meanwhile, Pookie and Scotty are planning how they will infiltrate Nino's crack enterprise. When Pookie infiltrates Nino's crack operation, he struggles not to use crack again, but he fails. Eventually, Nino's gang discovers that he is an informer and that he is wired. They quickly murder him and blow up the lab and apartments; thus, the plan to bring down Nino and his gang is ruined for lack of evidence. The commissioner is furious with Scotty and his fellow police officers, and he tells them that the operation is over. Scotty does not agree and decides to take the law into his own hands.

Following Pookie's funeral, Scotty tells his partner Nick Paretti, a White Italian police officer, "Drug dealer is the worse kind of brother, man. He won't sell it to his sister. He won't sell it to his mother, but he'll sell it to one of his boys on the street. I don't know about you, but I'm ready to kill Nino Brown. Are you with me?" His partner Nick replies, "I'm ahead of you." Scotty then raises his bottle of alcohol and clinks Nick's bottle in agreement. Next we see Scotty and Nick infiltrating Nino's operation, and Scotty pretends to be a high-level cocaine trafficker.

We see again how ruthless Nino is when he and his associates are attacked by rival Italian traffickers following a wedding reception. They are just leaving the reception when Italian gangsters pull out machine guns and shoot at Nino and his associates. In the middle of the shooting, Nino picks up a little girl and uses her as a bullet shield and then tosses her to the ground as he runs to safety. Later Nino retaliates and the camera cuts to a group of elderly Italian men sitting outside a coffee shop who are brutally gunned down.

At the same time that Nino is busy at the wedding, Scotty's partner Nick is shown illegally breaking into Nino's home and opening his safe. There he conveniently finds a small box with computer disks neatly stacked in a row, labeled "Financial Report." He steals them. The plot thickens as Scotty sets up the drug transaction with Nino, and Scotty arrives with his attaché case full of clear plastic bags of powder cocaine. However, as he opens the attaché case, one of Nino's gang members recognizes him. A shoot-out occurs and the police arrive but Nino escapes. We then see Nino murder Gee Money for betraying him by cutting a side deal with Scotty.

Nino is beaten up and arrested by Scotty following a chase scene. Scotty then aims his gun at Nino, but he is constrained in the nick of time by his partner. The court scene that follows has Nino's girlfriend, Celine, act as a state witness against him. At one point in the trial, Nino says to the young black female prosecutor and the court:

> I'm not guilty, you're the one that's guilty, the lawmakers, the politicians, the Colombian drug lords, all you who lobby against making drugs legal, just like you did with alcohol during the prohibition. You're

the one who's guilty. . . . Ain't no Aussies in Harlem. I mean, not one of us in here owns a poppy field. This thing is bigger than Nino Brown. This is big business. This is the American way.

The female prosecutor responds, "I'm sure the court was enlightened by your geopolitical tirade, Mr. Brown." This scene is interesting because it opens the door to examining the drug trade and who is profiting, but it also links legalization with the interests of violent traffickers like Nino. This, of course, makes no sense because a regulated market would do much to end the illegal trade and traffickers' profits, as happened at the end of alcohol prohibition in the United States.[21]

During the trial, Nino rats on all of his associates, claiming that they are the kingpins, not him. The judge sentences him to one year in prison. As Nino leaves the courtroom, the press asks him what he thinks of his sentence. He replies, "Think the American justice system is the greatest in the world. Proud to be an American." Then the camera cuts to the elderly man who was beaten up by Nino's associates. He yells out to Nino, "Your soul is required" as he shoots Nino on the stairs of the courtroom. Nino's body falls to the ground and retribution and justice have been accomplished. The next scene, and the end of the film, shows the following caption on the screen: "Although this is a fictional story, there are Nino Browns in every major city in America. If we don't confront the problem realistically—without empty slogans and promises—then drugs will continue to destroy our community."

The film *New Jack City* is reminiscent of earlier morality tales made with the help of justice officials and H. J. Anslinger, the U.S. commissioner of narcotics. Drug dealers are represented as the ultimate violent threat to communities and the nation. Here, the community is represented as Black rather than White, and Black space is represented as criminalized, where Black-on-Black violence and illegality prevail. In contrast to the racialized and criminalized space represented in the film, moral White space is ever present due to a few significant scenes such as one where a young White man looks out of place as he enters Nino's crack house. The film makes a few initial references to poverty and the impact of the Reagan era on inner-city residents, but greedy Black drug dealers are situated as the enemy and the root of community breakdown. There is no critique of punitive federal and state responses to social problems, including a heightened war on drugs, which includes new mandatory sentencing, harsher penalties for crack than for powder cocaine, and police and DEA race profiling that lead to rising incarceration rates and drug-trade violence.[22] In this film and others, the criminal-justice system is represented as lenient, and police and civil vigilante justice is celebrated. The Reagan Contra/cocaine scandal, in which the U.S. government under President Regan supported antidemocratic Nicaraguan Contra factions and drug trafficking in the 1980s, is absent from the film narrative; thus, cocaine and ultimately crack are associated only with racialized inner-city space. Surprising for the time, the HIV/AIDS crisis is also absent from the film narrative, which may have to do with its focus on crack rather than heroin. From the 1980s on, HIV/AIDS changed the face of illegal-drug use because it is a blood-borne disease making injection-drug users at risk for transmission of the virus. Rather than address the HIV/AIDS epidemic, U.S. politicians focused on crack use and associated it with poor Black urban dealers in the public imagination.

The Spike Lee film *Clockers* (1995), with a soundtrack of hip-hop and R&B, also weighs in on crack dealing. The film is set in the projects in Brooklyn, and it begins with a photomontage of dead young Black men cordoned off with yellow police tape that says "crime scene." The camera cuts to graffiti and wall murals of youth with guns and memorials to young men who have died from gun violence. Then the camera cuts to a scene of two Black men selling crack on the street. The central narrative focuses on male Black-on-Black violence, street-level drug dealing, and gun and gang culture. Guns and visible wealth are depicted as important signifiers of drug dealers' identities in the film. Although the film portrays crack dealing as a form of male capitalist entrepreneurship in the face of race and class barriers, it also strongly condemns it. In one scene a mother admonishes her son and his friends for their participation in the crack trade. She says, "You all ain't nothing but a bunch of good-for-nothing, death-dealing scum." Similar to the narrative by the old man in *New Jack City*, she says "you are selling your own people death." As well, reminiscent of representations in *Boyz n the Hood*, Black youth, especially those who participate in the drug trade, are under constant police surveillance, and the ghetto is represented as inescapable. The police are lawful, even though they are racist, and they are in sharp contrast to the excessive violence associated with the Black drug dealers in the film—who, despite their violence, are not demonized like the characters in *New Jack City*. It is the crack users who are ridiculed, and crack is represented as leading to addiction and death. Drug laws are not problematized in the film. Unlike *Boyz n the Hood*, *Clockers* ends on a happy note with Strike, one of the main characters, getting on a train and leaving the inner city behind.

Spike Lee and numerous film producers have attempted to capture the crack scare of the 1980s on screen. There is no doubt that crack use and selling, and associated drug trade violence, did have a negative impact on some inner-city communities; however, federal, state, and city cutbacks in economic and social supports, racial profiling, and drug-war policy also shaped the lives of people in these communities. Rather than looking more closely at these factors, crack was presented as the most dangerous and "contagiously addicting" drug known.[23] These sentiments and hastily crafted new drug legislation led to an increase in arrests and convictions. Black and Hispanic people accounted for 96.5 percent of crack prosecutions between 1992 and 1994. Rather than the drug kingpin, poor street-level dealers and users are most at risk for arrest and conviction.[24] Poor and racialized women have also been disproportionately impacted by the Rockefeller laws and federal drug law. Since 1973, when the Rockefeller laws were passed, the female state-prison population increased from 400 women to over 3,000 by 2002.[25] The criminalization and imprisonment of so many poor and racialized drug offenders has had a negative impact on families and has harmed their communities, but *New Jack City* and *Clockers* do not explore these issues.

Harsher laws to penalize crack use and trafficking and rising prison rates in the United States stem from specific events. In 1989, in a much reported speech, the first President Bush held up a bag of crack that he claimed was bought across from the White House. He claimed that crack was killing children and turning cities into "battle zones." He laid out his plan to achieve "victory over drugs." Bush Senior promised to double federal funding to state and local police and to increase prison capacity. In 1988 and 1989, the press and politicians devoted more time to the "drug war" than any other issue.[26] From the mid-1980s to the early 1990s, the media and a number of politicians helped fuel an anticrack-drug scare in which crack was blamed for numerous social and political problems.[27] Although President Reagan, and his successor President Bush Senior, were intent on creating a "drug free America," it was not achieved during or following their presidencies even though immense resources have been diverted to the cause at the expense of funding to schools, health care, housing, and social supports. Of course, drug-free America ideology does not refer to our most toxic drugs, which lead to far more health problems—alcohol and tobacco. Nor does it refer to the copious amounts of legal over-the-counter and prescribed drugs people take everyday.

In fact, during the crack scare in the United States, there was no empirical evidence to support Bush Senior and media claims that crack was threatening every community in the United States. Contrary to Bush Senior's claims about buying crack easily a block away from the White House, the sale was staged by DEA agents, who were not able to successfully buy crack in the vicinity. The DEA resorted to enticing a young Black high-school student to travel to the park across from the White House so that a claim could be made that the sale was made there.[28]

Clear and Present Danger: White House complicity

Although the emphasis in *New Jack City* and other illegal-drug films is most often on individual immorality, violent dealers and gangs, and their threat to communities, some films look outside the inner city and point to the White House as complicit in and profiting from the drug trade and covert foreign wars.

The opening scene of *Clear and Present Danger* (1994) depicts a U.S. flag with its stars and stripes undulating in the wind. The camera closes in on a U.S. Coast Guard boat to which the flag is attached. The boat has a huge gun attached to the deck, and it is pointed directly at a pleasure yacht occupied by Spanish-speaking people. Here the use of English subtitles provides us with clues as to their foreign identities. It appears that the owners of the boat were murdered in their sleep by members of the "Cali cartel" who allegedly took over the boat. One of the murdered men was a friend of the president, and the Coast Guard has two men in custody for the murders. The president says to Jack, a top level CIA officer played by Harrison Ford: "Promised the American people I would do something about the drug problem and drugs pouring into this country. Course of action I suggest is a course of action I can't suggest. The drug cartels represent a clear and present danger to the national security of the United States."

The President writes a letter authorizing covert "paramilitary action against cartels." An agent visits a paramilitary who is contracted in Colombia with twelve U.S. soldiers to help wipe out the cartels. Meanwhile, Jack investigates the president's dead friend, who appears to have received huge amounts of cash, US$650 million, to be exact, and the president wants the lost money to be recovered. The question is whether he was laundering money for the cartel.

The twelve U.S. soldiers chosen for the covert action against the cartel are left to die so that no evidence remains. However, in true Hollywood fashion, they are rescued almost single-handedly by Jack. When the last soldiers are rescued, Jack shouts to them with emotion, "Let's go, sons. We're going home, boys!" The film illuminates White House complicity in the drug trade and illegal covert activity in foreign countries, yet it glamorizes the armed forces, rugged individualism, and nationalism.

When Jack arrives home, he confronts the president and yells at him, "American soldiers and innocent people are dead because of you!" Jack says he will report everything to a Senate committee, and the president threatens him, saying Jack will take the blame along with his old (now deceased) boss. Bravely, Jack responds, "Sorry, Mr. President, I don't dance." The film ends with Jack standing alone before the Senate committee swearing under oath that his testimony is true.

Clear and Present Danger offers a critique of corruption and drug trafficking with a focus on the link between political power and covert actions. The president and his justice officials, all White and powerful, are corrupt and benefiting from the drug trade and covert military actions. However, cartel members are represented as sadistic killers, perpetuating racialized stereotypes. The lone defender of the constitution is Jack. He single-handedly exposes the corruption of power in the U.S. government, but collective action is not contemplated in the film.

Clear and Present Danger (1998) both disrupts conventional representations of drug-trade kingpins and also feeds into ideological narratives about U.S. nationalism and the enlisted men who defend it. The film does not problematize the military or the war on drugs. However, we shouldn't be surprised by that, because the film was made with the support of the

U.S. Department of Defense (DoD). Major Georgi of the DoD worked on the script and made recommendations. In his final report to the DOD, he writes: "Military depictions have become more of a 'commercial' for us, more than damage control, and the production offers good public information values."[29] Major Georgi goes on to say that if the script had changed during filming he would have said, "Well, I'm taking my toys and I'm going home. . . . I'm taking my tanks and my troops and my location, and I'm going home. And that would draw the attention of the producer."[30] The film received support from the DoD because it depicted patriotism and brave soldiers.[31]

Many movie producers work with the Pentagon in order to have access to military equipment (planes, tanks, submarines, and uniforms), film footage, bases, and troops for free or minimal fees. However, the military will only provide these goods if the film is considered "feasible and authentic," "informs the public about the military," and helps "military recruiting and retention."[32] Thus, films must always show military missions accomplished and antiwar films are not supported. What is deemed "feasible and authentic" is defined by the military not the producer. Thus, those producers who wish to tell a story that differs from the military's version are turned down and burdened with the exorbitant cost of creating or renting equipment elsewhere or are not able to produce their film.[33] The military uses public funds and resources to shape Hollywood films. Since 1927, the U.S. military has been rewriting Hollywood scripts and inserting propaganda into films in exchange for filmmakers' use of military equipment, troops, and bases. David Robb, the author of *Operation Hollywood*, questions how the Pentagon censors films and concludes that "no society is free that allows its military to control the arts."[34]

Traffic: the Mexican threat

As discussed in the book's introduction and chapter 3, *Traffic* (2000) was produced in the United States, and cocaine is the illegal drug being used and sold, rather than heroin. The U.S. version, in contrast to the earlier-produced British film *Traffik* (1989), does not include the story of a rural poppy farmer and family; rather, the film is from the points of view of a Latino American cocaine dealer, his pregnant wife and child, the Drug Enforcement Administration (DEA)—two men, one Black and one Hispanic—the Mexican police, the U.S. drug czar, his wife, and daughter, who is using crack. Mexico is represented as the drug-source country.

Traffic was directed by Steven Soderbergh, and it won four Academy Awards in 2001 for Best Director, Best Supporting Actor, Best Film Editing, and Best Adapted Screenplay. It also received the New York Film Critics' Best Picture of the Year and received five Golden Globe awards. A number of politicians and the U.S. media praised it for its accurate depiction of the war on drugs; in fact, a few politicians actually participate in the film.[35]

The racist imagery in the U.S. production of *Traffic* is shocking. Similar to earlier drug movies, racialized people depicted in the drug trade are vilified, as is Mexico, represented as the source country for cocaine later sold in the United States. The country is depicted as uncivilized and the military is seen as violent and active in drug trafficking. The inner city in the United States is depicted as racialized space where a White girl's, in this case the drug czar's daughter, downfall and degradation are facilitated by Black men and crack. In case viewers have difficulty distinguishing between criminalized and racialized space in contrast to White, Western civilized moral space, the director employs a different colour filter for Mexico, a grainy brown lens to contrast with the wealthy suburbs, and the inner city of the United States. The head of the Mexican military is portrayed as greedy, violent, and sadistic. Violence and punishment of drug traffickers is normalized in the film and the rule of law is ignored by U.S. DEA agents in their pursuit of Western justice. Illegal tactics are celebrated at the end of the film when a DEA officer risks his personal safety by planting an illegal bug in the home of a suspected drug trafficker after he is acquitted of drug trafficking following the murder, instigated by his wife, of his associate, who was about to provide state evidence against him. His defense lawyer is also portrayed as complicit and profiting in the cocaine trade.

Throughout the film, Mexico and the authorities there (except for one lone police officer) are represented as a threat to the United States, and the viewer is informed in the narrative of the movie that "in Mexico law enforcement is an entrepreneurial activity." In the film, the North American Free Trade Agreement (NAFTA) is depicted as opening the U.S.–Mexico border, fueling "a free for all" for foreign cartels. *Traffic* offers no critique of how NAFTA has increased social and economic deprivation, decreased jobs, and lowered wages for the majority of Mexican people at the same time that a small percentage of Mexican society becomes richer and foreign investors profit.[36] Nor does *Traffic* explore how U.S. drug policy and intervention contributes to violence and instability in Mexico. Instead, *Traffic* perpetuates official National Drug Control Strategy and DEA discourse— the U.S. border and the nation are represented as under threat from foreign Others. This is a convenient policy similar to the domino theory and subsequent foreign policy during the "red scare." Guarding the U.S. border means controlling drug, economic, and terrorist policy in foreign nation-states that are viewed as "drug-source" countries.

The U.S. Office of National Drug Control (ONDCP) states that "Internationally, we and our allies will attack the power and pocketbook of those international criminal and terrorist organizations that threaten our national security."[37] In 2002 in the United States, President Bush Jr. made a public announcement during the Super Bowl that "terrorists use drug profits to fund their cells to commit acts of murder. It you quit drugs, you join the fight against terror in America,"[38] which sent a message that the war on drugs was going to heighten. Mexico, Afghanistan, Colombia, the Caribbean, and Canada (among others) are represented as key drug-source countries.[39]

Both U.S. Customs and the DEA assisted in the making of *Traffic*. This was ignored by critics as they hailed *Traffic* as a critique of the war on drugs, ignoring its American-centric themes of racism (including fear of the mixing of the races and defending White womanhood), fear of foreign others, the celebration of vigilante-justice officials, and the failure of the court system. *Traffic* never seriously asks, "Who is the drug dealer?" The answer is that the U.S. government protects and supports drug trafficking when it suits its political goals and benefits corporations, politicians, international and domestic pharmaceutical companies, and local police departments and officers.

Maria Full of Grace: U.S. innocence

Maria Full of Grace (2004) also brings our attention to drug-source nations and their supply of cocaine to U.S. consumers, while emphasizing the plight of poor women drug couriers from Colombia who bring cocaine into the United States. Similar to *Traffic*, *Maria Full of Grace* won a number of awards and recognition in North America for telling a different story about the war on drugs. *Maria Full of Grace* provides an alternative to the mythical drug smuggler and more closely represents the type of women who end up working as drug couriers, or drug mules, as they are commonly called. Women, like the character Maria in the film, are the most vulnerable in the drug trade and subject to long prison terms if caught.[40]

The main character Maria is characterized as a poor young woman living in Colombia. She resides with her family, which includes her grandmother, mother, and her sister (a single mom with an infant son). Maria works in a rose factory, which is represented as a guarded plantation. Because Maria is spirited, she is fired from her job and is left with few prospects—for she is also pregnant by a boyfriend who shows little interest in her. She eventually meets a young man who says he can hook her up with a job where she can travel and make money to spare. It turns out that she has been recruited to work as a drug mule. All she has to do is swallow a large amount of latex pellets containing powdered cocaine and then travel by air to the U.S. and later expel them.

Maria takes the job. She is coached by Lucy, a seasoned drug courier who works for the same people, on how to swallow the latex pellets. They travel on the same flight to the United States. In the film, U.S. custom agents at the airport Maria passes through are represented as responsible and concerned, and when they hear Maria is pregnant they choose not to detain her. The director of the movie states in the film notes on the DVD release that help offered by U.S. Customs was "pivotal" in the making of the film because he was instructed by them. He states that they told him that racial profiling does not occur at customs because they are afraid of being sued. He claims that the customs agents he spoke to stated, "We look

Maria Full of Grace. Source: HBO/Fine Line/Photofest. © HBO/Fine Line.

for everyone." This is a stunning statement, given that numerous studies demonstrate that racial profiling is alive and well at U.S. airports, especially following 9/11.[41]

For those readers who saw the film, you know that Maria's fellow drug courier and friend, Lucy, dies once they arrive in the United States, because the drugs she swallowed have leaked into her body. In the film, Lucy's stomach is cut open by two young men who must account for all of the cocaine pellets. They too fear retribution from the drug dealers higher up in the organization that they are accountable too. Frightened for their safety, Maria and another friend flee to Queens, New York. In one scene, Lucy's sister, who is pregnant and a recent immigrant to the United States, tells Maria: "I stay for my baby, more opportunities, none in Colombia" In the film, Colombia is portrayed as mired in civil war, corrupt, with no hope of recovery. After a number of adventures, at the end of the movie, Maria makes the choice to stay in New York and to not return to Colombia.

The director claims that the movie is seen through the eyes of Maria, because he wanted to tell a personal story. Yet Maria is a fictional character, as are all the other characters in the movie; and embedded in the narrative and imagery on the screen we can see the United States represented as a land of opportunity and a haven from economic deprivation and violence. The director fails to deeply explore what C. Wright Mills would perceive as the link between history and biography and the relationship between the two in society, our personal troubles, and the social structure.[42] Specifically, the director fails to make clear the U.S. complicity in the war on drugs in Colombia and its ties to paramilitaries there. There is no critique of how Colombia's economy is shaped by the United States or how the U.S.-led World Bank's neoliberal restructuring comes at the expense of social supports and ensures that some people will remain poor and exploited. Women's involvement in the drug trade must be examined against the backdrop of the global economy. Poor and racialized women are exploited in both the drug economy and the global economy.[43] Yet *Maria Full of Grace* fails to fully reveal these realities that shape the lives of women.

The film does not mention the rich oil fields and other resources that U.S. corporations exploit in Colombia and guard with the help of private armies. Nor are the U.S. government's increased military spending through Plan Colombia and the war on terrorism referred to or their battle with the Revolutionary Armed Forces of Colombia (FARC), now classified as terrorists by the White House. These social, economic, and political realities are rarely represented in Hollywood films, including *Maria Full of Grace*, even though U.S. intervention in Colombia is an official and well-known fact.[44]

Similar to the U.S. film *Traffic*, which fails to address how NAFTA increased poverty and enriched a small sector of society and foreign investors, *Maria Full of Grace* fails to interrogate U.S. involvement in political, economic, and drug policy in Colombia. Colombia (similar to Mexico in *Traffic*) is portrayed as backwards and corrupt. The United States is depicted as the only nation that honours opportunity, justice, and democracy. It is represented as a society that others desire and envy and as vulnerable to drug-source nations. Thus, protecting the border from racialized others remains a top priority in the war on drugs and terror. Given the input of U.S. Customs in the filmmaking process, it is not surprising that the subtext of *Maria Full of Grace* communicates conventional drug discourse.

It is readily observed that the war on drugs and its intersection with the war on terrorism are vehicles for U.S. imperialism and colonization. U.S. intervention in Colombia is well known. In fact, the term "Colombinization" has become a popular term referring to nations outside of the United States that are subject to the U.S. war on drugs/terrorist intervention and imperialism. However, in most Hollywood illegal-drug movies, representations of U.S. innocence prevail. It can be argued that fictional films are not documentaries, and scriptwriters and producers are interested in more than just portraying the "facts" or "history." It can also be argued that the omission of U.S. complicity allows the viewer and the directors of *Traffic* and *Maria Full of Grace* to erase history and to celebrate White U.S. political and economic interests by its representation of Mexico and Colombia as criminal spaces and potential threats to the nation.

Hollywood illegal-drug movies celebrate Whiteness, imperialism, and colonization without ever mentioning them. In most U.S. movies, protecting the nation from savage drug traffickers and terrorists (who are one and the same) justifies intervention, increased militarization, and police power. A critique of U.S. imperial and military expansion around the world is absent from *Clear and Present Danger*, *Traffic*, *Maria full of Grace*, and other Hollywood films. Rather, films like *Scarface* and *New Jack City*, *Traffic*, and *Maria full of Grace* remind viewers that new immigrants, refugees, and poor inner-city racialized men are violent drug dealers and a threat to the nation.

Allen Feldman refers to the term *criminalized space* to examine the criminalization of illegal-drug use and public space.[45] He brings our attention to how the global phenomenon of criminalized space (ghettos within ghettos) is both economic and ideological, " . . . through which new strategies of policing and expert knowledge . . . are legitimized. In turn, these policing and treatment strategies are being exported to geopolitical zones that are undergoing neoliberal economic restructuring—there they are the building blocks of new public safety norms, policies, and procedures".[46]

Illegal-drug films represent specific spaces, the opium den, the jazz club, and inner-city streets as criminalized and racialized space. Nations such as Bolivia, Colombia, Cuba, and Mexico are depicted as non-Western space and therefore even more criminal and threatening to the nation.

SHAPING ILLEGAL-DRUG FILMS

Drug films are scripted and the parameters of the stories are narrow and exclusionary, especially in U.S. productions. Since the 1920s, the Hays Commission and the Pentagon have been censoring and shaping films.

Hollywood approves of films that punish dealers, sending out the right message. The military will only support drug movies if they show the war on drugs/terror in a favorable light.[47] Today, the local police, politicians, the DEA, and U.S. Customs (to name a few) are also in the business of shaping and censoring film. It is not surprising that their "official" stance on illegal drugs permeates the movies that they have been consulted on. As mentioned earlier, since 1989, the Office for Substance Abuse Prevention (OSAP) offers guideline materials about alcohol and drugs for television and film writers.[48] The National Institute on Drug Abuse (NIDA), the research arm of the U.S. government, with the Entertainment Industries Council (EIC) also helps to shape Hollywood films. They present a PRISM award for accurate portrayals of drug issues in film each year. They state that this award is given so that Hollywood networks, studios, scriptwriters, and directors will be more responsible in their portrayal of drugs. They also offer "script-to-screen" guidance, and film and TV scriptwriters can refer to their publication *Spotlight on Depiction of Health and Social Issues* in order to make sure that their scripts will meet approval with the U.S. government. Since 1997, the PRISM award has been given to TV and film that accurately portray drug issues. *Traffic* received a PRISM award in 2001 for best feature film.

Film producers' and movie viewers' ideas about illegal drugs may also be influenced by the U.S. government's antidrug ad campaign. In 2000, it was made public that the U.S. government spent over $1 billion in a five-year propaganda effort to convince citizens that the war on drugs is a good policy. Antidrug ads were placed in U.S. and Canadian magazines.[49] Since 2001, the Bush administration has spent from $100 to $180 million a year trying to convince citizens that marijuana will lead to insanity and that marijuana smokers and terrorists are one and the same. These TV and magazine ads support tough war-on-drugs/terrorism policy. However, the White House's attempts may have created a "boomerang" effect by which youth who view the ads may develop more positive attitudes to marijuana.[50]

The convergence of government, print media, and film is not new, although it has taken on new proportions since 9/11. Since 9/11, Hollywood filmmakers have rushed to offer their assistance to U.S. intelligence specialists and the White House. Hollywood's filmmakers claim that they have "expertise" to offer the U.S. Army in relation to planning for terrorist attacks.[51] One could easily argue that there is little need for censorship or propaganda offices when Hollywood does the job for free with the help of the U.S. military, DEA, Customs, and police.

It is in this political environment that filmmakers who wish to rupture convention and mythic representations of illegal drugs, criminal justice, militarization, and the nation must navigate. Embedded in the majority of mainstream illegal-drug films are narratives similar to President Bush Jr's. address to the nation in 2005, in which he claims: "There is only one course of action against them, to defeat them abroad before they attack us at home."

CONTAINMENT

Film is one of many mediums that produce knowledge and discourse about drug dealers, punishment, colonial and imperial longings, subjects, and nation building. In many ways the conventional stories that we tell about criminalized drug dealers today are not very different from early morality tales. Where early films were blatant about the evil lure of dealers and the city and the threat of the opium dens and foreigners to the safety of the nation, contemporary films, especially from the 1970s on, represent the inner city as racialized, violent, ready to explode, contagious, and unredeemable. Black and Hispanic men and women embody the threat to the nation, and when drug dealers are portrayed as White, race is not brought forward in the film. Illegal-drug dealers are represented as ultraviolent, no matter what drug they sell (see methamphetamine [*The Salton Sea* (2002)] and ecstasy [*Go* (1999)] traffickers).[52] Sympathy for lone dealers, the exception to the rule, is most often shown against the backdrop of corrupt and murderous police, civilians, and higher level traffickers who either want them to stay in the game or who are intent in punishing them for past or current transgressions, imaged or otherwise (i.e., *Easy Rider* (1969), *Superfly* (1972), *Atlantic City* (1980), *Tequila Sunrise* (1988), *Drugstore Cowboy* (1989), and *Light Sleeper* (1992)).

Police containment of the epidemic or the drug threat is a prevalent theme. Although filmmakers sometimes make a nod to poverty and race inequality and how it might shape the lives of those most affected, little attention is made to local, state, and federal policies that shape the lives of people, such as drug-law, criminal-justice, immigration, health, housing, economic, social, and education policy. Thus, the internal threat to the nation is embodied by poor young Black and Hispanic men and women in the inner city. The threat is essentialized, just as it was in early illegal-drug films. The threat to the nation intersects with external threats depicted in film discourse by images of porous borders and immigrant and refugee hordes. Later films depict corrupt foreign governments, police, and military engaged in drug trafficking and drug cartels as so powerful that the U.S. military is barely able to contain them. Since the 1980s, film depictions of drug cartels and terrorists groups involved in the drug trade perpetuate the image of the United States under siege from without and from within. Harsh drug laws, prison terms, policing, and militarization are advocated as solutions in illegal-drug films. Less lenient courts, judicial restraints (such as mandatory minimums), violence, and illegal tactics (see also *Rush* [1991] and *Narc* [2002]) are also advocated.

Michel Foucault proposes that "prison is the only place where power is manifested in its naked state, in its most excessive form, and where it is justified as moral force."[53] Prisons are the site of constant surveillance. Foucault argued that the invention of the penitentiary in the late eighteenth century was intended to regulate and discipline immoral and criminal bodies rather than subject them to corporal punishment, but prisons have never left the business of punishment. The ideas of rehabilitation or saving immoral souls compete to no avail in these law-and-order times. Yet there is a societal disconnect. Fear of the drug trafficker and societal and film representations clamouring for harsher drug laws are rarely problematized. For these questions are rarely raised: Where will all those bodies go? What bodies will be sent to prison? Who will pay for prisons? What resources and tax dollars will be diverted to build and maintain prisons? What evidence exists to demonstrate that punishment and prohibition are effective?

Prisons and prison experience remain largely invisible in illegal-drug films. Often, when prison is referred to in illegal-drug films (but not represented), homophobia reigns and the fear of male-on-male rape is represented as more terrifying than the loss of freedom and incarceration (see *25th Hour* [2002]). The U.S./U.K. production *Midnight Express* (1978) and the U.S. production *Brokedown Palace* (2000) are the only films in the sample that depict lengthy prison scenes, and these take place in Third World nations: Turkey and Thailand. In both films the justice system in these nations are portrayed as corrupt. The prison is a site of violence in *Midnight Express* and in both films racialized people are essentialized and represented as non-Western and uncivilized. In contrast, Western justice is viewed as just and civilized, and so too are its prisons. The absence of in-depth representations of Western prison experience allows viewers to remain in a continual state of innocence about U.S. criminal justice and the prison–industrial complex. Viewers do not have to wonder where the millions of criminalized bodies go. Neither do viewers have to worry about how drug offenders will be treated in prison or what happens to families and communities when suspected drug users and sellers are convicted and incarcerated.

U.S. incarceration rates are higher than any other nation in the world, and outside of traffic violations, drug offenders make up the largest category of arrests.[54] Yet it is not the cartel or high-level drug trafficker who is at risk for arrest and imprisonment. In 2005, 81.7 percent of all drug charges were for possession, and marijuana arrests exceeded all other drug categories.[55] Trafficking, production, and importation offences only make up 18 percent of all drug charges. Watching illegal-drug films, we don't have to think about the fact that more than seven million people are moving through the U.S. prison system right now, in prison, on parole, or on probation. Over two million people are in prison, and poor and working-class illegal-drug users and low-level street sellers make up a significant portion of drug offenders, and black and Hispanic people are disproportionately overrepresented.[56] In addition, since the 1970s, women's prison rates have tripled, the majority for nonviolent drug offences.[57] The prison–industrial complex is increasingly privatized, selling the right to punish to the highest bidder in a human experiment of which we have never before seen the likes. Relatedly, police and military powers increase at the same time that civil liberties decrease. One can wonder deeply about the absence of visual and narrative representations of prisons in U.S. illegal-drug films.

Of course, drug films are produced for entertainment and above all else profit. Illegal-drug films provide a vehicle for comedy, action, and dramatic stories about life and death, moral dilemmas and tension, pleasure, degradation, and redemption and punishment. Yet we might ask ourselves if drug law and policy would be different if we saw and heard stories different from those that celebrate punishment and perpetuate racism and U.S. imperialism. We might also ask if illegal-drug users, producers, and sellers themselves might be treated differently if we could hear more about their diverse lives. We might ask if the ever-expanding prison–industrial complex would exist. And finally, we might ask ourselves why we are entertained by film representations of nationalism, militarism, and violence directed against a large segment of the population as it is played out in the war on drugs/terrorism at home and abroad.

6 Vilified Women and Maternal Myths

Illegal-drug use and trafficking are most often depicted as a male domain. In contemporary illegal-drug films, women tend to be on the periphery and their characters are often not fleshed out. Contemporary criminal gangsta and male buddy films have little use for female characters outside of window dressing for the male sexualized gaze. However, a number of early and contemporary films depict moral White women who fall from grace. Early films focus on innocent women being lured into illegal-drug use by villainous men. Their moral and sexual downfall are often shown by their proximity to racialized men. Opium dens and jazz clubs are represented as the sites of their moral degradation.

However, not all White women are portrayed as innocent. In *The Cocaine Fiends* (1935), Fanny lures Eddie to try cocaine, and Blanche in *Reefer Madness* (1936) is constructed as a temptress who lures Bill into the drug culture. Yet even though these women are depicted as deviant, they move towards redemption in the films. Redemption comes with a price, though; Fanny and Blanche both end up committing suicide in the films. Women are punished for engaging in illegal-drug use and dealing, which is equated with pleasure, compulsion, unproductivity, disorder, criminality, and abandonment of responsibility and gender-role norms.[1] Illegal-drug discourse about women is quite different from that applied to men. Drug discourse is gender specific and women's morality, sexuality, their capacity to become pregnant, and mothering and conventional gender-role expectations shape cinematic representations.

Emily Murphy, one of Canada's early nineteenth-century moral reformers, educated readers through her magazine articles and her 1923 book *The Black Candle* about the dangers moral women might encounter. Murphy's representation of the male drug trafficker was a non-White, deranged villain bent on destroying the Anglo-Saxon way of life, corrupting the morality of White women, and taking over the world. While Murphy constructed male drug traffickers as devious people who were "active agents of the devil,"[2] the mixing of the races and the moral downfall of White women were central to her argument. She targeted Chinese and Black men for enslaving White women and contributing to "race suicide." Women's

Reefer Madness. Source: George A. Hirliman Productions/Photofest. © George A. Hirliman Productions/Twentieth Century Fox.

moral downfall was measured by their proximity to, and enslavement by, men of colour. Beneath a photo of a White woman and a Black man lying in what looks like an opium den, Murphy wrote, "When she acquires the habit, she does not know what lies before her; later, she does not care."[3] Murphy went on to assert that all women who are seduced by men of colour become addicted and degraded, and all become liars. She claimed that "Under the influence of the drug, the woman loses control of herself; her moral senses are blunted, and she becomes 'a victim' in more senses than one."[4] Foremost, the corrupted female drug user was depicted as immoral, promiscuous, and contributing to the breakdown of the family and Anglo-Saxon society.

In Britain, concern about women and drugs also began to emerge in the early 1900s and culminated in a panic by the mid-1920s. Following the high-profile overdose death of the well-known actress Billie Carleton in 1918, stories about female drug use, sexual immorality, and the mixing of the races became central themes in the news and helped to push forward drug regulation.[5] In the United States, Sara Graham-Mulhall, a former employee of the Department of Narcotics Drug Control in New York State, saw her book *Opium the Demon Flower* published in 1923. This book, newspaper articles, citizen groups, and later discourse generated by H. J. Anslinger and the U.S. Federal Bureau of Narcotics informed the public about the horrors of some drugs and women's vulnerability and immorality.

Although their histories differ, Britain, Canada, and the United States share a history of colonization, and their drug policy and regulation draw on similar ideologies about morality, gender, class, race, family, and the nation-state. The image of White women as fragile and vulnerable to moral corruption sharply contrasts with racialized women as promiscuous, unruly, prone to public displays of drunkenness (especially aboriginal women), and drug use and in need of confinement. If White women were in need of protection, racialized women were seen as culpable, and racialized men were represented as profiting from the drug trade and subculture. Protecting White women from racialized others in the nation and from encroachments at the border remains a dominant theme in official drug discourse. Film discourse reflects similar concerns. White women's drug use is often represented as a failure of nation building and moral and religious transformation. In illegal-drug-film representations, power and wealth are most often reserved for nonracialized subjects and Whiteness is naturalized.

Although men in illegal-drug films are represented as suffering too, through their participation in the drug trade and violence associated with it, the repercussions for their drug use and dealing are portrayed quite differently from women's. In addition, they are portrayed as profiting greatly from the drug trade. Significantly, their drug use is not sexualized. In illegal-drug films, women must pay for their drug use, and there is rarely any escape from their destiny: sexual degradation, pregnancy, suicide, and drug overdose accompany women's drug use. Often they are portrayed as the witless victims of criminal and greedy men. Quite a number are depicted supporting their boyfriends' drug habit. Although many early and contemporary film representations centre on White moral "victims," some women are depicted as beyond redemption. They are portrayed as more deviant than their male counterparts. They are depicted as being more addicted and unwilling to stop using drugs than their boyfriends and husbands, more sexually promiscuous, and more ruthless drug traffickers and killers. They are also represented as active agents in subverting their boyfriends' sobriety and commitment to leave the drug trade behind. In addition, they are depicted as failing as mothers and even worse, becoming pregnant while using drugs. Where men in illegal-drug films endure hardships and pain, they are granted more agency and their fate is less determined. The early film *The Cocaine Fiends* (1935) exemplifies how the plight of some women differs from men's. In the film, Jane is depicted as a moral young White woman who is seduced by a lying and treacherous man. Addicted to cocaine and estranged from her family, she is depicted as a "mobster's moll" now. Her brother Eddie comes to the city to find her, but he too is introduced to cocaine and then opium by his girlfriend Fanny, and he soon finds himself destitute and addicted. Jane discovers him smoking opium in a den. When he sees her he calls out her name, "Jane." She replies, "No. Not Jane. There isn't anymore Jane. I'm Lil, a gangster's discarded mole. Do you understand that, Eddie? No one must ever connect me to. . . . You must get away, back to the country and sunshine." "It isn't too late for you," he says. She replies sadly, "No, it's too late for me. Girls can't go back. But you can." In illegal-drug films, ruined women cannot escape their destiny.

Representations of women on screen reproduce the pleasure of the male gaze, and their characters are sexualized and one dimensional. Women and young girls are often characterized as sexually aggressive and promiscuous when they use illegal drugs (see *Narcotic* [1935], *Marihauana, the Weed with Roots in Hell* [1936], *High* [1967], *Valley of the Dolls* [1967], *I Love you, Alice B. Toklas* [1968], *Performance* [1970], *Postcards from the Edge* [1990]; *Jesus' Son* [1991], *Trainspotting* [1996], *Another Day in Paradise* [1998], *Traffic* [2000], *Blow* [2001], *Igby Goes Down* [2002], *Spun* [2002], *Thirteen* [2003], and *Mount Pleasant* [2006]) and even after they stop (*Sherrybaby* [2006]). *Trainspotting* and *Traffic* provide contemporary examples of this phenomenon. In *Trainspotting*, the female character Alison is introduced at the beginning of the film. She is a young White mother who uses heroin. We see her hanging out with the other main characters, all men, including a young man named Sick Boy, at Mother Superior's, their local heroin dealer's squat. Mother Superior's is depicted as run down and dirty. The camera zooms in on Alison's baby, Dawn, playing on the floor. Alison is sitting nearby with a belt wrapped around her upper arm. Sick Boy is sitting directly in front of her slapping her arm, looking for a vein to inject heroin into. He licks the tip of the needle and inserts it into her vein. She breathes in and out and moans, staring into his eyes, and says, "That beats any fucking cock in the world." Even contemporary male buddy "stoner" films depict female characters as objects of desire and the sexualized male gaze. In *Up in Smoke* (1978) and *Harold and Kumar Go to White Castle* (2004), women are incidental to the plot. The female characters in both films are sexualized and not fully fleshed-out characters.

The Canadian 1967 black comedy *High* provides a good example of a sexualized young woman becoming more deviant than her male partner. In the film, Vicky, a young White Canadian graduate student, has her drug use sexualized and linked to criminality and violence. Vicky quits her studies and her job in order to hang out with Tom, who introduces her to marijuana. Tom rejects the "straight world" and is involved in credit-card fraud and other criminal acts. Soon Vicky is helping Tom by stealing wallets from drunk men in bars. Later, Tom reprimands her for roughing up the men. He says, "Don't operate that way! Think we are street-corner thugs!" Now Vicky only attends to her personal grooming and criminal activities rather than intellectual pursuits. She is depicted smoking marijuana and blowing smoke in Tom's face. He is no longer her mentor to altered states of consciousness, sexuality, and crime. Now she takes the lead.

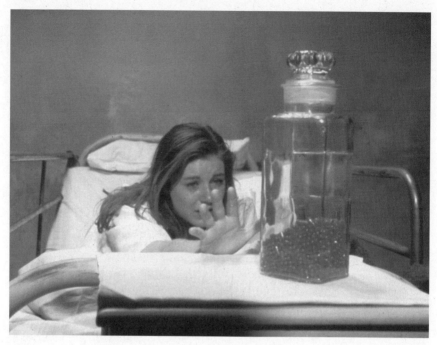

Valley of the Dolls. Source: Twentieth Century Fox/Photofest. © Twentieth Century Fox.

Postcards from the Edge. Source: Columbia Pictures/Photofest. © Columbia Pictures.

Eventually, Vicky hooks up with a wealthy married man. She prepares to leave on a car trip with him and at the last minute Tom joins them. Tom lights a joint in the car and Phil tells him to get rid of it. In the next scene they are shown driving in the countryside. Phil stops the car and they all get out. Phil wants to leave Tom behind. Vicky shouts at him, "You lousy bastard! Just because you drive a big car . . . you think you can push people around." She hits him with a metal bar that she picks up from the ground. Tom turns around and sees her raising the bar above her head; she has a gleeful manic look on her face as the bar comes crashing down on Phil's head. Later, Tom and Vicky are shown sitting in a bar. Vicky grabs the car keys and wallet of the dead man from Tom's jacket, and then she proceeds to walk out of the bar and drive down the highway alone.

Women are often depicted as falling from grace and working in the sex trade in order to support their habits (and their boyfriends; i.e., *The Cocaine Fiends* [1935], *The Panic in Needle Park* [1971], *My Name is Joe* [1998], *Requiem for a Dream* [2000], *Traffic* [2000], *On the Corner* [2003], and *Mount Pleasant* [2006]). Others offer their sexual services for a hit (i.e., *Boyz n the Hood* [1991]) or for favours (i.e., *Sherrybaby* [2006]). In addition, addicted women are portrayed as failing to support their boyfriends and husbands when they decide to stop using illegal drugs. In contrast, the nondrug-using supportive women depicted in films like *The Man with the Golden Arm* (1955) and *Monkey on his Back* (1957) reaffirm conventional female gender roles and postwar sentiments. Later films, representing backlash responses to women's independence and gendered drug-use representations, depict women as "drug pigs." Women are portrayed as having a larger appetite for illegal drugs than their male partners (See *The Panic in Needle Park* [1971], *Scarface* [1983], *Drugstore Cowboy* [1989], *Jesus' Son* [1991], *Sid and Nancy* [1986], *Another Day in Paradise* [1998], *My Name is Joe* [1998], *Protection* [2000], *Requiem for a Dream* [2000], *Trainspotting* [2000], *Blow* [2001], and *Clean* [2004]), and they are portrayed as unwilling to stop using when their boyfriends/husbands decide to cease using drugs and straighten up. In a number of films, girlfriends and wives are suspect and not to be trusted—they either rat on, or are suspected of ratting on, their boyfriends/husbands (i.e., *The Panic in Needle Park* [1971], *Scarface* [1983], *Blow* [2001], *25th Hour* [2002]) and hooking up with their boyfriends/husbands' best friend, business partners, and associates (See *The Panic in Needle Park* [1971], *Scarface* [1983], *Drugstore Cowboy* [1989], *Jesus' Son* [1991], *New Jack City* [1991], and *Blow* [2001]). Mothers of drug users cannot be trusted either. The mother in *Blow* is depicted as cold, unmaternal, and willing to call the police on her son knowing that he will serve prison time for drug trafficking. In *Scarface* (1983), the top trafficker's hardworking mother calls her son Tony an animal and throws him out of the house, refusing to see him or take money from him. Bob's mother in *Drugstore Cowboy* (1989) refuses to let him in the house when he comes to visit. She calls him a "dope fiend" and slams the door.

Drugstore Cowboy provides a good example of a White female character, Diane, who is unwilling to stop using illegal drugs when her husband
Bob does. Instead, she moves in with Rick, one of their crew, when Bob
decides to leave the criminal life behind him. In the film, which takes place
in 1971 in Portland, Oregon, Diane is depicted as the long-term girlfriend
and wife of Bob, and both are depicted as "full-time dope fiends." Bob
runs a crew that includes Diane and a younger couple, Rick and Nadine.
They rob drugstores to feed their habit. Following a close call burglarizing
a drugstore and Nadine's fatal drug overdose, Bob starts to think about
getting off drugs. He says to Diane, "Thinking about heading back home.
Getting on the 21-day methadone program. Cleaning up my hand. Diane,
I can't do it anymore." Diane responds, "Well, I'm not going on any withdrawal program. So what's gonna happen to me?" Bob asks her to come
with him and she says, "No thanks, Buster. Not a fucking word do you
mention about this. Right out of the clear blue sky you say your gonna
clean up your hand. And you know I can't."

Bob is shown leaving Diane. He goes back to Portland and gets on a
methadone-maintenance program there. He is also shown getting a job at
a drill factory and attending Narcotics Anonymous (NA)–style meetings.
He tells his fellow NA mates that his "old lady is still out there now. I told
her to come. She didn't want to come." Later, Diane visits Bob; he is still on
methadone, working and living in a squalid single-occupancy hotel room.
Looking around the room, she asks him, "What kind of dump is this?" She
also asks him how the methadone "thing" is working out and whether he is
really serious about staying off drugs. Bob says that he is. Diane then places
a brown paper bag filled with pills on the table. She says, "That's from Rick
and the rest of us. Thought you might need a taste every once in a while."
She asks him if she did something that made him want to stop using. Bob
tells her no. Then he asks her to spend the night with him. She tells him that
she has "another old man now. I'm Rick's old lady now." She makes clear
that she might be a dope fiend, but she has never been sexually loose. Then
she leaves his room.

In the film *Drugstore Cowboy*, Diane is unwilling to stop using drugs
and hooks up with Rick as soon as Bob leaves and quits their crew. However, unlike other illegal-drug films, Diane is also depicted as multidi-
mensional, and she remains a sympathetic character throughout the film.
Diane is represented as truly caring for Bob. It is her commitment to or
inability to stop using narcotics that shapes her choices. In the film she
never deceives Bob.

The character Mirtha, in *Blow* (2001), provides a narrative different
from *Drugstore Cowboy*. The film is roughly based on the true story of
George Jung, who is depicted as a young White working-class man who
says he made millions by supplying cocaine to American users in the late
1970s and early 1980s. In the film, George is initially characterized as an
innocent young man who literally stumbles into the drug trade and begins

Blow. Source: New Line Cinema / Photofest. © New Line Cinema.

selling marijuana. His first girlfriend, Barbie (the name accurately reflects the character), works as an flight attendant, and she helps him transport illegal drugs. She is depicted as a White blonde, supportive and moral. Their work in the drug trade is viewed as innocent and as a positive opportunity rather than as criminal. However, Barbie soon dies from cancer, and George's participation in the drug trade shifts radically as he develops ties with ruthless South American cocaine dealers. At a wedding reception for one of his drug-smuggling associates, George meets Mirtha. Mirtha is a Colombian woman who is married to a high-level drug dealer named Cesar. Upon meeting George, she dumps Cesar and moves in with him. In the film, Mirtha, similar to other racialized representations of Latina women, is depicted as "promiscuous and dishonorable," exotic and wild.[6] In a voice-over, George informs us that Mirtha could "party like a man and love like a woman." Their sexual relationship is viewed on screen through a red filter. We are subjected to a kaleidoscope of scenes, including one where Mirtha dances seductively, another where she is decked out in S/M gear, including a studded dog collar, leash, and revealing black lingerie. She is shown holding a whip and, finally, wielding a gun. They both use copious amounts of powder cocaine.

Mirtha and George marry and live in a huge mansion. Mirtha is George's door to Colombia, the "primitive" south and drug-source nation. When Mirtha becomes pregnant, she gives up cigarettes, but not cocaine, and she is depicted snorting lines. George reprimands her, "Put that shit [away], you're pregnant, for God's sake." She does not heed his advice. George is still actively using cocaine too. Their daughter Kristina is born and she is healthy, and we are told in a voice-over and a quick succession of images that George is a caring and loving father. He has quit the business and stopped using illegal drugs. In contrast, Mirtha has little interest in mothering, and she continues partying and using cocaine. In one scene, Mirtha is shown at George's birthday party holding up a silver dish filled with cocaine; she yells out to her guests, "Let's have some fucking fun!" It is implied that she is using too much cocaine when a guest comments to George about the weight she has lost, "What does she weigh, 80 pounds?"

The DEA raids George's birthday party and he and Mirtha are arrested. Even though it is clear in the film that the cocaine in the house is for Mirtha's use, George takes the rap in exchange for Mirtha's release from jail and Kristina's release from protective custody. While he is out on bail, George discovers that his millions of dollars in drug-trafficking profits have been confiscated by the Panamanian government, where he had an account set up. Now George and his family are shown without financial support. Mirtha is shown screaming at him about their lack of money in front of their daughter. In fact, throughout the film Mirtha has only two modes of expression, that of the screaming bad mother and wife and the sexualized "Latin" seductress.

Shortly after the arrest, we see George driving a car with Mirtha in the passenger seat, snorting cocaine. She turns to George and calls him a "faggot" and lunges at George, screaming, "Why don't you fuck me any more?" The car swerves and the next thing we see is a police cruiser pulling them over. Mirtha is still in a rage and she continues screaming as the cops pull her away from the car. She screams out that Bob is a drug dealer and that he has "a kilo in his trunk right now." Bob is arrested and he does three years in prison.

In the film *Blow* (2001), all of the women are treacherous, except for Barbie, whose memory remains pure. George's mother is depicted as selfish, nonmaternal, and cold. Early on in the film, she phones the police on him when he visits her. Mirtha is depicted as a Latin seductress who is greedy and more interested in partying than being a "good" mother or wife; she jeopardizes George's plans to lead a different life and she is presented as the agent of his final downfall. Throughout the film, George is shown doing business with and hanging out with men who are depicted as violent Colombian drug traffickers. We witness several different Colombian traffickers beating him up, shooting him, and murdering an informer in front of him. The film makes clear that racialized drug smugglers are immoral and murderous. George is soon portrayed wielding a gun too, and he is shown threatening his drug-smuggling partner with death. He is gone for years at a time while he is in and out of prison. He is unable to provide any child support or alimony. Yet throughout the film we are told by George in voice-over that he is a good father. We hardly see his daughter Kristina on the screen, yet the few times we do, George is briefly depicted holding her or gazing at her. Kristina's character is not developed, yet regardless of this, the central theme of the film is George's need to get back his "baby girl, his heart."

Although *Blow* is about marijuana and cocaine trafficking, it also plays as one big father's-rights-movement infomercial.[7] At the end of the film, George is drawn into the illegal trade again one last time in order to get enough money to take his daughter away with him. However, he is set up by an old friend and the FBI and DEA. George is arrested and sent to prison for 60 years in a federal penitentiary. At the end of the film we see him in the prison yard as the postscript reads: "George Jung is sentenced to Olisville Federal Corrections Institute until 2015. Kristina Sunshine Jung has not yet visited her father." Since the film only fictionalizes George's memories, we have no idea how his daughter and ex-wife felt about the fictionalization of their lives and their private troubles becoming public. Although the film may be seen as critiquing harsh drug laws, its critical stance does not extend to gender roles.

TRAFFICKERS

Trafficking in illegal-drug films is clearly laid out as a male domain. However, there are a few exceptions, such as Ann, the genial upscale dealer in *Light Sleeper* (1992); Angie in *Dirty* (1998), who grows marijuana without exhibiting criminal or immoral behaviour; Ronna in *Go* (1999), who is depicted as devious and dishonest but less so than the men in the film; Grace in *Saving Grace* (2000), who is depicted as a kind, law-abiding, and strapped-for-cash older White woman who grows marijuana in her greenhouse following her husband's death; and Maria in *Maria Full of Grace* (2004), who is shown as a poor young Colombian woman with no future prospects who agrees to ingest and transport cocaine into the United States. Where all of the preceding women are portrayed as no less moral than their male counterparts, and in some cases more moral, these are an exception. A number of illegal-drug films portray female drug dealers and girlfriends and wives of drug dealers as more deviant and violent than their male counterparts. Feminist criminologists such as Karlene Faith, Meda Chesney-Lind, and Helen Birch have pointed out how women in conflict with the law are represented in film. Mirroring conventional criminological theory and practice, a few of these women are constructed as moral, fallen women who are worthy of redemption, while most others are represented as doubly deviant for transgressing the law and gender expectations.[8] Some women drug dealers are constructed as more deviant than their male counterparts. They are depicted as callous, cold, scheming, and more willing than their male partners to commit acts of violence in order to carry out their criminal enterprises.

In *Marihuana, the Weed with Roots in Hell* (1936), Verna, a young, spirited but innocent White woman, is introduced to marijuana by an

Marihuana, the Weed with Roots in Hell. Source: Roadshow Attractions/Photofest. © Roadshow Attractions.

older man named Tony and his partner Nicky. She graduates from smoking marijuana to injecting heroin, and she also becomes a ruthless drug dealer, selling cocaine and heroin to her customers instead of just marijuana so that she can reap the benefit of more profit. A few years earlier she gave her child up for adoption and took up drug trafficking with a vengeance. Tony calls her "Ice Queen" and in the film we see her scheming to make more money. Now she calls the shots rather than her partners in crime, Tony and Nicky. In *Cleopatra Jones* (1973), the character Mommy is depicted as violent and overbearing. She is portrayed as a notorious white "queenpin" who works with her gang of sons whom she controls. She is also represented as a lesbian who employs a number of young beautiful women to take care of her needs. In *New Jack City* (1991), the top drug dealer's first girlfriend is unable to have children and she is depicted as more violent than the men in the film. When an elderly Black man chastises her and the top dealer Nino for corrupting innocent children and killing their own people, she turns to Nino and suggests that she should kill him, but he only allows the man to be beaten.

Similar to the female characters in *Marihuana, the Weed with Roots in Hell* (1936) and *New Jack City* (1991), women drug dealers and women who live with dealers are often represented in illegal-drug films as lacking maternal instincts and having no interest in domestic life. In fact, their sexual morality is suspect, and they are portrayed as promiscuous or frigid and infertile. In the film *Scarface* (1983), Elvira is depicted as the top dealer's girlfriend. Her cocaine use is linked to her infertility. Before we ever see her in the film, her high-level drug-dealing boyfriend tells a bunch of men in the room, "Half her life dressing, other half undressing." She enters the room in a green satin backless evening gown slit up to the top of her leg. She is a young, thin, White blonde, the token cultural symbol of Western male capitalist success. After Tony takes down her boyfriend, he wakes her up in her bed, telling her "Get your stuff, you're coming with me." Elvira is represented as a commodity, the spoils of war, and she moves in with Tony. Tony is depicted as a Cuban refugee who is intent on gaining wealth and power in the United States through the drug trade. He marries Elvira and hopes to have children with her. However, throughout the film, Elvira's character makes clear that she disdains him. On first meeting Tony she remarks, "Just got off the banana boat?" She is depicted making other racist comments to him, later calling him an "immigrant, Spic, millionaire." Elvira is not interested in sex with Tony; her only interests extend to cocaine in the day and quaaludes to sleep at night. Tony calls her a "fucking junkie" and tells his partner "her womb is so polluted I can't even have a fucking little baby with her."

Throughout the film, Tony idolizes his younger sister, and he is portrayed as having incestuous feelings towards her. At the end of the film, in a jealous rage he murders her boyfriend, his best friend and trafficking partner. In her grief, his sister enters Tony's office. She is wearing a long silk robe and it is open and her breasts are bare. She walks towards Tony and says, "Is this what you wanted, Tony? Can't stand for another man to be touching me?" She then says, "Fuck me, Tony. Fuck me" as she shoots him. Before she can kill him, rival gang members shoot and murder her and then Tony.

In *Another Day in Paradise* (1998), hustler and drug dealer Mel is hooked up with Sam, a middle-aged, blonde White woman whose interests in life extend to heroin, shopping, and gossiping. Sam is depicted as infertile; however, their recruitment of two youths into their crew is portrayed as partially fulfilling her need to mother—until the young girl overdoses and Mel turns on the young man attempting to murder him.

In both *Traffik* (1989) and *Traffic* (2000), the male kingpin traffickers are married to women who take over their business after they are arrested and imprisoned. In both films, the wives are portrayed as more murderous than their husbands. In order to maintain their privileged lifestyle and to free their husbands from the criminal-justice system, they transgress the law and conventional gender roles by carrying on their husbands' drug trafficking business and planning the murder of an associate who is about to provide state evidence against their husbands. In the British production *Traffik*, when the husband is released from prison his wife resists his attempts to go on a vacation and to have sex with him. She is no longer interested and she has no time for these more domestic activities. Her only interest is setting up the next big deal.

MATERNAL UNFITNESS

Where some women drug traffickers are depicted as doubly deviant in film, breaking the law and gender codes, women who use illegal drugs while pregnant or mothering are depicted as even more evil, especially racialized women. As noted above, illegal-drug use and trafficking are constructed as incompatible with mothering, conventional gender roles, and a women's capacity to become pregnant. Historically, women's capacity to become pregnant and their role as mothers made them particularly vulnerable to social-control efforts and moral regulation. As moral reform movements emerged in Britain, Canada, and the United States, women lost what little control they had over reproduction. Prior to the nineteenth century, women were not restricted by law from obtaining abortions or birth control, and most births were attended by midwives and female healers.[9] The newly established medical profession condemned the practice of midwifery and sought to strengthen their position by appropriating pregnancy and birth from "nonprofessionals." Legislation was enacted to criminalize the practice of midwifery in Canada and the United States; in all three nations, abortion was also criminalized.[10]

Moral reformers in the late 1900s also scrutinized poor and marginalized women's mothering. In all three nations, child abuse and neglect emerged as social problems during this era of industrialization and child labour.[11] Child-saving ideology assumes that parents can be transformed into "proper" and moral parents.[12] Because "some" women are considered ignorant in the areas of pregnancy and mothering, surveillance and regulation were justified.[13] Early moral reformers were interested in instances of child neglect and protecting children from cruel treatment, especially by violent fathers who drank to excess, thus subjecting their families to a life of poverty. Early moral reformers conflated alcohol use with abuse and rallied for prohibition. Temperance ideology framed their practice, as it does today. Self-control, abstinence, and sobriety became the template for White middle-class Protestant respectability.[14] Moral reformers in this era regarded White middle-class women as innately sober and moral and, by extension, responsible for the morality of society. Women moral reformers saw themselves as defenders of the home, community, and the nation. Rather than looking more closely at the impact of industrialization and economic and social structuring of society, moral reformers blamed alcohol and opium and later other drugs for a host of social problems.[15] They did so by establishing religious aid societies and civil projects that culminated in legislation and the social-services agencies that we recognize today.

The main focus of early child savers and later social workers' power to regulate women lies in their ability to label women "deserving and undeserving," unfit, and deviant.[16] In keeping with the intersection of the eugenics, temperance, and antiopiate movements with child saving, immigrants, the working class, and those deemed immoral became subjects of regulation. Central to the role of early child savers and later social workers is an assessment of mothering and "proper" female behaviour.[17] The regulation of sexuality, reproduction, family norms, and mothering are central to social work (and other professions such as criminal justice and medicine). Traditionally, child savers and social workers were White middle-class women. The White middle-class heterosexual family was and continues to be represented as the norm. White moral women are constructed as the moral barometer of Western society; their downfall, especially related to unsanctioned drug use, is linked to the breakdown of the family and society.[18] Since prohibition (of alcohol and other drugs), women who are suspected of using drugs became vulnerable to social service intervention. Whereas early child saving focused on poor and working-class Anglo-Saxon society, today welfare regulation centres on poor and racialized families.[19] Temperance ideology still permeates contemporary social-welfare policy, as it is shaped by a "political conservative anti-drug ideology" that reflects legal and medical interests.[20] Child apprehension is one of the most powerful tools that social workers wield over all women, but especially poor and marginalized women suspected of drug use. These concerns are represented in the films discussed in the following sections.

Intolerance: moral reformers and child apprehension

For many people, D. W. Griffith is best known for his 1915 White-supremacist film *Birth of a Nation*. Griffith was a prolific film producer of both short films such as *For His Son* (1912) and *Broken Blossoms* (1919), which were discussed in chapter 2, and feature-length films such as *Intolerance* (1916). The silent film *Intolerance* includes four different stories set in different eras. The "modern" segment of *Intolerance* explores White working-class tensions, industrialization, the activities of White moral reformers, and the regulation of mothers who are deemed unfit and suspected of using drugs, in this case alcohol. *Intolerance* also attempts to show how hatred and intolerance battle against love and charity through the ages.

The modern story is set in the United States, and it highlights the life of a young White working-class couple (the boy and The Dear One) and their newborn child. A group of moral reformers, mostly affluent women, are also central characters. The film caption explains that the moral reformers are "ambitious ladies [who] band together for the 'uplift' of humanity." Most of their funding comes from a wealthy industrialist, Mr. Jenkins, whose unmarried sister joins the "uplifters" in their moral-reform activities. The moral refomers disapprove of the pleasure activities engaged in by workers in the city. They are intent on cleaning up the city with the help of the police, closing down dance halls, rounding up sex-trade workers, and closing down home stills. The film also shows some of the tensions between workers and the industrialist Mr. Jenkins; a strike at his mill is central to the story. Here we see peaceful strikers gunned down and dispersed by the police, ordered to do so by the wealthy industrialist. Many of the workers, including the the boy and The Dear One, have to leave town following the strike. Separately, they move to the city. The Dear One lives with her father, but he dies shortly after they arrive. The boy becomes involved in criminal activities, working for a criminal boss, but he goes "straight" once he meets up again with The Dear One.

The boy and The Dear One marry and settle into a happy domestic life. But the criminal boss is angry and he wants the young man to continue working for him. He sets out to punish him by setting him up, planting a stolen wallet on him. The boy is arrested by the police, convicted, and sent to prison. He is to be executed for his crime. The Dear One is shown sitting by herself in their one-room home. She is now raising their little baby by herself. She sews for a living, being able to do piece work in her home. The moral reformers (or "uplifters," as Griffith calls them) in the film turn their attention to "negligent mothers." We see The Dear One in her room smiling at her baby, who looks happy and well-nourished. She sneezes and the film caption reads: "A cold sends our little mother to an old-fashioned remedy, condemned publicly yet privately used by many physicians and hospitals." She steps across the hall and her kind and elderly male neighbour gives her a small bottle. Returning to her room, she finds the moral reformers are there. They decided to investigate her when they heard that her husband is in prison. They find the baby alone and when The Dear One enters the room they seize the small bottle she is holding and exclaim, "Whisky! We are afraid you're no fit mother . . ." The Dear One argues with them and finally she grabs a broom and threatens them with it. The moral reformers flee from her room, but they reconvene with other members and decide that they will "seize" the baby.

Later, the friendly elderly neighbour brings over some food and a glass of beer for The Dear One. She takes it and thanks him. As the kindly neighbour walks away from The Dear One's door, the moral reformers arrive in the hallway. They cry out, "Did you see that? A man visitor!" They open the door to The Dear One's room and state, "We have a warrant to take your baby!" The Dear One pleads and argues with them. She holds her baby in her arms. The moral reformers grab the baby and she fights with them only to lose. As they leave with the baby, she is lying on the floor and her hand touches her baby's knitted bootie which was left behind in the ruckus.

In the next scene, The Dear One visits the Jenkins Foundation building, which holds apprehended babies. She looks in and sees a large sterile room with rows of cribs with babies in them. There is a woman in the room, dressed like a nurse. She says to herself, "Perhaps they are right and baby is happy after all." Intimidated, she walks away. The following caption says, "Of course hired mothers are never negligent." The next scene shows two of the staff dancing; others are talking to each other ignoring the babies in the cribs. Later, we see The Dear One looking longingly at other children and families. The Dear One eventually brings evidence to the governor showing that her husband is innocent. He is on the scaffold and the noose is already around his neck, but he is saved in the nick of time. The following scene shows the penitentiary where he was imprisoned turning into a field of blooming flowers.

In the film *Intolerance*, we see an early effort by a feature-film director to capture the tensions between working-class people and moral reformers who sought to regulate them. The film not only critiques moral-reform efforts and the regulation of working women's sexuality, mothering, and substance use; it also critiques criminal justice, prison, and capital punishment.[21] The film affirms the sanctity of the White nuclear family and paints some moral reformers as affluent elderly spinsters, representing early maternal feminists. The film also links reform movements to industrialists' concerns and to the institutions they support, including the Jenkins Foundation, as a site for apprehended infants of wayward substance-using mothers. Today we may be surprised by the neighbour's offer of whisky as a remedy and beer as a beverage; however, much to the disappointment of temperance advocates, in the early 1900s beer was still the drink of choice for most people, and whisky and other distilled beverages were taken for their medicinal properties.[22] In the United States, federal alcohol prohibition would be enacted in 1920 and it would not be repealed until 1933.

The Cocaine Fiends: a baby born to a hophead

In 1935, another early feature-length film, *The Cocaine Fiends* (1935), portrayed pregnancy and illegal-drug use on the screen. As mentioned at the beginning of this chapter, Jane is portrayed as unwittingly becoming addicted to cocaine and then living as a gangster's moll. Her brother Eddie comes to the city to look for her. Once there, he hooks up with a blonde young White woman named Fanny at his workplace, depicted early in the film as a "temptress," who falls from grace due to her addiction and her love for Eddie. She introduces Eddie to cocaine. She eventually loses her job due to her sloppy work habits and her inability to care for her "personal appearance." Eddie is also fired. He ends up sleeping in the park before finally going to Fanny. They are shown living together in a one-room flat. They are now portrayed as poor and addicted. Fanny is working but she does not make enough to support them. It is implied that Fanny is now also working in the sex trade. In contrast, Eddie stays at home and paces waiting for Fanny to bring him money and drugs. In a following scene, Fanny is shown walking into their one-room tenement looking tired. She is crying and she lies down on the bed without taking her coat off. Eddie asks her, "What's wrong, Fanny? What happened? No luck today?" She replies, "We have to get off the dope; we've got to go straight." She then whispers in Eddie's ear and he cries out, "NO! NO! It can't be!" NO! It can't be. It mustn't be. You're a disgrace. My mother!" She replies, "Eddie, think of me." He yells, "Think of you? What do I care about you? No. I never really loved you. Now a baby born to a hophead on the street!"

Fanny gently puts her hand over his mouth and pleads, "Don't. . . . Whatever I've done it's because I loved you." She hands him some money and says, "Here, take this." She asks for a kiss and then says, "Goodbye, Eddie." He leaves their flat. The camera shows her sitting with her head in her hands; the kettle is boiling away on a gas burner. She removes the kettle, but she does not turn off the gas flame. She stands and gently touches her stomach with her hand and looks in the mirror, and then at the gas burner. She then picks up a piece of cloth and places it at the bottom of the door frame. She turns out the light and sits on the bed and waits for the gas fumes to kill her. When Eddie finally returns home, the landlady and the police are in his apartment, and they do not see him in the doorway. Fanny is dead. "Accidental," the policeman says.

In *The Cocaine Fiends*, women cannot be redeemed. Fanny is rejected by Eddie when he finds out that she is pregnant. Rather than concern for Fanny, he immediately worries about what his mother (represented as moral and maternal) will think when she finds out. Even though Fanny has allowed Eddie to move in with her, sacrificing her own safety and health by supporting their drug addiction through working in the sex trade, Eddie is quick to abandon her and brutally tells her he has never loved her. Even at the end of the movie, when his sister Jane discovers him at an opium den, he relies on her to provide money for him to return home to his mother in the countryside.

White women who use illegal drugs during pregnancy are consistently represented in early illegal-drug films as immoral, fallen women who signify "social decay" and "deviance" and "the end of modernity's civilizing mission."[23] Even when we sympathize with the plight of fallen women in these early films, we are set up to be horrified at the thought of their giving birth to "social problems." It is assumed that they will be "unfit" mothers and that their infants will be of limited mental and moral character, thus weakening the nation. Moral reformers during this era perceived White children as the foundation of the nation, the next generation of soldiers and workers.[24]

Historically, poor and racialized women have fought to have control over their own bodies, to bear children, and to keep the children they have. Slavery and the residential school system, contemporary social-service child-apprehension practices, and class inequality serve to separate mothers and children. Whereas the Western ideology of mothering embraces

White moral women as maternal, caring, and self-sacrificing, racialized and poor women have most often been excluded from this conception. Rather, poor women and racialized women are seen as sexually promiscuous, having one baby after another. They are also presented as inadequate mothers, incapable of nurturing and socializing their own children.[25] Discourse about maternal drug use contributes to and intersects with ideologies about mothering, reproduction, and drug prohibition.[26]

New Jack City and *Losing Isaiah*: unfit mothers and maternal harm

The horrors of pregnant women and mothers who use substances still concern moral reformers, as well as scriptwriters and film directors, although their concerns have shifted slightly. Early films tended to highlight how women who used substances were unfit mothers and immoral in character; later films include narratives about prenatal and permanent problems related to fetal exposure to illegal drugs. The shift in focus reflects the medical profession's pursuit of more knowledge about the fetus and the availability of new technology. It also reflects contemporary conflicts over women's reproductive rights and fetal rights. In her book *Using Women*, Nancy Campbell discusses how "pregnant addicts, their babies, and their children play a significant role in political discourse."[27] Campbell examines political discourse about infants labelled "crack babies" in the mid-1980s in the United States. She notes that all women are constructed through the lens of law as "potentially pregnant";[28] thus, their behaviour can be scrutinized by the state, moral reformers, and the professions. Although the medical profession and moral reformers expressed some interest in fetal exposure to heroin in the 1960s, it was not until the "crack scare" in the mid-1980s that maternal drug use became a public and national concern.[29]

The film *New Jack City* (1991) is set in 1986 in Harlem during an era of blaxploitation films. As discussed in chapters 3 and 5, the movie depicts the emergence of crack use and selling in an inner-city neighbourhood, and although the film is primarily about drug trafficking, its representation of women is revealing. The film begins with an aerial view of New York City, with radio voice-over. We hear the radio announcer say, "Hospital officials say that the number of addicted infants born in Manhattan-area hospitals has risen steadily over the past few years. Hospital officials say the care required by these, the smallest victims of the cocaine epidemic, has severely impacted the resources for pediatric care."

In another scene, the camera zooms in on a White woman at an NA meeting in a mandatory-treatment centre who says, "It's crazy 'cause I did everything. I whored. I ripped my family off. I was so scandalous I would even sell my baby's Pampers." The camera quickly closes in on the face of a Black woman. She says, "I have a crack baby. He was born blind. I know why he's blind. Everyone knows why he's blind. I kept telling myself I was gonna kick. And I never did. I'm a junkie. I'll be a junkie the rest of my life." In the film, "addicted" women are depicted as "crack whores" and instruments of fetal damage.

Similar to *New Jack City*, *Losing Isaiah* (1995) opens with an aerial view of a city. We see skyscrapers, city lights, and we hear police sirens in the background. Then we hear a bottle smashing and the scene cuts to Khaila, who is holding a small infant named Isaiah. As mentioned in chapter 3, she is homeless and is living in an abandoned building. Khaila walks out onto the street and puts her tiny baby into a cardboard box and tells him that she will be "right back." We hear Isaiah crying. The camera then cuts to a close-up of Khaila lighting a crack pipe; the camera zooms in on her mouth as she puffs desperately. He eyes are closed and she leans her head back and says, "Oh. Oh, yeah."

In the next scene, a garbage truck is shown pulling up to a pile of rubbish on the sidewalk. Two Black men hop out of the truck and start throwing rubbish into the back of it, including the cardboard box holding the baby Isaiah in it. Just as the blade descends and is about to crush the garbage and the baby, the men hear Isaiah cry. Next we hear the sounds of an ambulance and the camera cuts to Isaiah in a hospital. He is attached to an IV and monitors, and he is surrounded by a number of medical staff and a White, blonde, middle-aged social worker named Margaret, played by Jessica Lange. We know that Isaiah's situation is serious, but just in case we miss the point, one of the medical staff shouts, "Not breathing on own"; another says, "Having seizure," "phenobarbital!" "ICU!" The film is problematic in the sense that the baby who plays Isaiah is plump and healthy-looking, yet we see him lying in an incubator.

Margaret takes an interest in Isaiah right away and she finds out that he is only three days old. A nurse tells her "mother and baby both crack-addicted." Margaret lives a comfortable life with her husband and daughter. Characterised as "high strung," she becomes Isaiah's advocate against his bad mother who abandoned him, and against social workers and judges who fail to understand the situation. We are led to believe that Isaiah lives against all odds and Margaret is intent on adopting him.

Margaret's husband is wary of bringing Isaiah into their home. He cautions, "A black crack baby . . . who could have problems that won't show up for years." Margaret will not be deterred; she sees in Isaiah "love" and a "spirit" and, selfishly, he represents a way to fill the void in her own life and her marriage. Margaret brings Isaiah home. In one scene, she tells her adolescent daughter to rock him but not to look at him directly in his face. She says, "Crack babies sometimes have trouble with that." Isaiah is shown crying and crying and crying. As the film progresses, we see Margaret tenderly caring for Isaiah, at the expense of her husband and daughter. The film then cuts to several years later, and Margaret has now adopted Isaiah. Even though Isaiah is about five years old, he is depicted as very demanding and he screams easily. He is shown having major temper tantrums. In the film, it is made clear that these behaviours are directly related to fetal exposure to crack. Isaiah is shown in his own bedroom, with middle-class consumer signifiers such as "kiddie" wallpaper.

Meanwhile, Khaila has turned her life around. She has been sober for many years. We learn that she is illiterate. The film shows her struggle to learn to read and create a home for herself. Her apartment is run down and stark compared to Margaret's home. Khaila has physically transformed; instead of wild hair, her hair is straightened and confined, her clothes modest, neat, and clean. She is working as a nanny for a professional White family.

Khaila sets out to find her son. It turns out that she never received official notice of her son's adoption, and she never signed away her parental rights. Khaila is befriended by a White social worker and a Black lawyer who help with her custody case. She intends to challenge Isaiah's adoption. During the trial, a doctor is depicted providing evidence about fetal exposure to crack. He lists the effects: seizures, intercranial bleeds, malformed kidneys, low birthweight, and crib death. He then states that many children will go on to have severe learning disabilities, moodiness, and poor coordination. He claims that stress exacerbates the situation; therefore, providing "calm, steady, dependable parenting" is key to parenting children exposed to crack and in the child's best interests.

At one point, during the family-court session, both Margaret and Khaila accidentally meet in the women's washroom. Margaret shouts at Khaila, "Any animal can give birth. That doesn't make it a mother!" The fact that not so long ago Black women in the United States were treated as animals, with no rights to their children during slavery, is not investigated in the film. In the film, contemporary Black women are essentialized, and the myth that Black women are animals incapable of mothering is perpetuated. The film does touch on the issue of interracial adoption, but any critical message is undermined by the ending of the film, where Margaret asks the judge (and viewers watching the film) to consider the subject of "love." She wants to know why "love" has not been spoken about in relation to Isaiah's custody. She argues that the court is more interested in being "politically correct" than really taking into account Isaiah's life. At the end of the film, Khaila does win custody of Isaiah, yet when she brings him home kicking and screaming he is depicted as mourning for Margaret and secretly hanging on to a hair clip of hers. He is shown being afraid of Khaila, and he refuses to talk at the day-care center he attends in the heart of the ghetto while Khaila works. The camera zooms in on the word "ghetto" spray-painted on the outside of the building—a visual symbol so there is no doubt in the viewers' minds where Isaiah resides now. In one scene, when Isaiah is shown having a temper tantrum, he bites Khaila and screams for his "mommy" as he runs out of their home. The next day, Margaret is shown arriving at the day-care center, and Khaila tells Margaret to go to Isaiah and "hold him until he's not scared anymore." Khaila agrees to let Margaret back into

Isaiah's life because "she loves him." At the end of the film, the two women are shown hugging. Isaiah sees Margaret and he runs towards her, crying out "Mommy, mommy, mommy." Margaret hugs him and exclaims, "Oh, my boy." In the final scene, we see Margaret and Khaila sitting on the floor together with Isaiah as he plays with wooden blocks.

Losing Isaiah perpetuates the notion that Black women who use illegal drugs cannot possibly raise their children without the aid of White women and middle-class virtues. In the film, "love" is presented as the most important factor in parenting, more important than biological parents' rights. However, love is presented as more than an abstract concept; it is depicted as providing material support, such as a middle-class home and other consumer trappings. In the film, Black women who are or have been addicted to illegal drugs are represented as a risk to their children and incapable of providing love. The film also perpetuates myths about fetal exposure to crack. These myths are quite enduring, given the fact that by the time both *Losing Isaiah* (1995) and *New Jack City* (1991) were produced, an array of research challenged early claims about crack and fetal development and crack and mothering.

Legal researcher Laura Gomez analyzed newsprint articles about pregnancy, drugs, and abuse in two California papers from 1985 to 1992. She claims that the "news media" played a significant role in constructing the "crack scare" and "crack babies." She also argues the print media shaped the public's opinion about these issues and affected California legislative debates, policy, and prosecutors' actions in criminalizing maternal drug use.[30] Drew Humphries also examines the American media frenzy related to "crack babies and crack mothers." Humphries's study focuses more closely on the media's construction of the derogatory terms *crack mothers* and *crack babies*. She notes that reporters "stressed the mothers' indifference to their suffering newborns."[31] Women and their "crack babies" were constructed as poor "black and urban."[32] Humphries examined national network TV evening news reportage by ABC, CBC, and NBC between 1983 and 1994. Similar to Reinarman and Levine's[33] study, she notes that news reportage increased from 1983 even though illegal-drug rates had been going down since 1979. Reportage on mothers and infants peaked in 1989, at the height of the drug scare or moral panic about "crack mothers."

Claims about the innocent victims of the crack epidemic were shocking. These infants were said to be born with "malformed arms" and "organ abnormalities." It was reported that they suffered "heart attacks and strokes, cerebral palsy and mental retardation."[34] Images of crack withdrawal were splashed across TV screens. "Tiny trembling newborn[s], incubated and attached to monitors" remains the favoured media representation of infants prenatally exposed to crack.[35] These infants were said to have severe developmental and disciplinary problems rendering them a drain on already strapped health, social-service, and criminal-justice institutions.

Early claims like those above, about infants exposed prenatally to crack, have been largely discredited.[36] Prenatal exposure to crack (or any form of cocaine) does not lead to neonatal withdrawal syndrome (or blindness). Many of the effects thought to be due to crack are also associated with poverty, such as low birthweight. Early research samples were comprised of poor women and their infants, and the effects of poverty were often mistaken for the effects of exposure to crack. In 2004, thirty doctors and scientists in Canada and the United States sent an open letter to the media asking that it stop perpetuating myths about infants prenatally exposed to cocaine. In their letter they point out that the label *crack baby* lacks scientific validity, and it only serves to stigmatize infants and their mothers. They also argue that there is no such syndrome or recognizable condition termed *crack baby;* by "definition, babies cannot be 'addicted' to crack or anything else."[37] Social factors such as poverty and lack of economic and social support have a negative impact on maternal outcomes. When nonjudgmental prenatal and social support is provided, maternal outcomes improve.[38]

Since the mid-1980s, feminist researchers have pointed out that women's bodies have become the newest terrain for the war on drugs. The war on abortion and women's reproductive rights converge and intersect with the war on drugs, culminating in a dangerous mix. The intersection of the war on drugs and the war against women's control of their own reproduction is referred to by feminist advocates as "maternal-state conflicts."[39] Ignoring evidence-based research, prosecutors in the United States have charged over 300 women with child endangerment, trafficking to the fetus, manslaughter, and homicide. The majority of these women were poor and women of colour.[40]

As welfare policy has became "leaner and meaner" in the United States following neoliberal cutbacks in the 1980s and the enactment of workfare in the 1990s, women are increasingly viewed as individually responsible for their poverty. Thirty states have fetal-homicide laws and over eighteen states have civil-welfare laws related to maternal drug use.[41] Prenatal drug use, and drug use when mothering, is defined as abuse and neglect. Women's drug use is consistently represented as more out of control than men's. Their drug use is also constructed as a more important indicator of their personal character than their maternal and parenting commitments. A similar set of discourses is not applied to men's drug use.[42]

Since the end of the 1980s, the number of infants in foster care dramatically increased, especially in urban areas like New York City. The crack scare and fears about maternal drug use and maternal fitness led to the amendment of and enactment of civil child-abuse statutes. Infants who tested positive for drugs at birth were defined as "neglected" and/or "abused." Mothers who tested positive for drugs were defined as "unfit." Following the crack scare, child apprehension exploded in many urban cities. By the end of 1997, 73 percent of the children in foster care in New York City were Black. For these reasons, feminist scholar Dorothy

Roberts refers to the foster-care system in the United States as "an apartheid institution."[43] Researchers and advocates like the National Advocates for Pregnant Women argue that women who use drugs can be adequate parents. A number of studies demonstrate that drug use in itself does not equal poor parenting.[44]

The black comedy *Citizen Ruth* (1996) focuses on parenting and maternal drug use, specifically alcohol, glue, and inhalant use, through the character Ruth Stoops, who is characterized as a poor, recidivist, irresponsible, uneducated, homeless, and addicted White woman with four children in state care. She is pregnant again and charged with a felony, criminal endangerment of her fetus. The judge tells her that she "sickens him," and outside of the courtroom he suggests that she have an abortion rather than face the charges. The film narrative quickly descends into a polarized and one-dimensional view of the pro-choice and pro-life movements, which want to use her to further their causes. The issue of maternal drug use and criminal charges against pregnant women is left unexplored. Nevertheless, Ruth's drug use is portrayed as negative and damaging to the fetus, and in one scene a pro-life leader tells her that she is "full of sin and disease." Ruth miscarries a few days after finding out that she is pregnant, and she quickly escapes from the clutches of the pro-choice and pro-life activists. Although Ruth is demonized to a certain extent in the film, it is done with comic effect, and she is not portrayed as negatively as Khaila in *Losing Isaiah*.

Filmmakers are quite wedded to negative depictions of maternal drug use. Yet not all women are represented the same. In *Jesus' Son* (1991), Michelle, a young White illegal-drug user, is depicted having an abortion after she finds out she is pregnant, thus saving her child from further mistreatment. Nikki, a young White methamphetamine user in *Spun* (2002), tells a friend that she had a child three years ago. She says, "I held him once . . . and then they took him away." Yet Nikki is characterized as the most gentle and caring person in the film. At the film's end, she gets on a bus and leaves the drug scene behind her. Sheryl, a single Black woman in *Boyz n the Hood* (1991), is characterized as a "bad mother" and a "crack whore" who fails to take care of her toddler. Similar to the women portrayed at an NA meeting in *New Jack City* (1991), Sheryl is depicted as more committed to her crack use than to her child. In one scene, her child wanders into the middle of the street. Tre, a young man who lives across the street, rescues the child and brings her home. Rather than being pleased to see her child, Sheryl asks him, "You got some rock? I'll suck your dick." Tre responds, "Just keep your baby off the streets and change her diapers. They almost smell as bad as you."

In contrast, Christina, an affluent White woman in *21 Grams* (2003), is portrayed quite differently from Sheryl, even though she too uses cocaine, along with prescription pills and alcohol, when she is pregnant with her first child and later after her children and husband die in a car accident. Unlike Sheryl, Christina is shown embracing NA and her identity as a good mother during her recovery. In the film, White moral female characters are often saved after falling from grace, but poor and racialized women are rarely constructed as worth saving. Their drug use and addiction is constructed as more compelling and out of control; therefore, they are depicted as unable to, or not interested in, mothering.

Trainspotting and My Name is Joe

Myths about illegal-drug use and maternal neglect are not limited to U.S. film productions. The British film *Trainspotting* (1996) also offers a vivid story about White working-class illegal-drug use and maternal neglect. The film is set in Edinburgh, although most of it was filmed in Glasgow. As noted above and in chapter 4, in the film, Alison is depicted as a heroin-using mother and the sometimes girlfriend of Sick Boy. Her baby Dawn is shown crawling around Mother Superior's trashed-out squat, where she and her male buddies hang out when they are using heroin. We never see Alison and Dawn outside of this space, although all of the men in the film are shown outside of it. Dawn looks healthy and happy at the beginning of the film. It is established at the beginning of the film that Alison's heroin use takes precedence over all other activities, including sex. After showing some of the good times associated with using heroin and other narcotics, the film takes a turn. In one scene, we see Alison, Renton, and the rest of their buddies nodding out, enjoying their heroin high. The scene shifts dramatically after we hear Renton's voice-over, "Good times couldn't last forever. . . . Alison's screaming all day. . . ." The camera cuts to baby Dawn in her crib. She is dead. It is understood that she died from neglect. Sick Boy starts to cry and Renton responds by stating, "I'm cooking up." Alison concurs, saying "cook us up a shot." Renton does, but only after shooting himself up first. The film depicts Sick Boy reacting to the death of Dawn by taking up petty crime with a passion, and Renton is shown haunted by images of the baby when he is forced to go through heroin withdrawal at his parents' home. Yet we are never told what happens to Alison following the death of her daughter. Having outlived her usefulness in the film, she never appears again.

In the film *My Name is Joe* (1998), the character Sarah is portrayed as a middle-aged White woman who works as a community nurse at a health centre in Glasgow. She works with mothers and babies and is shown educating parents about how to clean and care for their infants. Sarah has a job, owns her apartment and her own car. In contrast, her clients are poor and living on assistance. One of her clients is Sabine, a young White woman who is on methadone when we are first introduced to her. Her young husband Liam is just out of prison and they are trying to keep their family together. Sarah visits the family and checks on their small son's development. She becomes intimately involved with Liam's football coach, Joe, a recovering alcoholic who is on the dole after being laid off during the wave of cutbacks, closures, and privatization under Margaret Thatcher. The first scene in the film depicts Joe at an AA meeting.

Soon Sabine is shown using heroin again and jeopardizing the safety of her family. Her mounting drug debts directly contribute to the vicious local drug trafficker, McGowan, threatening Liam and then Joe. Desperate, and in order to keep Liam and his family from being hurt by McGowan, Joe takes up McGowan's offer to write off the drug debt by helping him with two heroin deals. All he has to do is drive the transport car. When Sarah finds out, she freaks out and condemns Joe's actions. She links heroin trafficking to damaged children exposed to the drug maternally. She cries out, "Listen, I have seen babies rattling. Sent up to intensive care with expected brain damage. Have you ever seen a 14-year-old child choke on his own vomit? He's there with his mother screaming, 'I only did it once!'"

Maternal drug myths have been perpetuated by politicians, media, and film directors representing diverse political perspectives. Film directors Ken Loach and Danny Boyle are known for their critical representation of working-class life in Scotland, yet when it comes to depictions of heroin-using mothers and their children, they too fall back on familiar tropes and perpetuate myths about maternal drug use. It is interesting that both films, *Trainspotting* and *My Name is Joe,* were filmed in Glasgow, the home of the Women's Reproductive Health Service. In 1983, Dr. Mary Hepburn established the service to provide reproductive care for women with major social problems, including drug use. The service is multidisciplinary, where doctors, midwives, social workers, nurses, and other staff work together to provide nonjudgmental medical, social, and economic support for women and their families. Drug use is only one of many risks that shape pregnancy and birth, and Dr. Hepburn notes that "adverse outcomes among babies of drug-using women are primarily due to underlying socio-economic deprivation."[45] Drug use is considered a risk, but one that is manageable. Hepburn also notes that there is no "good evidence of teratogenesis" by heroin and other illegal drugs commonly used by women such as cocaine and marijuana.[46] The evidence shows that maternal heroin and cocaine use does not cause infant brain damage, adolescent vomiting, missing limbs, or any other anomalies attributed to it.

Poor women who use heroin, and other illegal drugs such as cocaine, have a higher rate of sudden infant death syndrome (SIDs), preterm deliveries, perinatal death, and low birthweight. The same incidence of these nonspecific effects are found in women who are poor and nondrug users and cigarette smokers.[47] The only specific effect from maternal heroin use is withdrawal. Withdrawal is transitory and it is not predictable, and not all babies prenatally exposed to heroin will experience withdrawal. At the Women's Reproductive Health Service in Glasgow, of 200 infants born to women who used drugs, only 7 percent required treatment for withdrawal.[48] Unlike film and news media representations of these babies, narcotic-withdrawal symptoms are similar to flu symptoms and range from mild to severe, and infant withdrawal can be medically managed if needed. There are no lifelong abnormalities associated with fetal exposure to heroin; in fact, it is quite a safe drug in that it causes no organic damage to even long-term users. In relation to adult use, outside of death due to drug overdose, which is most often related to unknown quantities and quality of drugs bought on the illegal market, negative effects associated with heroin are due to social and economic deprivation and drug-associated risks like transmission of disease through the use of unclean needles.[49][50]

A wide range of studies, including a number of U.K. ones, note that women who use illegal drugs can be good parents, especially when provided with economic and social supports.[51] Yet as we will see in the next section, child protection remains a central concern for social workers, in and outside of illegal-drug films.

Protection and *Clean*

Two Canadian productions also examine mothering and illegal drugs. These films are more concerned with fitness to mother rather than the effects of maternal drug use on the fetus. In the film *Protection* (2001), we are introduced to Betty, a poor young White woman with two children who is addicted to heroin. She lives with her boyfriend, who deals drugs. He is also physically abusive to her and her children, and he is thought to be sexually abusing Betty's young daughter. They live in a small rundown house in Surrey, in the lower mainland of British Columbia, which is represented as an industrial wasteland where "white trash" live. The landscape is bleak and it seems to be populated by only people addicted to illegal drugs, sex trade workers, and dealers. Although the film is about Betty, the story is told through the eyes of Jane, a social worker. Bruce Spangler, the director of the film, drew from his own experience as a social worker when making the film. Jane is constructed as a burned-out social worker who is caught between her irrational and unreasonable clients and the bureaucracy of the Ministry of Children and Families, which does not provide her the resources she needs to do her job well. In the film, Jane is shown smoking marijuana and drinking wine. All of the characters in the film are White except for an ex-social worker, who is Asian Canadian.

Although Betty has custody of her two children, she has an open file. She is now under investigation by social services after her son arrives at school with a black eye. When Jane and another social worker visit Betty's home, they bring along two police officers. Betty looks impoverished and wasted compared to the social worker's clean-cut clothes and pulled-back hair. They question Betty about her son's black eye and the possibility that Joe is molesting her daughter. Jane makes clear that she is worried about the safety of the children, but Betty sees her as interfering and says Joe would never harm her daughter. She says that she has done everything social services wants; she has taken the classes they wanted her to take, and she went on the methadone program and now she is off it. Jane tells her that "when her drug and alcohol abuse affect the safety of children it becomes my concern." She asks if Betty is using again and Betty says no. Jane decides nevertheless to apprehend her two children. Betty is shown screaming and then she says, "I'm gonna report this. I'm gonna call the media. I'm gonna tell them how you pick on poor people. You know, if I wasn't on welfare, if I had some big lawyer, there is no way you would take my kids!" She goes on to question what Jane, who does not have children, would even know about "being a mother." Jane's character remains calm and she stresses that the issue is the children's safety. She argues that until Betty makes changes, she considers the children at risk. Jane says, "It's up to you, Betty." Jane then tells the children that she is "going to take [them] to a nice home, with some nice people and they're going to take care of you for awhile." She tells them they are called foster parents.

The social workers take the children as the police hold Betty down. She cries and pleads with them to not take her children. Later, we see Jane in the park talking to her friend who used to be a social worker, and she tells him that she thinks she is beginning to "hate some of my clients." The next day at the office, Jane tells her newer coworker that the ministry is not a "very good parent." Later, Jane laments that Betty's kids will probably be back in six months anyway, and then they will be knocking at her door again, "that's the way it is." The camera cuts to Betty, she is shown destroying her house, breaking things and crying. The next time we see Betty, she is sitting in front of the TV, all alone. She is preparing to shoot up heroin. Afterwards, we see her lying flat on the floor and the camera fades out. At the end of the film, the viewer is not sure whether or not she has overdosed and died.

The juxtaposition of the rational and moral social worker and the volatile, violent, and bad parent is a thread throughout *Protection*. In the film, there is no real questioning of the practice of child apprehension. Nor is foster care problematized as a possible site of abuse and neglect for children. Given the grim history of British Columbia's care of foster children, this is a tremendous oversight. In the film, illegal-drug use is associated with child endangerment, physical and sexual abuse, violence, criminality, and neglect. Inadequate welfare rates and the unpaid labour of mothering are not problematized. The film does provoke some questions about the purpose of social services and the impact of the job on social workers. However, throughout the film, the problems that Betty encounters are seen as her "choice." Her choices are largely decontexualized from the social, economic, and political factors that shape her life. Betty is represented as using more heroin than her boyfriend and unwilling to make "proper" choices for her children.

Clean

In the Canadian/French/British-produced film *Clean* (2004), the female lead, Emily (played by Maggie Cheung), is depicted as a British Chinese woman who is possibly in her 30s or early 40s. In the film, we are introduced to her at a Canadian club where the indie band Metric is playing. Emily is dressed in punklike fashion, chewing gum, wearing a leather jacket with the collar up, and she has wild teased hair; wild hair often represents women's illegal-drug use and degradation. Her husband Lee is a 42-year-old White rock musician who is trying to stage a comeback with a new CD. At the club, Emily argues with Vernon, Lee's music agent, who might have a deal with a small indie label. Emily wants Lee to sign with a bigger label. They argue and Vernon yells at her, "We're in the real world," as opposed to the "psychedelic junkie fantasy world" she lives in. Vernon claims that it is "not my fault his [Lee's] reputation is shot." It is made clear during the club scene that Emily's "ego" is a problem as is her illegal-drug use. It is believed by people in the music industry that her behaviour has hampered her husband's career. One of the band members playing at the club says, "She's a junkie to the bone. That girl's a curse. Hear that she dumped her kid with Lee's parents. What's the point of having kids if you just dump them?"

After leaving the club, Emily scores some heroin before returning to the hotel room where she and Lee are staying. When she enters the room, Lee asks her, "You got what you wanted?" She says yes as she walks into the washroom. There she leaves some of the heroin she purchased in a toilet bag. Lee and Emily argue and she asks him if he wants to talk about their drug use, but he shouts "No! That's all we ever talk about!" In frustration, she leaves the hotel room and drives to the edge of a lake in an industrial area. She parks the car and takes out a small plastic bag of heroin. The camera zooms in on the rubber tourniquet she holds in her lipsticked mouth. We see a needle fall from her hand as she leans back in her seat, with her eyes closed. In the next scene, it is dawn and Emily wakes up and returns to the hotel. When she arrives at the hotel, the police are there; she tries to run away but they grab her. Her husband is shown lying face down on the floor and we see the police lift him into a body bag. The police search Emily's purse and find some heroin; they arrest her and bring her to jail. There she is interrogated by a police officer. He asks if she supplied Lee with the heroin. She says no, that she got the heroin from Lee. She is convicted of heroin possession and sent to prison for six months, an unlikely sentence for a first-time offence in Canada.

Vernon, her deceased husband's music agent, visits Emily in prison. He lets her know that he has signed a record deal now because there is more interest in Lee's work now that he is dead. He makes it very clear that he did this for Lee, not Emily. He tells her that her lawyer's fees and debt will be paid off. "You won't have to pay for a thing. And in return, I don't want you to ask me for anything ever again. When I walk through this door, I no longer exist." Then he asks,

"Just tell me this, were you there when he died?"

"No."

"Had you been fighting?"

"Yes."

"Did you buy the stuff?"

"No."

Thus, in a very short time, the film narrative establishes that Emily is not only a lying "junkie" and a mother who has abandoned her son, but she is complicit in her husband's overdose death. The film narrative also makes clear that Emily's heroin habit is larger than her husband's and that she was jeopardizing his career. Although we witness the brief visit, Emily's prison time is not represented on the screen.

After leaving prison, Emily visits Lee's father (played by Nick Nolte) and tells him that she is on methadone, a heroin substitute. Lee's father, Albrecht, and his wife Rosemary have permanent custody of Emily's son. Albrecht tells Emily that the court decision was handed down the day before, "father dead, mother in prison," and though she can visit they would prefer that she did not do so for a couple of years so that they can provide some stability for her son. She agrees to this arrangement.

Emily moves to Paris, where she used to live before meeting Lee. She continues to take methadone and other drugs while she is living there, unregulated by a clinic or doctor. She is depicted working in her uncle's restaurant, but she quits after he confronts her about her drug use. She leaves the restaurant and gets on a train. She looks quite desolate. She is shown throwing her methadone pills out of the window of the train. We never see Emily go through withdrawal, although in one scene she is depicted lying on her bed crying.

Later, Emily visits her son. He is now five years old and he asks her about his dad. "How come he needed drugs?" Emily says, "They gave us some really good times. But afterwards you always have to pay the price. And it is very high. Look at me. I am still paying." In the film, prison time and overdose death are not directly linked to prohibition, so we are left to assume that heroin addiction in itself incurs a price that one must pay.

Emily is shown struggling in the film. She is rejected by old friends in the music business and she has lost her standing with them. However, she is also portrayed as supported and protected by friends and family who have economic resources, such as homes, restaurants, music-recording businesses, and affluent lifestyles. By the end of the film, it looks like Emily's own music career is about to take off and she is reunited with her son, although she does not have custody. *Clean* is refreshing because, unlike many other drug films, Emily herself does not die of an overdose as do the women in *Marihuana, the Weed with Roots in Hell* (1936), *Clean and Sober* (1988), *Drugstore Cowboys* (1989), *Jesus' Son* (1991), *Another Day in Paradise* (1998), and *Protection* (2001). Her child does not die as does the baby in *Trainspotting* (1996), nor is he apprehended or under social-service surveillance as are the children in *Intolerance* (1919), *Losing Isaiah* (1995), *My Name Is Joe* (1998), and *Protection* (2001), given up for adoption (*Marihuana, the Weed with Roots in Hell* [1936]), or aborted

(*Jesus' Son* [1991]). Nor does she commit suicide to atone for her sins as do the women in *The Cocaine Fiends* (1935), *Reefer Madness* (1936), *The Man with the Golden Arm* (1955) and *Valley of the Dolls* (1967). Nor is she murdered as is the female character in *Reefer Madness* (1936), *Scarface* (1983), *New Jack City* (1991), and *Light Sleeper* (1992), and she does not die from the illegal drugs she has ingested like Sabira in *Traffik* (1989) and the young drug mule Lucy in *Maria Full of Grace* (2004). Rather, by the end of *Clean* we actually begin to empathize with Emily. Similarly, in *Sherrybaby* (2006), we begin to sympathize with the character Sherry, a young White woman struggling to reconnect with her daughter after spending three years in prison for drug-related crimes.

On the Corner

Whereas *Clean* depicts heroin users who are middle- and upper-middle-class with access to resources, the film *On the Corner* (2003), another Canadian production, depicts life for poor and marginalized aboriginal women in the Downtown Eastside (DTES) of Vancouver, Canada's poorest urban neighbourhood. The film stands out in the illegal-drug-use genre because it is the only one that represents the life of aboriginal people. In the film, the social factors that shape the main character's heroin use are explored. Angel is a young aboriginal woman living in poverty, represented by the tiny room she rents in a rundown hotel and her work in the sex trade. We also meet her two aunts at the local bar, drinking beer. We are told that her mother abandoned her at a very young age, as did her father. Her mother is depicted later in the film as a recovering "addict" who has been sober for over a year. Her mother comes to the DTES in search of her adolescent son, and she wants Angel and her son to come home with her to Port Rupert, their rural reserve. We learn that Angel's father died of a drug overdose years ago in the DTES.

The residential-school experience, racism, and poverty are explored to some extent in the film. Angel's younger brother comes down from the reserve to find her, and he starts using illegal drugs too. Angel's dealer, an older White man, is depicted as brutal and sadistic. Stacey, Angel's best friend, who also works with her on the street, disappears after she is shown getting into a car with a john. Stacey's disappearance is a reference to the ongoing danger and vulnerability of women, especially aboriginal women, living and working in the DTES and elsewhere in Canada, and the 69 women who have "officially" disappeared from the DTES since 1983. As I write, Robert Pickton's trial proceeds. He is currently on trial for six of the 26 counts of first degree murder in relation to women missing from the DTES.

In the film, following a violent scene where Angel is pushed down a set of stairs, she ends up in the hospital, where she is offered methadone, which she takes. She eventually leaves the hospital and tries to get her brother to go home with her. She wants him to leave the city with her and go back to the country, to their reserve. She sets up a time for them to leave, but as she waits for him on the corner, we see him shooting up, and it is unclear at the end of the film whether Angel actually leaves the city or whether her brother lives.

On the Corner examines the lives of aboriginal people and the class-biased, racialized trajectory of negative drug use, whether illegal or legal, and it makes clear the links with colonization and dislocation. In the 1950s and 1960s, the anticolonial writer Franz Fanon brought our attention to the dislocation derived from the colonial experience.[52] Aboriginal researcher Pat Monture-Angus also examines dislocation and the negative impact of colonization of aboriginal people in Canada.[53] Drawing from the social-political environment of global neoliberalism, addiction researcher Bruce Alexander explores how "dislocation" is linked to the impact of global market forces. Negative addiction (for addiction is not necessarily negative) is linked to dislocation, although it is not predetermined, nor is it the only response. Alexander makes clear that addiction, drug policy, and practice must move outside the medical/criminal models because, in a free-market economy, "the spread of addiction is primarily a political, social, and economic problem."[54] He examines historically how the rise of early capitalism, negative addiction, and dislocation are linked. He also argues that negative addiction is not a "drug problem" but a response to prolonged dislocation in which global market-driven societies destroy culture and social relations, as occurred with aboriginal peoples in Canada.[55]

Colonization is often achieved through laws that criminalize spiritual, social, political, and economic practices. Forced removal from land, suppression of knowledge of one's language, and residential school accompanied colonization of aboriginal people in the United States and Canada. Gilbert Quintero explores how colonization was also accompanied by negative constructions of Native American drinking, which "serve to reinforce and reproduce colonial images" of aboriginal people, and he explains that colonization is accompanied by the "control over people's images of themselves and others."[56] Beginning in the early and mid-nineteenth century, laws were enacted to criminalize aboriginal people drinking alcohol in the United States and Canada. Similarly, the war on drugs and the prohibition of alcohol and illegal drugs is accompanied by the production of negative representations of poor and racialized people, illegal drugs, users, and addiction. Film narratives and visuals, along with the music industry and criminal justice, medical, social service, agencies, and so on, reinforce and shape punitive policy and practice and occasionally rupture illegal-drug discourse.

Of all the illegal-drug films that I viewed, *On the Corner* is the only film that focuses on aboriginal people, especially the plight of aboriginal women.[57] The film also features quite a number of aboriginal actors and actresses. In these ways, it is an anomaly. The film's producer, Nathaniel Geary, is familiar with the neighbourhood, having worked there as a mental-health social worker for many years. He humanizes all of his characters; even the brutal drug dealer is depicted as scared and vulnerable at the end of the film. Although central themes, such as dislocation, loss, and addiction, are illuminated in the film, he is careful not to demonize his characters. In fact, in another anomaly for an illegal-drug film, his characters are represented as capable of love and caring.

CONCLUSION

In Britain, Canada, and the United States, women suspected of using drugs are separated from their children through child apprehension and rising prison rates. Similar to their male counterparts, film depictions of illegal-drug-using and -dealing women rarely show prison scenes outside of bookings and/or brief visitation scenes (see *Lady Sings the Blues* [1972], *Light Sleeper* [1992], *Clean* [2004]). The exception to the rule is when women are arrested and incarcerated far from home. In the sample for this study, only the U.S. production *Brokedown Palace* (2000) portrayed lengthy prison scenes with women, and they take place in Thailand. The film focuses on two young White women who are imprisoned in Thailand for smuggling heroin. Thailand's criminal-justice system is portrayed as corrupt. When a lawyer tells the women that he is familiar with Thailand's justice system, one of them replies, "Now there's an oxymoron." Later, she tells the judge, "This trial is a joke. A shitty Third World joke." Rather than call attention to the real plight of women in prison around the world imprisoned for drug smuggling (who are most often poor and women of colour), the film serves to delineate corrupt Third World justice systems from fair and just Western justice systems.[58] The myth that justice prevails in the West is left intact.

Overall, illegal-drug films erase women's imprisonment for drug offences in Western nations. In the United States, women's prison rates have skyrocketed since the 1970s, largely due to drug offences. For example, following the Rockefeller drug laws enacted in 1973, the female prison population in New York State increased by 825 percent, and poor and racialized women are vastly overrepresented in prison, and the majority of them are mothers.[59] Black and Hispanic women make up almost 80 percent of women incarcerated for drug offences in New York State.[60] In Britain, Canada, and the United States, women's prison rates are increasing faster than men's, and the female prison population has tripled since the 1970s.[61] However, we are never bothered with these details when watching illegal-drug films. Of the 120 films in the sample, only five were directed by women (4 percent), and there is little difference in their portrayals of female characters. Illegal-drug films situate women outside of prison. However, they are punished, through representations of violence, rape, murder, suicide, overdose deaths, and child apprehension, and their children are portrayed as permanently damaged due to the effects of maternal drug use and neglect.

7   Challenges to the Drug War
1980 to 2006

This chapter explores ruptures in drug-war discourse, focusing on films produced since the late 1980s that are referred to as stoner flicks, including the Cheech and Chong film *Up in Smoke* (1988) and *Harold and Kumar Go to White Castle* (2004). These films normalize and exaggerate recreational illegal-drug use, especially marijuana; and most significantly, drug use is associated with pleasure and play. Alternative films, including the Canadian production *Trailer Park Boys* (2006) and the Showcase series of the same name, are also examined because they exemplify normalized illegal-drug use, production, and selling. Other alternative films discussed here include *American Beauty* (1999), *Withnail and I* (1987), and *Drugstore Cowboy* (1989), as well as films that rupture drug-dealer narratives such as *Saving Grace* (2000) and *Buffalo Soldiers* (2001). *Valley of the Dolls* (1967), *Garden State* (2004), and *Layer Cake* (2004) lead to a discussion of the illusionary line separating legal and illegal drugs. The final section highlights the British miniseries *Traffik* (1989) because it is the only film in the sample that looks in depth at the global war on drugs and the poppy grower.

STONER FLICKS

Films labelled "stoner flicks" provide comic relief from the relentless violence and racist imagery of serious illegal-drug films, especially those that focus on trafficking. In contrast to narratives about turf wars, violence, addiction, degradation, and redemption, stoner flicks are all about pleasure, play, and antiauthoritarianism. It is easy to understand why these films are so popular, especially amongst young men. Popular films like *Up in Smoke* (1978), *Cheech and Chong's Next Movie* (1980), *Fast Times at Ridgemont High* (1982), *Dazed and Confused* (1993), *Fear and Loathing in Las Vegas* (1998), *Half Baked* (1998), *How High* (2001), *Jay and Silent Bob Strike Back* (2001), and *Harold and Kumar Go to White Castle* (2004) focus primarily on male buddies and their adventures, excessive marijuana use, and ridiculous, exaggerated effects. Through parody, the film narrative and imagery reveal the absurdity of illegal-drug regulation and narratives that represent illegal-drug use as *"essentially* damaging."[1] The cult status of early films like *Reefer Madness*, which was considered a serious educational film at the time it was produced, reveals how temporal propaganda is. Later stoner flicks also encompass what Fiona Measham refers to as the tension between escapism from "regulatory consumer-oriented society through self expression and liberation . . . [and] 'head space' as leisure space."[2] "Drugs, then, represent both the escape from contemporary capitalist consumer society and are themselves the object of consumption."[3]

Up in Smoke

Up in Smoke (1978), directed by Lou Adler, focuses on two marijuana-smoking buddies, Pedro and Anthony Stoner, played by Cheech Marin and Tommy Chong, a stand-up comedy team. Pedro, Mexican American, fluent in Spanish, displays Mexican-flag stickers on his low-rider car and listens to Latino bands such as Santana and El Chicano. Whereas the low-rider car driven by Tony and his buddies in *Scarface* is derided and rejected by the top dealer's White girlfriend as evidence of racial inferiority, in *Up in Smoke*, racist cultural symbols of difference are turned on their head and celebrated. At the beginning of the film, Pedro is shown picking up Stoner while he is hitchhiking. Stoner is disguised as a woman with large breasts as a ploy to get a ride. Together they share a huge joint and bond with each other. The car fills up with smoke until they can no longer see out the windows. They are arrested by the police and become fast friends. Following their release from jail they are picked up by immigration police and deported to Mexico. They arrange to drive Pedro's uncle's vehicle back to get into the United States. Alas, they pick up the wrong van and unknowingly drive across the Mexican/U.S. border with a van that is made of marijuana. They make it across the border and join a Battle of the Bands contest, playing their hit song "Earache My Eye." At the end of the film the van is accidentally lit on fire and it combusts, filling the Battle of the Bands with marijuana fumes and inadvertently deterring the police, who are looking for the owners.

Up in Smoke is the first of ten films with Cheech and Chong as stoned-out, free-loving hippies (see *Cheech and Chong's Next Movie* [1980] and *Still Smoking* [1983], amongst others). Illegal-drug use is celebrated and drug smuggling is comedic, with conventional society represented as oppositional to the freewheeling hippie lifestyle of the main characters. Although marijuana is their main drug of choice, quaaludes, speed, cocaine, and acid are consumed too. In *Up in Smoke*, marijuana smuggling is portrayed by a police officer as "the last vestige of free enterprise left" for poor people in Mexico. The drug trade is not associated with violence, even though there are encounters with the police, who are represented as incompetent and interfering rather than as agents of law and order. Whiteness is not normalized in the film, and, even though Whiteness is linked to authority, it is satirized and undermined, with the multiethnic subculture positioned against the White establishment courts and police. As a male buddy film, the women characters are all White, marginal, and viewed through the male gaze as objects of pleasure.

Harold and Kumar Go to White Castle

Harold and Kumar Go to White Castle (2004) also exemplifies the stoner-film genre. Similar to *Up in Smoke*, both films turn ethnic stereotypes on their heads and critique drug prohibition. *Harold and Kumar Go to White Castle*'s main characters are two young men, Harold, a Korean American, and Kumar, a South Asian American. The film begins in an office building with rows of cubicles. In one cubicle, two young White men are talking about going out partying instead of doing their work. One of the men decides to unload his unfinished work on Harold, and he threatens to tell the boss that Harold is "slacking" if he does not complete it over the weekend. The two White men leave the office gloating about how "Asian guys love crunching numbers." The next scene introduces Kumar, who is shown applying to medical school at Princeton when his cell phone goes off in the middle of the interview. It is Harold. Kumar tells him, "I just got a quarter of the finest shit in New York City and I'm not smoking it alone." Overhearing the phone call, the university Dean throws him out, which is exactly what Kumar wants. Both his father and his brother are physicians and he is desperately trying to escape his destiny even though he aced his MCATs.

Harold is portrayed as the "hardworking," preppy, and quiet Asian man, and Kumar is shown as a hoody-wearing irresponsible slacker, although we know that he obtained top scores at university. When Harold drives home after work and tries to park, a bunch of White youths in a truck drive into the space before he can, and the driver yells at him: "This is America, learn how to drive!" Harold enters the apartment he shares with Kumar, and the camera cuts to Kumar's bedroom: it is in total disarray. In contrast, Harold's room is neat and tidy. The music lyrics blare in the background "let's get retarded," and they settle down to watch TV and to smoke a lot of marijuana. A parody of a "just say no" ad appears on the screen of their TV. In the ad, two White youths smoke marijuana, one of them so high he picks up a rifle and kills himself. Harold laughs softly and says with admiration, "I love that ad!" The ad is followed by a White Castle commercial highlighting their square hamburgers. Spurred on by the thought of having a burger, but not just any burger, Harold and Kumar take off and drive to the local fast-food restaurant. However, the nearest White Castle is closed, so they take off for one further away. This action takes them on a wild journey through New Jersey in search of White

Harold and Kumar Go to White Castle. Source: New Line Cinema/Photofest.
© New Line Cinema.

Castle, a symbolic allegory for the holy grail and the American Dream. Their adventures include being hassled by the police and obnoxious White youths and a number of encounters at Princeton University. They also stop in at the hospital where both Harold's father and brother work. On seeing his father, Kumar hugs him and takes his ID to gain access to the hospital's "medical marijuana." This is the only film in the sample that ever refers to medical marijuana, but the plan fails because it is not available at the hospital. Nevertheless, they find it elsewhere as they continue on their quest to find a White Castle. The green leaf and bud appear as a sort of icon, inspiring an attitude of reverence by the youth in the film. There is also a surreal "love scene" between Kumar and a human sized bag of pot, and a scene where Harold and Kumar smoke pot with a cheetah.

During their adventures, Harold's car is stolen. At Kumar's urging, since the road is clear, Harold steps onto the street when the light is red in order to go to a pay phone across the road to report his stolen car to the police. As soon as he steps onto the street, a White police officer pulls up and tickets him for jaywalking. Upon hearing Kumar's name, the White police officer says, "What happened to good old American names?" Harold is so mad at Kumar that he takes a swing at him, but he accidentally hits the police officer and he is arrested and dragged down to the police station. When he arrives at the jail, he sees a young White man who earlier sold marijuana to Kumar at Princeton University; the young man is now arrested for possession of a large plastic bag of it that is now sitting on the police officer's desk. We see the young man's mother hand the police officer a cheque as she thanks him and tells her son to get into the car. The camera cuts to a middle-aged Black man sharing a jail cell with Harold who is reading a book titled *Essays of Civil Disobedience*. When Harold asks him what he is in for, he responds, "For being Black." He tells Harold he was just walking down the street when the police drove up and beat him and arrested him.

Kumar, attempting to rescue Harold, phones the police station, falsely reports a crime, and all the police officers leave in their cars. Kumar finds the keys to unlock the cell and grabs Harold's police file. He sniffs the air and discovers the bag of marijuana. He grabs it, and to the backbeat of the lyrics "Crazy about You," Harold slips into a surreal fantasy of loving and living with the bag of pot, represented as life-size and female. At this point, the police return with another Black man in custody who is proclaiming his innocence. Seeing the keys in the prison door, the police run into the cell and start to beat up the middle-aged Black man for attempting to escape; meanwhile, Harold and Kumar escape with the pot. Eventually they wind up at a gas station/store where they steal a truck from the White youths who have been harassing them throughout the film. They drive away but are soon pursued by a police cruiser. They pull off the road and drive down a ridge until they stop at the edge of a cliff and climb out of the car. We can hear the police sirens in the background, and it seems they will be caught any minute. As Kumar looks over the cliff and the camera cuts to a brightly lit White Castle in the distance, Kumar points it out to Harold, saying that they can still make it because there is a hang glider on the top of the stolen truck. Harold says there is no way he is risking his life hang gliding for a burger, but Kumar says this is not just about burgers. Looking out at the brightly lit White Castle on the horizon, he says:

> It's about far more than that. Our parents came to this country to escape persecution, poverty, and hunger. Hunger, Harold. They were very very hungry. They wanted to live in a land that treated them as equals, a land filled with hamburger stands and not just one type of hamburger, hundreds of types with different sizes, toppings and condiments. That land was America! America, Harold. America. This was about achieving what our parents set out for. This was about the pursuit of happiness. This night was about the American dream.

The camera cuts to them hang gliding through the air and they land in a field right across from the White Castle. Bruised, cut, and exhilarated, they walk into the fast-food restaurant and order 30 burgers, drinks, and fries only to discover that they have no money to pay for their food. They are rescued by a man they picked up hitchhiking earlier in the film and who later stole Harold's car. He apologetically pays for their meal. Meanwhile, the police discover the truck and the bag of pot and assume it belongs to the troublesome young White men.

At the White Castle, Harold and Kumar eat to their hearts' content. Kumar has an epiphany and decides that he will go to medical school after all, and Harold stands up to his workplace colleagues when they enter the restaurant. As the credits roll, we see Harold and Kumar watching TV again, and a newscaster is reporting about the Black man who was in jail with them. It turns out that he is a Rutgers University professor, and he is suing the New Jersey police for racial discrimination and police brutality. We see the White police officers being arrested and brought into custody, and then the newscaster says that the police are looking for two fugitives, and they show sketches of the fugitives, which, the newscaster says, are "extremely accurate." The camera then cuts to stereotypical and racist line drawings of a bearded Chinese man with buckteeth and a straw hat and a South Asian man wearing a turban. In the background, we hear Kumar remark softly, "Nice," and the film ends.

Harold and Kumar Go to White Castle deconstructs the racialized discourse that young men of colour live with every day. It also points to the absurdity of drug laws and makes clear the institutionalization of violence associated with racial profiling. The White police are represented as ignorant, uneducated, corrupt bullies. It is also a buddy film and the characters play with the tension between homophobia and homoeroticism while the young women in the film are objects of desire. It is here, to a certain extent, that the critical narrative fails. However, the sexualized representation of women in the film is turned on its head during a scene in the women's washroom where the object of desire is grossly humanized. The American Dream and consumer culture are satirized and marijuana use is seen as positive and fun, a normalized activity of educated youth, a pleasurable, mystical, and transcendental experience.

In *Up in Smoke* and *Harold and Kumar Go to White Castle*, the main characters and storyline provide a different image of the illegal-drug users and sellers than official narratives. These films also evoke what Measham refers to as "the performance of carnival" to explain how drug use can incorporate both "transgression and accommodation [in capitalist consumer society] in weekend leisure-time excess."[4] Paul Manning's work examines the relationship between "drug consumption and popular culture." He notes how difficult it is to explain recreational-drug use and widespread use of illegal drugs like ecstasy and marijuana amongst youth in terms of biological and behavioural models.[5] Manning and others also reject "pharmacological determinism." "It is the cultural aspects that shape the use of drugs rather than the other way around."[6] In those terms, recreational illegal drug use can be understood as providing users with a path to pleasure, transcendence, healing, and exploration of the meaning of life outside the material world and consumer culture.

American Beauty: waking up from a coma

In contrast to the young men portrayed in most stoner flicks, the main character in the U.S. film *American Beauty* (1999), Lester, is a 42-year-old White man trying to flee from his straight suburban middle-class life. He is depicted living in suburbia with his wife Carolyn and teenage daughter Jane. In a voice-over, he tells the audience that he is waking up after 20 years in a coma, informing us that he is going to die in less than a year, but it hardly matters because, in a way, he has been "dead already." Yet Lester starts to "wake up" after he smokes some marijuana with his 19-year-old neighbour, Ricky. Threatened with losing his professional job, he quits instead and starts to smoke marijuana regularly, supplied by Ricky. He trades in his Camry for a 1970 Pontiac Firebird and he takes a job at a fast-food restaurant flipping burgers. He works out and takes up jogging (because he wants to look good naked for a young teenage friend of his daughter that he lusts after). In contrast to the increasingly laid-back Lester, his wife Carolyn is depicted as a joyless, "money-grubbing," neurotic, suburban control freak who works as a real-estate agent. She has not had sex with him for years, although she is having an affair with a rival agent. She is shown looking very uptight and listening to inspirational tapes.

Lester's newfound love of marijuana and rejection of suburban values is juxtaposed with his tense neighbour, a homophobic colonel in the U.S. Marines who believes in zero drug tolerance. The colonel enforces this with a vengeance in his own home, and in one scene he tells his son Ricky he needs a urine sample for drug testing. When he suspects his son of going into his locked cabinet, he breaks down his bedroom door and beats him until blood runs down his face. He yells at his son, "Fight back, you little pussy." We learn that when Ricky's father caught him smoking marijuana when he was 15 years old, he sent him to military school to learn how to be disciplined and drug free. It did not work out and he was kicked out of school when he threatened another student. Ricky tells Lester's daughter, Jane, that his father committed him to a psychiatric hospital where he was drugged for two years. He is now home and selling marijuana, top of the line stuff that he says is "genetically engineered" by the U.S. government.

Later, fearing that his son is gay, the colonel confronts Ricky. Again, he resorts to violence and hits him and tells him he would rather see him "dead than be a fucking faggot." The colonel kicks him out of the house, and Ricky's mother is oblivious to the violence and her son's plight. She is depicted as near catatonic throughout the film, and as Ricky leaves home for good she tells him to "wear a raincoat." In a following scene, the colonel, mistakenly believing that Lester is gay, tries to kiss him, but Lester tells him that he has the "wrong idea." The audience now understands that the colonel's suspicions related to his own son's sexuality may derive from his own repressed desires. Horrified, the colonel walks home in the rain. Meanwhile, at home, Lester finally resolves his crush on his daughter's friend, and he is shown sitting at the kitchen table feeling good. He holds an old photo of his family when they were all happy. We then see a gun pointed to the back of Lester's head and we hear a gunshot. The camera cuts to the colonel back at home, covered in blood, his gun missing from the wall.

As the film ends, Lester says in voice-over, "Hard to be mad when there is so much beauty in the world." The credits role and the Beatles song "Because," covered by Elliot Smith, can be heard: "Because the world is round, it turns me on. Because the wind is high, it blows my mind. Love is old, love is new."

American Beauty speaks to simple beauty in the world, the desire to be free, and drugs as a door to altered states and shifts in perception. It is an existential film that explores legal- and illegal-drug use, sexuality and repression, violence and love, family, and consumer society. The film's focus is on individual freedom, rather than collective action or a closer examination of gender roles and capitalism. In fact, when Lester's daughter Jane yells at him for staring at her friend and making his inappropriate desire for her so blatant, he turns on her and says, "Turn into a real bitch just like your mother," and he reasserts his patriarchal status as the film progresses. The film explores homophobia and homosexuality, but linking murder with repressed desire plays on worn-out narratives.

In the film, repression of illegal-drug use is critiqued, and Lester's marijuana use is viewed as a positive element in his search for meaning in his life. In contrast, the use of legal drugs to "regulate" Ricky during his forced stay in the hospital is portrayed as negative and damaging to him. By the end of the film, it is uncertain whether Ricky can escape the patriarchal violence that has been imposed on him, but his considerable earnings from selling marijuana will enable him to start a new life in New York City. Lester is punished terribly for his quest towards freedom and beauty, but director Sam Mendes sought to present positive experiences of illegal-drug use on the screen. Similar to other films discussed in this chapter and chapter 3, drugs are portrayed as conduits to explore life beyond the material, to closely examine consumer culture, and to move towards personal and cultural change and altered states of consciousness.

Garden State: legal drug use

Although this book is about illegal-drug films, I emphasize the illusionary line between legal and illegal drugs. Drug users themselves are fully aware of the potential of legal drugs to enhance performance, pleasure, and mood. Jim Hogshire, the author of *Pills-a-Go-Go: A Fiendish Investigation into Pill Marketing, Art, History and Consumption*,[7] examines modern society's love of pills. Unlike natural plants such as marijuana, poppy, and coca, which have long been associated with racialized people and non-Western nations, synthetic drugs—pills—are viewed as therapeutic and civilized, yet their status can shift, as happened with Valium and later Prozac and OxyContin. These drugs were initially praised and then demonized by the press and medical profession, although official narratives about their worth seem to have little impact on rates of prescribing and use. Hogshire notes that pills are the "quintessential icon of Western Civilization,"[8] the majority being brightly coloured synthetic consumer products that promise happiness and health.

In the 1950s, Milltown[9] parties sprung up, and later, pills like Librium, Seconal, and Valium became known as party drugs. The early film *Valley of the Dolls* (1967) captures the lives of three White women (one notably played by Patty Duke) and the underside of illegal- and legal-drug use, sexual expression, and ambition. In this film, and its sequel, *Beyond the Valley of the Dolls* (1970), drugs like the barbiturate Seconal are central to the film's narrative. Both films are melodramatic, but *Requiem for a Dream* (2000) is the ultimate contemporary nightmare of legal- and illegal-drug use (for a fuller examination of this film, see chapter 4). Dramas aside, a number of comedies such as *Kids in the Hall: Brain Candy* (1996) and *Garden State* (2004) explore the pharmaceutical drug industry as they attempt to push the boundaries about drug narratives rather than reassert conventional stories.[10]

The U.S. production *Garden State* (2004) is a romantic comedy set mostly in New Jersey (the Garden State) focussing on the life of a 26-year-old White man named Andrew, a struggling actor in Los Angeles. Similar to Lester, the middle-aged man portrayed in *American Beauty*, Andrew is waking up from a long sleep. In the opening scene, Andrew wakes up to his telephone ringing and a message from his father telling him his mother has died by drowning in the bathtub. We see him lying under a crisp white sheet in a white bed, in a sterile white room. It is unclear whether or not he is in a hospital room until he gets up. The camera follows as he walks to the medicine cabinet in the bathroom; he opens it and we see that it is filled with rows of prescription drugs. Soon he is on his way home to New Jersey. It becomes clear that Andrew is overly medicated on lithium and other antidepressants, which have been prescribed by his psychiatrist father. He is nearly paralyzed and shows no emotion or reactions to questions asked of him by old friends and family back in New Jersey. His mother's death and his visit home make him determined to go cold turkey, and he stops taking his prescribed drugs; he has decided to examine his inner pain and conflict in order to move on in his life. He tries ecstasy at a party with old friends, and unlike the depressive effects of the legal drugs he has been consuming since he was ten years old, he begins to open up and enjoy himself. Soon he hooks up with a local girl, and by spending time with her and his old friends, he begins to wake up from his long sleep and to reconnect with his feelings. Marijuana and ecstasy are represented as positive and fun, and they are associated with transcendence, in contrast to legally prescribed psychiatric drugs that are depicted as stifling life and emotions.

Layer Cake: a promise that falls into familiar discourse

The British film *Layer Cake* (2004) is notable for initially providing a scene in which criminalized drugs are legally available and for sale at pharmacies. The film also questions drug prohibition in its opening scene. It is also a good example of a film that appears promising and then falls into conventional drug-war narratives, in many ways mirroring Tony Blair's leadership. In a voice-over, we hear a man describe his rejection of violence and his drift towards the hippie scene in London during the summer of love. He tells us that he was born into a simpler world than today: it was just "cops and robbers" then. We see him walking through a white, sterile pharmacy with rows and rows of shelves with containers and bottles of legal drugs stacked on them. The containers are labeled, "fcuk, intensify your life," and it is made clear that they contain cocaine. We also see rows of bottles that contain ecstasy. There are also a number of small white boxes stacked on the pharmacy shelves and they are separately labeled: intoxication, orgasm, addiction, and delusion. Slowly, the rows of bottled drugs and boxed "desires" are replaced by a colourful array of "recognizable" pharmacy products. The man walking through the pharmacy, referred to as XXXX, is a White middle-aged man (played by Daniel Craig) who says:

> Drugs changed everything. Always remember all this drug monkey business will be legal. They won't leave it to people like me. Not when they finally figure out how much money there is to be made. Not millions. Fucking billions. Recreational drugs . . . giving people what they want. Good times today, stupid tomorrow. But this is now, so until prohibition ends, make hay while the sun shines.

The film associates illegal-drug use with hedonism and escape. XXXX states, "I'm not against it. I'm a businessman whose commodity happens to be cocaine." Quite quickly, the story shifts towards conventional drug-trafficker discourse.

After being threatened by the top dealer, XXXX picks up a gun and takes to violence like a long-time pro. He goes on a killing spree, murdering the top dealer (who turns out to be an informer) and taking his place in the drug-trade pyramid (the "layer cake" of British society). He is no longer cool and rational; instead, he is dangerous and unpredictable. Unlike the fun-loving ecstasy users shown in *Garden State* (2004), the recreational "love" drug is associated with violent local dealers and even more treacherous and murderous Serbian traffickers. XXXX is brought down at the end of the film. As he walks away from his empire and the trade, with his girlfriend at his side, her jealous ex-boyfriend shoots him. The film's ending confirms that "crime does not pay," that violence, mayhem, and foreign criminal organizations typify the illegal-drug trade, and that underneath the urban, educated, White male drug-dealer veneer, a true killer exists.

Layer Cake. Source: Sony Pictures Classics/Photofest. © Sony Pictures Classics. Photograph by Daniel Smith.

Trailer Park Boys

The Canadian film *Trailer Park Boys* (2006) offers a view different from that of *Layer Cake,* of drug producers, dealers, and illegal-drug users. Whereas XXXX is affluent and urban, and middle-aged Lester in *American Beauty* resides in the suburbs and wishes to transcend it, and Harold and Kumar are university-educated and represented as upwardly mobile youth in the United States, the men in *Trailer Park Boys* are no longer youths but not yet middle-aged; they are portrayed as uneducated and downwardly mobile White English-speaking Canadians. The *Trailer Park Boys* came on the scene in 1999 as a series on the cable network Showcase,[11] and the film of the same name was produced in 2006. The film and series are done in documentary fashion following the day-to-day adventures of three buddies, Ricky, Julian, and Bubbles, who live at a trailer park called Sunnyvale, in Dartmouth, Nova Scotia. They are atypical male characters and lack Hollywood star characteristics of muscled, sculpted bodies and "WASP" looks, and instead are stereotypically "white trash." For readers not familiar with Nova Scotia, it is "officially" represented as the Celtic homeland of the East, a Scottish and Protestant bastion of bagpipes, short-bread, kilts, and fiddles. Not so in the *Trailer Park* film and series. Sunnyvale Trailer Park is home to a bunch of lovable misfits, including the trio Ricky, Julian, and Bubbles, who are represented as poor small-time crooks with hearts of gold. Their illegal activities, such as stealing parking metres, growing marijuana (in the backseat of a car), and selling grams of hashish, are played with comic effect. Julian is portrayed as the brains of the trio, always shown with a rum and Coke in his hand. Like modern-day Robin Hoods, they work with friends and take from those who are a little better off and give to their fellow Sunnyvale residents; they are generous to a fault but most often their schemes fail to pan out. Their marijuana growing fails and they deal in nickels and dimes, giving away most of their drugs. Their criminal and antiestablishment lifestyle and their on-and-off-again romances are juxtaposed with Lahey, the caretaker of the trailer park, and the local police, who are portrayed as ineffective and absurd. Occasionally, Julian and Ricky do get caught by the police, and they are shown in and out of prison for their minor offences. Fellow prisoners are friendly; in contrast, one of the guards they encounter is depicted as vindictive and capable of violence.

A 2004 Showcase episode titled *Trailer Park Boys X-Mas Special* (2004) exemplifies the spirit of the series and the film. The story begins a few days before Christmas and the "boys" are getting ready for the holidays. Bubbles is shown in his home, a roughly made one-room shack that leans against a trailer, wearing a winter coat and toque, and he is knitting as his numerous cats play with balls of yarn on the floor. His large eyes, magnified by his Coke-bottle eyeglasses, are directed at the camera as he says that Christmas is a stressful time. When the criminal enterprises of the "boys," stealing Christmas trees and gifts from parked cars, fall apart, their antics illuminate the true meaning of Christmas. On Christmas Eve, the trailer-park residents go to church for midnight mass, and Ricky stands outside of the church calling out to people, "Weed and hash. Ten bucks a gram." Julian walks up and reprimands him, calling his actions disrespectable. But Ricky is not deterred and he shouts to people entering the church, "I know people smoke dope. The sermon makes a lot more sense if you're stoned." In the next scene, the congregation is seated, and the priest, standing in front of a podium at the front of the church, begins his sermon. He says that some people are "desperate and given to crime," but, before he can really get going, Ricky bursts into the church and interrupts him, hoping to win back his on-and-off-again girlfriend Lucy. He fails and she storms off. Meanwhile, the trailer-park caretaker, Lahey, who is terribly drunk, enters the church. There is a scuffle and then Ricky walks to the front of the church and the podium and asks the priest to step aside. He addresses the congregation:

> Sorry to interrupt. I just had one of those brain-learning things that wasn't there a second ago . . . What is Christmas? I just got out of jail, which was awesome. In jail, we don't have presents, lights, and trees. We just got stoned and drunk. It's the best time. And I got out here and I'm all stressed out. My girlfriend breaks up with me, and that's not how Christmas should be. You should be getting drunk and stoned with

your friends and family. People you love. Who here is drunk right now? How many people are drunk besides Julian?

Ricky looks out at the congregation and about three quarters of them raise their hands. Then he says with reverence: "That is so awesome." He continues, "And dope. God doesn't give a shit if you smoke dope. You're in church so you can't lie. How many people here are stoned right now?" More then half the congregation raise their hands. Ricky exclaims, "That's what I thought! That's Christmas. None of this presents and lights and stress and shit. Just getting drunk and stoned with friends and family and people that you love." Ricky leaves the church to go back to the trailer park to be with Bubbles and his friends and family and to get more stoned. He tells everyone they should do the same. We then see Bubbles, Ricky, and Julian gathered around a burning campfire. Bubbles, who was abandoned by his parents when he was young, realizes (once again) that Ricky and Julian are his true family, and he says to them, "I love you guys." They all walk away together and we hear the other two boys respond, "Love you too."

The *Trailer Park Boys* film, series, and X-Mas Special play on class, race, and religious tensions in Nova Scotia. The history of the marginalization of poor Catholic settlers, Black settlers, slavery, and violence against aboriginal people is erased from the official marketed history of the area. Through parody, *Trailer Park Boys* exposes the Celtic Canadian myth. The film and series (as does an earlier, less humourless Canadian production, *Dirty* [1998]) also deconstruct the official view of the illegal-drug user and marijuana grower. Since the 1990s, the Canadian police, the RCMP, and U.S. law officials have warned citizens about the threat of the marijuana-grow operator.[12] We are informed almost daily, through the media and police and RCMP reports, that these enterprises are large, sophisticated, and hazardous operations, run by dangerous and organized racialized gangs, refugees, immigrants, and foreigners. These themes are evident in the U.S. film *Homegrown* (1998) and the Canadian film *Pig's Law* (2001), which show marijuana as a cash crop linked to organized crime and violence. The *Trailer Park Boys* tells a different story. Drug growers, users, and sellers are "regular" people having fun, trying to make a few dollars, coming together with family and friends and spreading the joy rather than committing crimes. In the film production, Ricky equates marijuana growing with settling down to provide for his family. When Lucy and Ricky get married in the film, he includes in his marriage vows, "Love you . . . start growing dope again and getting my life back on track." The final shot in the film shows Ricky, Lucy, and their daughter sitting down to a meal in their trailer, and we see them through the leaves and branches of green marijuana plants, exemplifying the loving nuclear family.

Unlike most stoner flicks, the women in *Trailer Park Boys* are more than one-dimensional. In fact, it is made clear that they are smarter than the "boys." Lucy and her friends do not cater to the boys, although they are willing to benefit from them when it suits their purposes. In one priceless scene, Ricky tries to convince his 9-year-old daughter to give up smoking cigarettes, telling her it is bad for her health, and they can wear the patch together in order to quit. In contrast, we know that he believes illegal drugs are positive and functions to bring about family and community cohesion. In contrast to the excessive use of illegal drugs and exaggerated effects portrayed in stoner flicks, illegal- and legal-drug use is normalized in the *Trailer Park Boys* film and series. Bubbles, Ricky, and Julian are depicted as oppositional to male gender norms and especially the ultramasculine actors of Hollywood action films. Although many buddy films show friendship and loyalty between male characters, *Trailer Park Boys* portrays affectionate men who express love and caring for each other and for their friends and family. Significantly, marijuana and hash bring them all together, in a very Canadian way.

Saving Grace and *Buffalo Soldiers*

The British film *Saving Grace* (2000), similar to *Trailer Park Boys*, provides an alternative story about the marijuana growers and sellers in a small country village in England. Grace, the main character, is depicted as a White upper-middle-class woman about 50 years of age. Her husband has just died and she discovers that their home is mortgaged to the hilt, leaving her with tremendous debts. She is represented as kind but naive and oblivious to the economic conditions of people who lack her comforts.

Grace lives in a small tightly knit community that becomes aware of her plight. Threatened with losing her home and having no other livelihood, she naively decides to grow marijuana with her young gardener Matthew after he brings her a few of his ailing plants to tend. Matthew is not depicted as a "dealer"; rather, his few small and ailing marijuana plants appear to be for his own use, and it is doubtful they would have made it to maturity without Grace's help. He has been working for free ever since Grace's husband died. He has no other source of income, yet he does not want to leave his home to look for other work. He is attached to the community and he has a local girlfriend named Nicky who works on her fishing boat. Matthew also does not want Grace to lose her home, and their joint venture to grow marijuana stems from economic necessity; it is a way to make some quick money because "desperate times call for desperate measures." Grace is an excellent gardener, and soon her greenhouse is turned into a hydroponic grow-op where healthy marijuana plants flourish under her care.

The local doctor is depicted as a close friend of Matthew's and they smoke marijuana together in the film, obviously enjoying themselves, but their use does not change their behaviour. Grace, who has never smoked marijuana, decides to try it since she is now growing it. Matthew and Grace share a joint sitting on a cliff side overlooking the ocean. After inhaling, Grace tells Matthew that she does not feel anything, and asks him, "Is this addicting?" He responds, "It's not crack." When she wonders if the drug really works, he assures her that it does and she starts to laugh. She looks at Matthew and says, "You're Scottish." She erupts into more laughter and he laughs too. The camera cuts to the ocean and the sky and Matthew comments, "God, I love it here." They both sit back and enjoy the beauty of the landscape and their high.

Unbeknownst to Grace, the whole town is aware of her marijuana grow-op, but except for Nicky, Matthew's girlfriend, they show no judgment. Nicky is concerned with their criminal activities, and she fears that Matthew will be arrested after she hears a radio news announcement, "Police victory in the war on drugs." The announcer reports how marijuana was found hidden in a barn and the growers were sentenced to fifteen years in prison.

In the meantime, Grace's creditors are closing in, and she has little time left before her house will be taken from her. The marijuana plants are mature now and heeding Nicky's concerns for Matthew, Grace does not want him to be involved with selling it. She dons a ridiculous white pants suit and matching hat and travels to London alone in search of a drug dealer to buy their crop. She approaches a number of people on the street, with sample "bud" to show her wares. One potential buyer is a brown-skinned man with dreadlocks, speaking with a Jamaican accent. She also stops a white punk couple and an Asian man, but she has no luck approaching these "outsiders." Everyone avoids her. In desperation she turns to Honey, her deceased husband's mistress, who takes her to visit a local dealer, a White ex-biker hippie. When she tells him that she has 20 kilos to sell, he lets her know the amount is way out of his league, but he agrees to introduce Grace to another dealer, warning her he is "a bit heavy" and he is "not laid back like us."

Meanwhile, Matthew and the doctor rush to London when they hear that Grace has journeyed out on her own, because they fear for her safety. We see Grace and Honey walking into a large club where they meet the dealer, a White Frenchman who is accompanied by a violent thug named Cookie. The dealer threateningly asks Grace where her marijuana is, telling her he will "cut off your fingers one by one till you tell me where it is." Matthew and the doctor come crashing in, and the thug grabs Matthew and places a knife on his throat. He also flashes a knife at the local dealer, who then asks, "Can I go now? I have to pick my daughter up from flute practice." The top dealer looks at Grace and says, "All people I deal with are scum. I'm a little scum myself. You're not scum. That worries me." They make their deal. They agree to over 3,000 pounds for each kilo of marijuana. The dealer then asks Grace if she would like a glass of wine, and he asks her if he "looks like someone who would cut someone's fingers off." She says that he does.

When Grace and the others return to the village, the banker who wants to foreclose on her home arrives, as does the top dealer's thug. Thinking that the thug is a poacher, the local sergeant calls for reinforcements. When the sergeant walks into Grace's greenhouse and sees all of her plants, he tells her that he had turned a blind eye to her "bit of home grown," but other police are on their way to apprehend the poacher. Everyone arrives at Grace's home at the same time, including a bunch of local women for their annual tea party. Lighting a match, Grace says "maybe no one should have it." The plants begin to burn and soon the greenhouse and then the whole property is filled with marijuana smoke. The top dealer arrives and Grace slaps him, saying, "Whatever happened to honour amongst thieves?" He protests and says he only sent his thug to protect Grace. The camera shifts to the lawn, where older women and the police are depicted under the influence of marijuana. They are dancing, twirling, and laughing. They are so uninhibited from the drug that a policeman is portrayed streaking nude across the lawn.

Grace goes on to write a best-selling novel about her adventures as a marijuana grower. She marries the French dealer, and later we see her on television receiving a book award for her novel. Reporters, curious about whether the novel is based on a true story, ask the local sergeant about alleged rumours. He makes it clear that there were no witnesses to the day's events: "No one could remember anything." The doctor muses, "It's strange that alcohol is legal while marijuana is illegal; it is an accident of history." When the reporters ask her husband about his past activities, he threatens them by pushing the camera away and telling them to get off his property. The film ends with everyone happy, including Grace, Matthew, and the villagers.

Saving Grace ruptures conventional narratives about marijuana growers and sellers while also confirming that some high-level "foreign" dealers may be prone to violence and willing to resort to it if pressured. Yet even this narrative is challenged by Grace's marriage to the French dealer. Scenes throughout the film playfully link marijuana consumption with inhibition and joy. From the 1960s on, marijuana has been associated with the rejection of conventional society and its perceived rigid values, and *Saving Grace* draws from this narrative to a certain extent. Yet Grace does not reject conventional society, and in the film, her upper-middle-class status is maintained. However, she does reject the criminal regulation of growing and selling marijuana, as well as the negative narratives about using the drug.

Another British film, *Buffalo Soldiers* (2001), looks at drug production; but rather than marijuana production, it looks at heroin production and the intersection of the war on drugs and terrorism, the cold war, and military complicity in the drug trade. The film is set on a U.S. military base in West Germany in 1989. The title of the film refers to freed slaves who were used to fight frontier wars against aboriginal peoples in the United States, and the director, Gregor Jordan, discusses on the commentary notes on the DVD that these soldiers were treated poorly by their White counterparts and by military superiors. They were disenfranchised and fought without purpose, much like the group of peacetime soldiers depicted in the film. Elwood, a young White man, a soldier and drug dealer, who possesses a detached humour and a "rebellious free spirit,"[13] is the main character, and we see the film through his eyes.

In the opening scenes of *Buffalo Soldiers*, viewers see the U.S. flag, but rather than seeing it waving loftily in the breeze, as in *Clear and Present Danger* (1998), the camera pulls back, and we see that the U.S. flag is painted on the ground of the military base and a group of soldiers are marching across it, singing "follow me to victory." Symbols of militarism and patriotism are invoked throughout the film. In Elwood's room, a poster bears the familiar slogan "Army: Be all that you can be." A missile on the parade ground has the slogan "In God We Trust" painted on it, and a staircase has the words "competence, spirit, professionalism" written on it. In order to provide the historical setting of the story, archival television footage is seen in the background of the film, showing iconic scenes including the fall of the Berlin wall and images of George Bush, Sr. It is also used ironically to contrast the hegemonic construction of the U.S. military during the Cold War with the deviant and corrupt military of the film narrative. Although the film is set at the end of the Cold War, we see that several of the U.S. soldiers are uncertain whether they are in East or West Germany.

One of the first scenes introduces the viewer to U.S. soldiers wrestling with one another. On the sidelines we see a Black man pushing a hypodermic needle into his stomach (of all places) and white powder, presumably heroin, hidden in a large battery. Elwood states,

> Vietnam was the thorn in everybody's side. They stopped the draft and asked for volunteers, except nobody volunteered. I mean, who wants to play for a losing team? So where did they go to find the new patriots? Answer: prison. Take convicted felons and give them a choice: serve time, or serve your country. . . . Soldiers with nothing to kill except time. They know war is hell. But peace? Peace is fucking boring.

Elwood's voice-over informs us about the kind of soldiers we will come to know in the film. Many of them are poor men diverted into military service.

Elwood works with other soldiers to refine heroin from morphine. His morphine supply is acquired from "Turk," a local dealer, and then cooked into heroin by him and his crew at a makeshift lab on the base. His crew of workers (a multiethnic group) are depicted as buddies. In contrast, Lt. Saad, an MP, who sells heroin to "addicted" soldiers on the base, is depicted as violent and unlikable. Both Turk and Saad are depicted as untrustworthy and potentially dangerous. The division of labour in the trade is made explicit, as are the different material rewards derived from it, for Turk displays more signs of drug-related wealth than the other men. Although heroin use is portrayed, the drug narrative of the film focuses on production, not use, and production and dealing are depicted as a means of gaining wealth, a form of capitalist entrepreneurship for Elwood and other soldiers.

Drug manufacturing and the sale of heroin is ignored by the colonel at the base, even when a toxicology report shows that heroin, speed, and cocaine were present in a soldier's body at death. All illegal-drug causalities, whether overdoses or violent turf-war murders, are deemed casualties of the "Cold War" by military officials at the base. However, the suspense in the movie is carried forward when a new sergeant, Top, arrives on base to look into corruption and the black market. He is suspicious, especially of Elwood, who starts to date his daughter Robin. She is depicted using ecstasy; however, she is a recreational user and she has no role in the male-dominated drug trade. Interestingly, her father's legal alcohol use and the harm it may cause others are portrayed through a discussion she has with Elwood after she shows him a huge disfiguring scar from a burn on her body. She says, "When I was a kid, my Dad was drunk and he dropped a cigarette on my nightgown and it caught fire." Throughout the film, Top harasses Elwood and attempts to uncover the drug trade by searching his room and the base and by planting an undercover agent to share Elwood's room.

In one scene, Elwood and his buddies discover a truck loaded with weapons in Red Cross boxes. Elwood approaches a White German man who deals in arms, and they haggle over the price and finally settle on 30 kilos of morphine for the guns. The tension in the film builds as Top continues to harass Elwood. Elwood's roommate (the undercover agent) is brutally beaten by his rivals, Saad and his gang of soldiers. After Elwood's best friend is murdered, he decides to stop the large drug deal; however, the German dealer says that it is too late because the guns have already been sold. He orders Elwood to sit down and he yells that the deal is on or "I'll fucking kill you!" Elwood and the German dealer are interrupted by Saad, who wants in on their business and is willing to kill; thus, Elwood is forced to partner up with him.

Later, we see Elwood's buddies at the drug lab. Saad is there too with his gang of soldiers. At the same time, Elwood is accosted and beaten up by Top. Top handcuffs him and tells him that he loved Vietnam and that he "did all sorts of things, everything you're doing here and more, lots more." Top drags Elwood into a building and tries to throw him out the window, but Elwood hangs on and they both fall out of the window at the same time that the military police arrive at the drug lab, shooting at the crew, causing the lab to explode.

Later, military officials at the base state that the explosion and deaths were due to a gas leak or possibly a terrorist bomb. Eight months later, we see Elwood; he has a cane and burns showing but he is alive and Top is dead. Elwood is talking to the new colonel, although clearly he is still in the drug business and unrepentant.

When *Buffalo Soldiers* was released in 2001, the threat of terrorism was elevated to new levels following 9/11. Apparently the film was held back for release due to its content and the fear that it would offend viewers. The film exposes military corruption at high levels, drug manufacturing, and the composition of the U.S. military—poor disenfranchised men. Elwood, rather than murdered or formally punished, as many drug dealers are, carries on, making the best of a bad situation with entrepreneurial spirit.

Withnail and I and *Drug Store Cowboy:* cautionary tales

A number of other films examine the legitimacy of the war on drugs. The British film *Withnail and I* (1986) questions the legal and illegal divide. Although the film was produced in 1986, the comedic story takes place in London during the last weeks of 1969. The film's main characters are two White men, actor hippies in their 20s or early 30s, who go to "the country" to straighten out from a life of hedonism, drugs (speed and marijuana), and alcohol. The film narrative can be read as symbolizing an era "coming down from its trip." Although the film centres on the two main characters, Withnail and I, Danny, the drug dealer in the film, called Headhunter by his friends, is also a significant character; he is a White male, scruffy and unshaven. Danny has a "rocker" look, complete with long shaggy hair, tattoos, and cheap jewellery, and he wears his sunglasses indoors. When we are first introduced to him in the film, he is smoking a joint. He sells both pills and marijuana. He is not depicted as violent, but as an experienced user and dealer, he communicates "drug wisdom" throughout the film.

Withnail and I have a number of adventures in the country in which they stay at Withnail's uncle's cottage, returning to their apartment days later looking healthier. It turns out that Danny has been staying there since they left the city and together they all smoke a large joint, made with 12 rolling papers. Danny calls it a Camberwell carrot. Danny says, "This will make you very high. This grass is the most powerful in the Western hemisphere." I smokes the joint, but then he feels paranoid and cries out, "Give me a Valium. I am getting the fear!" Danny calmly says to him, "You have done something to your brain. You have made it high. If I lay 10 mils of diazepam on you, it will do something else to your brain. You will make it low. Why trust one drug and not another? That's politics." I says, "I'm gonna eat some sugar!" Danny calmly advises I:

> I recommend you smoke some more grass. This is an unfortunate decision reflecting on these times. . . . London is a country coming down from its trip. We are 91 days from the end of this decade and there is going to be a lot of refugees. If you are hanging on to a rising balloon, you are presented with a difficult question: let go before it's too late, or hang

on and keep getting higher. How long can you keep a grip on the rope? They're selling hippie wigs in Woolworth's, man. The greatest decade in the history of mankind is over, and we failed to "paint it black."

The film *Withnail and I* reminds us that trusting one drug over another is "politics" and, I would add, cultural. The film speaks to the promise of the 1960s era and its failure to bring about social revolution. It also speaks to how the movement was co-opted and taken up and sold as a mainstream commodity. Yet contrary to Danny's final statement about the 1960s, and contrary to conventional media reflections on the times, significant shifts occurred in relation to hierarchical authority, the state, militarism, economic and race relations. The Beat and counterculture movements challenged conventional society through action, literature, and art. Protestors challenged the war in Vietnam and the proliferation of nuclear weapons. Human-rights groups formed as advocates for children, prisoners, aboriginals, Latino/as, and virtually all vulnerable minorities. The women's movements changed Western culture, as did the movements for gay and lesbian rights and environmental protections.[14] As an outcome of the civil-rights movement, the Black Panther and' African-Canadian organizations emerged. As well, nuclear-family arrangements and the primacy of patriarchy and heterosexuality were challenged, and many people lived and worked collectively. Drugs and altered states of consciousness were explored and, for many, were associated with new art forms and a cultural revolution. All these movements challenged the capitalist state and authority. Though participants were not necessarily revolutionary, all this activity in the late 1960s and 1970s had a "revolutionary impact" in respect to civil liberties and human rights in Britain, Canada, and the United States.[15] Without romanticizing the era, this is the reality that official discourse attempts to render invisible along with positive narratives about criminalized drugs.

The film *Drugstore Cowboy* (1989) also ruptures official discourse about the war on drugs, the illusionary line separating legal and illegal drugs, and ideas about people who use and sell illegal drugs. Similar to *Withnail and I*, the film problematizes the line between good and bad drugs. In addition, *Drugstore Cowboy* ruptures discourse about the source of illegal drugs. Rather than all-too-familiar scenes of "drug-source" nations (like Colombia or Bolivia), inner-city racialized dealers, or top kingpins, *Drugstore Cowboy* introduces viewers to pharmacies as the primary source of drugs and drugs made and produced legally right at home. In the DVD notes, the film director, Gus Van Sant, notes: "We thought that previous films about drugs, conventional anti-drug films, if you will—were too simplistic and one-dimensional, and failed to fully explore the power and desperation of this world." Van Sant claims that he did not create a "prodrug" film; rather, he sees it as antidrug because the film allows audiences to see the attraction of drugs, understand the lifestyle, and see the consequences of "destruction and loss" that accompany addiction. *Drugstore Cowboy* allows audiences to understand what it is like to live under prohibition. Van Sant is not the first director to claim that drug films are one dimensional, yet unlike many, he is successful in producing a multilayered film.

The film takes place in Portland, Oregon, in 1971. The film opens with Bob on a stretcher in an ambulance. Through a montage of pictures, we see that he was shot during an attempted drug robbery at his apartment. We see Bob and his crew—his long-time girlfriend Diane and Nadine and Rick—fooling around. Their friendship is apparent. In a voice-over, Bob says: "I was once a shameless, full-time dope fiend. Yeah, me, Bob. This sweet mother's son. Me and my crew rob drugstores. Don't get the idea that it was easy. It's hard being a dope fiend and it's even harder running a crew. . . . I guess deep down, I knew we could never win."

The film, through comedy and drama, follows the adventures of Bob and his crew as they plan drugstore robberies to feed their drug habits and hang out together. Rather than buy street drugs like heroin, Bob and his crew rob pharmacies to get legal narcotics like morphine and Dilaudid. Bob and his crew are depicted as working-class White youth who reject the straight-and-narrow life. In one scene, Bob's mother calls him a thief and a dope fiend and refuses to let him in the house when he visits. She feels pity for both Bob and Diane and says, "You're grown up now but you still act like children who run and play." However, their play includes a number of serious encounters with the police and violent speed users and dealers. Bob and Diane are not violent and they do not become so as the film progresses. Rather, we sympathize with them and their plight to obtain drugs under prohibition. We see surrealistic montages of drug paraphernalia and drug-consumption imagery, such as close-ups of blood entering a syringe, spoons, flames, and pills. The film *Drugstore Cowboy* provides insight into the lives of people who use drugs that are not considered "mind expanding."

In the film, Bob attempts to stop using and lead a "straight" life. He leaves Diane and moves into a shabby room in a rundown hotel. One of his neighbours is Father Murphy, an ex-priest, played by William Burroughs (the Beat writer and author of *Junkie*). Father Murphy tells Bob that there is "no demand in the priesthood for an elderly drug addict" and that he has shot "a million dollars" into his arm. Bob tells him he is on methadone, trying to go straight. Later, Father Murphy tells Bob: "Narcotics have been systematically scapegoated and demonized. The idea that anyone can use drugs and escape a horrible fate is anathema to these idiots. I predict, in the near future, right-wingers will use drug hysteria as a pretext to set up an international police apparatus."

The film was produced in 1989 and Father Murphy's prediction is entirely accurate. *Drugstore Cowboy*, through imagery, narrative, and the character of Father Murphy, boldly questions the legitimacy of the global war on drugs. Today, the global war on drugs intersects with the global war

Drugstore Cowboy. Source: Artisan/Photofest. © Artisan Entertainment.

on terrorism; neither has an end in sight and neither accomplishes the task allegedly set out: stopping the use and sale of illegal drugs and stopping terrorism. Instead, a global police and military apparatus, repressive laws, civil wars, and a prison-industrial complex have emerged at the expense of human lives, civil liberties, and billions of tax dollars that could be better spent on public health, housing, education, drug treatment, and social and economic supports. Numerous reports and groups conclude that drug prohibition is an expensive failure, and illegal-drug use and drug production have remained steady.[16] Prohibition is accompanied by repressive laws, increased police and military enforcement, and more prisons and prisoners, discrimination, racial profiling, an unregulated illegal market, drug-trade violence, high prices, unsure quality and quantity, health risks due to transmission of disease and overdose death, and social and economic marginalization. Law-enforcement efforts have never been evaluated with scrutiny in the same way that health and harm-reduction programs are. Countless researchers, policymakers, civil-liberties organizations, politicians, and concerned citizens make clear that drug prohibition is a dismal failure, and legal regulation rather than prohibition is advocated.[17] Many harms associated with illegal drugs are actually the effects of prohibition, such as violence associated with the drug trade, rising rates of HIV/AIDs and Hepatitis C. Narcotics, outside of sanctioned medical uses, are demonized in Britain, Canada, and the United States. Yet a century ago, people could obtain narcotics legally and fully participate in conventional life.[18] As noted above, in the film *Drugstore Cowboys*, Father Murphy says the "idea that anyone can use drugs and escape a horrible fate is anathema" to drug-war advocates. Yet for the majority of drug users prior to prohibition, narcotic use did not equal destruction, addiction, or degradation and prison time.[19] Many view the ongoing war on drugs as a means to suppress altered states of consciousness not sanctioned by the state and to police marginalized populations and nation-states.

Traffik: the global drug war

I end this chapter and book with a discussion of the 1989 British miniseries *Traffik* because it provides alternative discourses about the global war on drugs, the drug producer, and drug-source nations, and it is the only production in the sample that represents in depth the lowest level international participant in the heroin trade—the grower—in this case, the poppy grower. The film also introduces viewers to a female drug courier (or drug mule), who is also situated at the bottom of the drug-trade hierarchy. It is a three-part television series that was produced and first shown on Channel 4 Television. The script was written by Simon Moore and portrays the war on drugs from three different vantage points. *Traffik* won a number of awards, including the International Emmy, British Academy of Film and Television, and Broadcasting Press Guilds Awards.

In *Traffik*, the viewer is introduced to Fazal (played by Jamal Shah), a poor rural poppy grower in Pakistan, and his family; Jack Lithgow (played by Bill Paterson), a U.K. member of Parliament who is newly appointed to head the Drug Abuse Committee, and his wife and daughter; and a German drug dealer and his British wife and children. The complex story focuses on the plight of Fazal and his family and rural poppy growers' limited choices in the face of a crop-eradication program, supported by the United Kingdom, that destroys their livelihood. Government representatives from Pakistan are pressured by the United Kingdom to carry out crop-eradication programs in order to continue to receive aid. As well, the viewer comes to understand that poor rural farmers have few acres and depleted soil and that poppies are grown because it is easier and more profitable to grow than other crops. Growing poppies and smoking opium are seen as different from the heroin trade, which is depicted as a Western construct, and most specifically a British and American problem. The United States is blamed for fuelling drug trafficking in Pakistan through its demand for and consumption of illegal drugs at home, and the CIA involvement in financing "freedom fighters" linked to the drug and arms trading.

In order to survive after Pakistani soldiers burn his poppy fields, Fazal goes to Karachi to find work. Like his fellow countrymen who are also moving to the city to look for work, he is unable to find employment, and he eventually begins to works for a ruthless Karachi trafficker named Tariq Butt, who converts opium to heroin and sells it to Western dealers. Through Fazal's eyes, and others, we witness how crop-eradication and other Pakistan antiopium policies are a farce played out to appease the British government. When Fazal is eventually arrested and incarcerated for transporting drugs, his wife Sabira appeals to Tariq to help in his release. Tariq consents if she will agree to transport heroin into the United Kingdom for him. Sabira hesitantly ingests a large quantity of heroin wrapped in plastic bags, and then boards a plane to the United Kingdom with her two small children. She dies right after arriving at the airport in the United Kingdom, poisoned by the heroin she has ingested, which has leaked out of the plastic bags. Her husband Fazal is released from prison, but he has lost his wife. Later, seeking revenge, he approaches Tariq outside a mosque. He hugs him and whispers in his ear. "I know where there's all the heroin you could ever need." Tariq greedily asks, "Where?" In response, Fazal jabs him in the neck with a hypodermic needle. Tariq staggers and we are left to assume he dies.

The second story, intertwined throughout the British miniseries *Traffik*, focuses on Jack Lithgow, his wife, and teenaged daughter Caroline, who is addicted to heroin and who quickly deteriorates after she is kicked out of her parents' home for stealing from them. We witness her decline as she moves in with a White working-class drug dealer, and eventually her father finds her in a hotel room, half undressed, with an older White man leaning over her attempting to wake her up. It is made clear that she has been exchanging sex for money.

The third story centres on Karl, a German drug dealer, his British wife Helen, their two children, and the German police, who are trying to convict him. He is arrested after a low-level dealer gives evidence to reduce his own sentence. Karl is imprisoned during his trial, and Helen takes over his drug-dealing enterprise and travels to Pakistan, meeting Tariq and setting up business with him. She is perceived as ruthless as she sets up the killing of the state informant when he plans to provide evidence against her husband, and her husband is released from prison after the death of the informant.

In Pakistan, Jack Lithgow actually smokes opium, and it is an unexpectedly pleasant experience. He comes to recognize that in Pakistan, opium is part of the cultural fabric of life. He also begins to understand that drugs do not lure people into addiction; rather, drug use is shaped by social, cultural, and psychological factors. Lithgow begins to question Western drug policy and colonial intervention in foreign nations. Smoking opium, as presented in the film, does not fit with the "Western notion of all drug use as *essentially* damaging."[20] We rarely see such scenes in illegal-drug films, nor do we see scenes about cross-cultural, spiritual, ritual, or medical uses of criminalized drugs.

The movie ends on an unexpected note. Due to his daughter's drug addiction, and his own personal and professional transformation, the British minister is depicted at the end of the series addressing his colleagues. Although he supports criminal-justice effort, he states that "we can't police the world." He continues: "We can not ultimately stop the supply of heroin and cocaine or any other drug. We can only limit the demand for it. And in the long term that will means making a decent life for people and producing a decent society that people want to live in, and not to escape from. And that, my friends, will not be easy."

The British miniseries *Traffik* explores how Western drug policy and the denial of aid contingent on eradication affect Third World countries. Throughout the miniseries, an attempt is made to demonstrate how the war on drugs shapes international relations, domestic policy, communities, and families. Although the series can be criticized for it conventional depiction of high-level traffickers, including Helen, illegal tactics by law officials, and working-class heroin dealers and users, the film also emphasizes the Western world's unquenchable thirst for drugs and the failure of the war on drugs. Illegal-drug use is viewed as a Western problem, not the problem of Pakistan but one that is changing the shape of drug use and the economy in Pakistan.

Traffik refers to the history of the Afghanistan war against the Soviet Union's invasion. During this period, the United States funded CIA covert operations that supported and protected drug traffickers in Pakistan and Afghanistan.[21] Backed by U.S. funding, the Pakistan border was opened to accommodate the CIA and millions of Afghan refugees during the war. From 1979 to 1989, the Pakistan military controlled $2 billion in CIA covert aid and arms, which they distributed to Afghan guerrillas during the war. The aid also supported training camps for Afghan guerrillas run by the Pakistan military,[22] and it was here that many Afghan men first came into contact with Taliban fundamentalist Islamic beliefs. After ten years of war against the Soviets, and CIA covert funds, Afghanistan guerrillas and the Pakistan military emerged as proficient drug traffickers.

In the 1970s, heroin use was not a significant problem in Pakistan; however, by the 1980s that would change as more people became addicted. McCoy[23] notes that the heroin trade flourished during the war even though seventeen DEA agents were stationed at the U.S. embassy in Islamabad, and during that time there was never one major drug arrest. In fact, "Heroin was shipped out in the same Pakistani army trucks that brought in covert U.S. aid to the Afghan guerrillas."[24] The U.S. ignored the drug trade and the rise of the Taliban because it served their own political purposes to limit Soviet expansion at the time. Once the Soviets were expelled from Afghanistan and civil war broke out, the United States refused to help.

Opium-poppy production and trafficking in Afghanistan are once again being linked to terrorist groups and domestic consumers, even though in the past, advocates of the war acknowledged that the Taliban originally sought to limit poppy production, and there is evidence that the Northern Alliance was complicit in production and trafficking.[25] Both U.S. and British politicians, and the public, appear to have forgotten the role of the CIA in Pakistan and its impact on the rise of the Taliban. Since the attack on the World Trade Center in New York City and the illegal invasion of Afghanistan and Iraq, poppy cultivation is once again viewed as central to the contemporary war on terrorism and international drug policy, including the eradication of poppy cultivation in Afghanistan.

Traffik was produced prior to the invasion of Afghanistan and Iraq by the United States, Britain, and the "coalition of the willing" as a cautionary tale about imperialism, the war on drugs, and terrorism. Today, British, Canadian, and U.S. troops are actively involved in suppressing poppy production in Afghanistan. However, their attempts have been a dismal failure, and poppy production is flourishing because, like the character Fazel in *Traffik*, for poor rural farmers who have little land and poor soil, poppy farming is more profitable than other crops and crop-substitution programs have failed. Although it has been advocated by Afghanistan farmers, Western politicians refuse to consider legalizing poppy production there as it is in other nations such as India, Turkey, and Australia, which are contributing to the legal production of opium-based medicines.

It is difficult to know whether the story presented in *Traffik* would be different today, given the events that have happened since 2001. It is over twenty years since the miniseries was first shown on British television. Crime control has always been a central feature of British drug policy, and it has historically been heavily influenced by the United States.[26] Nevertheless, Britain is still perceived as a nation that offers public-health and harm-reduction initiatives rather than just crime control. Activists and drug workers in North America continue to view Britain as having more practical and less moralistic drug policy, and British policy does not resemble "the disastrous control regime pursued in the USA."[27] However, critics note that drug policy has turned from past public-health practices due to Thatcher's "get tough on crime" mandate, and continued under the leadership of Tony Blair and the Labour party. Since 1997, there has been a shift away from public-health policy to linking drugs with crime. Blair has supported the war on drugs and used drug-war language like "menace," "threat," and "scourge" to link drugs with crime and family and community breakdown. His "Respect Campaign" and Task Force that crack down on behaviours labeled "antisocial," early identification of families that use illegal drugs, and crime-prevention legislation speak to significant shifts in policy, and his law-and-order stance has been critiqued by researchers as having a negative impact on drug services.[28] Blair's drug policy parallels his active support of the war on terrorism and the invasion of Afghanistan and Iraq, and his loyalty to Bush, Jr. Yet contrary to his law-and-order stance, cannabis was reclassified in 2004 from a Class A to a Class B drug; thus, penalties are more lenient. During the writing of this book, it is too early to know whether Gordon Brown, the new Labour Party leader, will pursue different drug policy. His 2007 announcement of a government review of the classification of cannabis is not encouraging.

POLITICS, DRUG PROHIBITION, AND FILM

Hollywood produces more films each year than the film industries in Britain and Canada, and it remains the most wedded to war-on-drugs, law-and-order, and prohibition narratives. Even though a number of alternative films discussed in this book were produced in the United States, it remains a significant global cultural producer of war-on-drugs narratives and imagery, and no other nation in the world has equal economic and military power.

British and Canadian films in the sample were more nuanced and less focused on law and order. However, British and Canadian filmmakers should not feel too smug because films like the British production *Layer Cake* (2004) and the Canadian production *Mount Pleasant* (2006) remind us that negative mythologies about traffickers and illegal-drug users, respectively, are enduring and not necessarily associated with the United States.

In contrast to the majority of conventional illegal-drug-film representations that focus on problematic heroin, cocaine, and methamphetamine use, marijuana is the primary illegal drug of choice for U.S., British, and Canadian consumers, and the war on drugs should be understood as a war against cannabis users, even though users of other criminalized drugs are punished too. In all three nations, marijuana and possession charges overwhelmingly outnumber trafficking charges, and poor and racialized people are overrepresented in arrest and prison populations, even though there is no evidence to support that they are more involved in the drug trade than White people.[29] As well, in all three nations, there has been a steady increase in the number of women serving time for drug sentences.[30] Nevertheless, the myth that law enforcement's main focus is on the high-level trafficker still exists and is reinforced in illegal-drug films. Our drug stats and prisons populations tell another story.

In Britain, in 2005 to 2006, 34.9 percent of adults surveyed reported having used an illegal drug in their lifetime.[31] In 2004, Britain reclassified cannabis from a Class A drug to a Class B drug. Prior to the reclassification, 90 percent of drug charges were for possession, and 70 percent of all charges were for marijuana.[32] There has been a steady decrease in cannabis use since 1998, and this trend continued after the drug was rescheduled.[33] A 2005 Home Office bulletin reports that in the year following reclassification of marijuana, 85 percent of all charges were for possession and 56 percent related specifically to marijuana. Drug dealing accounted for 14 percent of all drug offences, and 12 percent of all drug offenders are women.[34] In 2007, there were 149 prisoners per 100,000 British residents.[35] Twenty-five percent of all foreign nationals in prison were convicted of a drug offence, and over 38 percent of the female foreign national prison population is from Africa.[36] Unlike high-level traffickers who transport large quantities of drugs by ship and planes, some poor and racialized women, exploited in the global economy and the drug trade, agree to carry or swallow drugs and transport them into other nations. As we understand from the films *Maria Full of Grace* and *Traffik*, the results can be deadly and the returns are negligible. Criminal justice is an agent in these women's plight, for those who are caught face long prison terms far away from family and friends.

In 2004, 44.5 percent of the adult population surveyed in Canada reported having used cannabis once in their lifetime, and other illegal drugs account for 16.5 percent of the lifetime national rate. Thus, 61 percent of Canadians surveyed report having used an illegal drug at least once in their lifetimes.[37] Drug offences in Canada have been rising since 1996, mostly due to increases in cannabis charges, although there was a 4 percent dip in 2005.[38] In 2006 in Canada, 60 percent of all drug offences are for cannabis and 75 percent of those are for possession.[39] Interesting for its absence, recent Statistics Canada *Juristat* publications fail to provide information on all drug possession charges; thus, it is difficult to access what percentage of cocaine and heroin charges are for possession. In 2004, there were 130 prisoners per 100,000 Canadian adult residents.[40] Drug offenders under federal jurisdiction comprise 25.9 percent of the total population and one-fifth (22.9 percent) of the federal prison population.[41] In British

Columbia, between 2006 and 2007, 42.2 percent of provincial prisoners in custody for drug-related charges were there for possession.[42]

In 2004–05 in Canada, 73 percent of the Federal Drug Strategy budget was allocated for law enforcement.[43] In 2007, the Conservative federal government announced it has created a new drug strategy; now re-titled "National Anti-Drug Strategy," the 2007 budget includes additional funding to crack down on illegal-drug production and selling and to combat illegal-drug production outside of Canada, especially Afghanistan.[44]

In 2007, more than 7 million people in the United States are under criminal-justice control: in prison, on probation, or on parole.[45] U.S. prison rates have quadrupled over the last 30 years due to ill-advised federal and state decisions about sentencing, punishment, and drug offences.[46] In 1974, there were 111 prisoners per 100,000 U.S. residents. In 2005, there were 737 prisoners per 100,000 U.S. residents.[47] The U.S. war on drugs is estimated to cost over $40 billion annually, and the running of prisons $60 billion, yet illegal-drug use continues.[48] Over 46 percent of the population surveyed in 2005 reported illegal-drug use at least once in their lifetime.[49] Regardless of this fact, the Bush, Jr. administration (like his predecessors) continued to aggressively pursue the war on drugs and terrorism at home and abroad. As discussed in chapter 5, In 2005, 81.7 percent all drug charges were for possession: marijuana arrests exceed all other drug categories. And of all criminal infractions outside of traffic violations, drug arrests were higher than any other crime category.[50] Thus, trafficking and importation offences only make up 18 percent of all charges.

Drug arrests have been rising steadily in the United States. Twenty-five percent of all prisoners in jail and 55 percent of prisoners in federal prison in the United States in 2004 were charged with drug offences.[51] Although men overwhelmingly make up the majority of drug offenders convicted and imprisoned, between 2005 and 2006 the increase of female state and federal prisoners was almost twice that of male prisoners, and the percentage of female prisoners held in jail increased by 40 percent compared to an increase of 22 percent of male prisoners.[52] Of the more than 2 million people in prison in the United States at the end of 2006, 41 percent of male prisoners are Black men. The incarceration rate for Black women is 3.8 times higher than the rate for White women.[53] Hispanic men and women are also overrepresented in prison.[54]

Illegal-drug use, arrest, and prison rates provide good evidence that drug prohibition is flawed. Harsh drug laws have not substantially decreased illegal-drug use or trafficking, nor have Western interventions in countries like Afghanistan lowered poppy production. As one commentator in a recent U.K. report on women in the criminal-justice system notes: "We are not winning the war on drugs but we are certainly taking a lot of prisoners."[55]

Since our first drug laws were enacted in Britain, Canada, and the United States, we have seen waves of drug scares almost every decade that have culminated in more and more laws to prohibit the use, sale, and production of drugs categorized as illegal. Moral reformers continue to clamour for harsher drug laws and more law-enforcement powers; there is little difference in their arguments whether it was against opium and alcohol regulation in the late 1800s and early 1900s, marijuana regulation in the late 1920s and 1930s, LSD regulation in the 1960s, harsher laws for crack cocaine in the 1980s, marijuana grow-ops in the 1990s, and methamphetamine in the 2000s. Each drug is singled out as being the most dangerous drug we have ever experienced, reaching epidemic proportions, destroying lives, families, and threatening the fabric of communities and the nation. Each drug is depicted as instantly addictive, robbing people of their will. Harsher laws for drug users and the evil seller and producer are then advanced and most often enacted. Consequently, in all three nations, prisons are filled beyond their capacity and the prison-industrial complex continues to expand. Whenever there is a more liberal shift in public opinion about drug regulation, a new demon drug emerges, and/or drug trafficking and manufacturing becomes the focus of criminal-justice officials, media, medical and social-service professionals, and moral reformers of every stripe who jump on the band wagon and call for harsher laws and regulation, as if draconian laws in the past have successfully stopped people from using criminalized drugs.

Illegal-drug scares arise out of unsupportable mythologies, but they generate fears even in the absence of scientific evidence. By contrast, there is more than ample evidence of the dangers of legal drugs such as tobacco, alcohol, and prescription drugs. Even though mind-altering plants and drugs were used throughout history in every culture around the world, minus the Inuit of the Arctic, most of us cannot imagine a world where drugs are not criminalized. The films discussed in this chapter remind us that the categorization of good and bad drugs is political. Such films serve as a template to shift our understanding about drug issues to one in which altered states of consciousness are no longer criminalized, racialized, sexualized, and pathologized. Rather, we can begin to view drug use as a legitimate activity accepted as part of the fabric of life. Alternative illegal-drug-film narratives illuminate the illusionary line dividing legal and illegal drugs and serve as a "counterpunch to the belly of authority."[56]

At the beginning of this book, drawing from the writer Thomas King,[57] I discussed the importance of the stories we tell and how film is a powerful medium for storytelling. The films discussed in this chapter portray illegal drugs as part of everyday life. Clearly, drugs, in and outside of Western nations, can be a "positive, integrative and functional contribution . . . to the social-health of particular communities of people."[58] Negative addiction does not stem from a particular drug; rather, the way we use drugs and our expectations of them are shaped by cultural, social, psychological, and biological factors. Most illegal-drug films provide a worldview of deviance, loss of control, the need for law and order, criminalization and militarization of civil society, violence, punishment, and imperialist ventures.

The films discussed in this chapter, and Western nations' arrest and prison statistics, tell another story about illegal-drug use and law-enforcement regulation and its negative impact on society and those suspected of using, producing, and selling criminalized drugs. Contrary to what we see in some conventional drug films, harsh drug laws can cause more harm than illegal drugs. A number of films discussed in this book that challenge conventional mythologies are characterized by normalized drug use, caring, pleasure, fun, transcendence of the material world, and cooperation. Missing are stories about spiritual/ritual use of drugs, alternatives to the war on drugs, utopias where state and personal violence are absent and peace prevails, and societies where people's needs are met and drug use is normalized.[59] A few films, like *Traffik* and *Drugstore Cowboy*, do question the legitimacy of the global war on drugs. King asks if the stories we tell reflect the world as it is or whether or not we have started off with the wrong story. We might ask the same question in relation to prohibition and war-on-drugs narratives and mythologies. Would our world look different if we began to tell other stories?

Appendix

ILLEGAL DRUG FILM SAMPLE
(Alphabetic, with female directors identified by (F))

Alice in Wonderland (1951). Dir. by C. Geronimi, W. Jackson, & H. Luske. USA.

Alice's Restaurant (1969). Dir. by A. Penn. USA.

American Beauty (1999). Dir. by S. Mendes. USA.

Another Day in Paradise (1998). Dir. by L. Clark. USA.

Assassin of Youth (1935). Dir. by E. Clifton. USA.

Atlantic City (1980). Dir by L. Malle. Canada/USA/France.

Barbarian Invasions, The (Les Invasions Barbare) (2003). Dir. by D. Arcand. Canada/France.

Basketball Diaries (1995). Dir. by S. Kalvert. USA.

Beyond the Valley of the Dolls (1970). Dir. by R. Meyer. USA.

Blow (2001). Dir. by T. Demme. USA.

Boyz n the Hood (1991). Dir. by J. Singleton. USA.

Bright Lights, Big City (1988). Dir. by J. Bridges. USA/Japan.

Brokedown Palace (1999). Dir. by J. Kaplan. USA.

Broken Blossoms (The Yellow Man and the Girl) (1919). Dir. by D. W. Griffith. USA.

Brother from Another Planet (1984). Dir. by J. Sayles. USA.

Buffalo Soldiers (2001). Dir. by G. Jordan. UK/Germany.

Chappaqua (1966). Dir. by C. Rooks. USA/France.

Cheech and Chong's Next Movie (1980). Dir. by T. Chong. USA.

Citizen Ruth (1996). Dir. by A. Payne. USA.

Class of 1984 (1982). Dir. by M. L. Lester. USA.

Clean (2004). Dir. by O. Assayas. UK/Canada/France.

Clean and Sober (1988). Dir. by G.G. Caron. USA.

Clear and Present Danger (1994). Dir. by P. Noyce. USA.

Cleopatra Jones (1973). Dir. by C. Bail. USA/Hong Kong.

Clockers (1995). Dir. by S. Lee. USA.

Cocaine Cowboys (1979). Dir. by B. Corben. USA.

Cocaine Fiends, The (The Pace that Kills) (1936). Dir. by W. O'Conner. USA.

Coffy (1973). Dir. by J. Hill. USA.

Come on Baby, Light my Fire (1970). Dir. by L. Campa. USA.

Cool and Crazy, The (1958). Dir. by W. Witney. USA.

Curtis's Charm (1995). Dir. by J. L'Ecuyer. Canada.

Dazed and Confused (1993). Dir. by R. Linklater. USA.

Dirty (1998). Dir. by B. Sweeney. Canada.

Doors, The (1991). Dir. by O. Stone. USA.

Drugstore Cowboy (1989). Dir. by G. Van Sant. USA.

Easy Rider (1969). Dir. by D. Hopper. USA.

Fast Times at Ridgemont High (1982). Dir. By A. Heckerling (F). USA.

Fear and Loathing in Los Vegas (1998). Dir. by T. Gilliam. USA.

For His Son (1912). Dir. by D. W. Griffith. USA.

French Connection, The (1971). Dir. by W. Friedkin. USA.

Garden State (2004). Dir. by Z. Braff. USA.

Go (1999). Dir. by D. Liman. USA.

Goodfellas (1990). Dir. by M. Scorsese. USA.

Gridlock'd (1997). Dir. by V. Curtis-Hall. USA.

H. (1990). Dir. by D. Wasyk. Canada.

Half Baked (1998). Dir. by T. Davis (F). USA.

Harold and Kumar Go to White Castle (2004). Dir. by D. Leiner. Canada/USA/ Germany.

High (1967). Dir. Larry Kent. Canada.

High School Confidential (1958). Dir. by J. Arnold. USA.

Homegrown. (1998). Dir. by S. Gyllenhaal. USA.

How High (2001). Dir. by J. Dylan. USA.

I Love You Alice B. Toklas (1968). Dir. by H. Averback. USA.

Igby Goes Down (2002). Dir. by B. Steers. USA.

Jesus' Son (1991). Dir. by A. Maclean (F). Canada/USA.

Joe (1970). Dir. by G. Avildsen. USA.

Johnny Stool Pigeon (1949). Dir. by W. Castle. USA.

Kids (1995). Dir. by L. Clark. USA.

Lady Sings the Blues (1972). Dir. by S. J. Furie. USA.

Layer Cake (2004). Dir. by M. Vaughn. UK.

Less than Zero (1987). Dir. by M. Kanievska. USA.

Light Sleeper (1992). Dir. by P. Schrader. USA.

London (2005). Dir. by H. Richards. UK/USA.

Losing Isaiah (1995). Dir. by S. Gyllenhaal. USA.

Man with the Golden Arm, The (1955). Dir. by O. Preminger. USA.

Maria Full of Grace (2004). Dir. by J. Marston. USA.

Marihuana, the Weed with Roots in Hell (1935). Dir. by D. Esper. USA.

Midnight Express (1978). Dir. by A. Parker. UK/USA.

Monkey on my Back (1957). Dir. by A. D. Toth. USA.

My Name Is Joe (1998). Dir. by K. Loach. UK/France/Italy/Germany.

Mystery of the Leaping Fish, The (1916). Dir. by C. Cabanne & J. Emerson. USA.

Naked Lunch (1991). Dir. by D. Cronenberg. Canada/UK/Japan.

Narc (2002). Dir. by J. Carnahan. USA/Canada.

Narcotic (1934). Dir. by D. Esper & V. Sodar't. USA.

New Jack City (1991). Dir. by M. Van Peebles. USA.

Night Zoo (Un Zoo la Nuit) (1987). Dir. by J. C. Lauzon. Canada.

On the Corner (2003). Dir. by N. Geary. Canada.

Panic in Needle Park, The (1971). Dir. by J. Schatzberg. USA.

Performance (1970). Dir. by D. Cammel. UK.

Permanent Midnight (1998). Dir. by D. Veloz. USA.

Pig's Law (Loi du Cochon, La) (2001). Dir. by E. Canuel. Canada.

Postcards from the Edge (1990). Dir. by M. Nichols. USA.

Protection (2000). Dir. by B. Spangler. Canada.

Psych-out (1968). Dir. by R. Rush. USA.

Pulp Fiction (1994). Dir. by Q. Tarantino. USA.

Ray (2004). Dir. by T. Hackford. USA.

Reefer Madness (*Tell Your Children*) (1936). Dir. by L. J. Gasnier. USA.

Requiem for a Dream (2000). Dir. by D. Aronofsky. USA.

Riot on Sunset Strip (1967). Dir. by A. Dreifuss. USA.

Rude (1995). Dir. by C. Virgo. Canada.

Rush (1991). Dir. by L. F. Zanuck. USA.

Salton Sea, The (2002). Dir. by D. J. Caruso. USA.

Saving Grace (2000). Dir. by N. Cole. UK.

Scanner Darkly, A (2006). Dir. by R. Linklater. USA.

Scarface (1983). Dir. by B. De Palma. USA.

Sherrybaby (2006). Dir. by L. Collyer (F). USA.

Sid and Nancy (1986). Dir. by A. Cox. UK/USA.

Skidoo (1969). Dir. by O. Preminger. USA.

Spun (2002). Dir. by J. Akerlund. USA/Sweden.

Still Smoking (1983). Dir. by T. Chong. USA/Netherlands.

Superfly (1972). Dir. by G. Parks Jr. USA.

Supergrass, The (1985). Dir. by P. Richardson. UK.

Sweet Sixteen (2002). Dir. by K. Loach. UK/Germany/Spain.

Teenage Devil Dolls (*One-way Ticket to Hell*). Dir. by B. L. Price, Jr. USA.

Tequila Sunrise (1988). Dir. by R. Towne. USA.

Thirteen (2003). Dir. by C. Hardwicke (F). USA/UK.

To the Ends of the Earth (1948). Dir. by R. Stevenson. USA.

Traffic (2000). Dir. by S. Soderbergh. USA/Germany.

Traffik (1989). Dir. by A. Reid. UK.

Trailer Park Boys: The Movie (2006). Dir. by M. Clattenburg. Canada.

Trainspotting (1996). Dir. by D. Boyle. UK.

Trash (1970). Dir. P. Morrissey. USA.

Trip, The (1967). Dir. by R. Corman. USA.

25th Hour (2002). Dir. by S. Lee. USA.

21 Grams (2003). Dir. by A. G. Inarritu. USA.

Up in Smoke (1978). Dir. by L. Adler. USA.

Valley of the Dolls (1967). Dir. by M. Robson. USA.

Veronica Guerin (2003). Dir. by J. Schumacher. USA/Ireland/UK.
Withnail and I (1987). Dir. by B. Robinson. UK.
Walk the Line (2005). Dir. by J. Mangold. USA/Germany.
Yellow Submarine (1968). Dir. by G. Dunning. USA/UK.

STILLS

Chinese Opium Den (1894). Dir. by T. Edison. USA.
Human Wreckage (1923). Dir. by J. Wray. USA.

SCENES IN FILM

Intolerance (1916). Dir. by D. W. Griffith. USA.

PHARMACEUTICAL INDUSTRY FILMS

Constant Gardener, The (2005). Dir. by F. Meirelles. UK.
Kids in the Hall: Brain Candy (1996). Dir. by K. Makin. Canada/USA.

Notes

NOTES TO THE INTRODUCTION

1. King, 2003: 9.
2. Ibid., 25.
3. Ibid., 26.
4. Ibid., 29.
5. Ibid., 32.
6. Boyd, 2002.
7. Ibid.
8. Purvis & Hunt, 1993.
9. Druick, 2007: 33.
10. *Sourcebook for Teaching Science*, 2006.
11. Ferrell & Websdale, 1999: 3.
12. Hayward & Young, 2004: 259.
13. Boyd, 2004; Hayward & Young, 2004.
14. Ward, 1998: ix.
15. Thobani, 2007a: 24.
16. Reinarman, 2005: 307.
17. Said, 2001: xix.
18. Ibid., 332.
19. Foucault, 1979, 1984.
20. Ibid., 333.
21. Ibid., 332.
22. Altheide, 2002; Barak, 1994; Best, 1995, 1999; Cohen & Young, 1981; Eldridge, 1993; Ericson, Baranek, & Chan, 1991; Dowler, 2003; Garofalo, 1981; Gerbner, Gross, Signorielli, & Morgan, 1980; Heath & Gilbert, 1996; Howitt, 1998; Lambertus, 2004; Mann & Zatz, 2002; McMullan, 2005; McMullan, 2001; McMullan & McClung, 2003; Surette, 1992; Thobani, 2007a, 2007b; Wykes, 2001.
23. Hall, 1981.
24. Ibid., 241.
25. Ibid., 242. Italics in original.
26. Young, 1981: 327.
27. Blum, in Young, 1981: 329.
28. Boyd, 2004: 32–38.
29. See Altheide, 2002; Best, 1999; Birch, 1994; Chesney-Lind, 1999; Clover, 1999; Faith, 1993; Ferrell & Websdale, 1999; Ferrell, Hayward, Morrison, & Presdee, 2004; Fowler, 1991; Hall, 1997; Hall et. al., 1987; Hart, 1994;

Homlund, 1994; hooks, 1992; hooks, 1994; Jewkes, 2004; Mann & Zatz, 2002; Manning, 2007; McCaughey & King, 2001; Postman, 1985; Rafter, 2000; Rapping, 2003; Smith-Shomade, 2003; Surette, 1992; Young, 1996; Valverde, 2006; Wykes, 2001.

30. Faith, 1993: 255–273.
31. Johnson, 2000.
32. Buchanan & Johnson, 2005.
33. hooks, 1994.
34. Dyer, 1999.
35. Numerous writers have contributed to our awareness about representation, racialization, and the media. In this section, my focus is on representations of crime and racialized people in film.
36. Dyer, 1999: 460.
37. hooks, 1992: 29.
38. Castro, 2002.
39. Dyson, 1993; Guerrero, 1993; Rome, 2002.
40. McCarthy et al., 1997.
41. Jones, 1991.
42. Eschholz, Bufkin, & Long, 2002.
43. See Branden, 1981; Coomber, Morris, & Dunn, 2000; Gomez, 1997; Greaves et al., 2002; Humphries, 1999; Reinarman & Duskin, 1999; Reinarman & Levine, 2000; Young, 1981.
44. Parry, 2000; Reinarman & Levine, 2000, 1997.
45. Reinarman & Duskin, 1999: 49.
46. Cape, 2003; Gerbner, 1990; Gitlin, 1990; Grist, 2007; Gunasekera, Chapman, & Campbell, 2005; Hirshman, 1995; Katovich, 1998; LaLander, 2002; Lensing, 2002; Shapiro, 2002. Norman Denzin's (1991) book *Hollywood Shot by Shot: Alcoholism in American Cinema* also provides an excellent analysis of films as cultural products.
47. See Starks, 1982; Stevenson, 2000; Shapiro, 2003.
48. Starks, 1982: 9.
49. Starks, 1981.
50. Stevenson, 2000.
51. Shapiro, 2003.
52. Another important study, although unpublished, is Jonathan White's (1997) doctoral thesis titled *Extreme Prejudice, Excessive Force, Zero Tolerance: Cultural Political Economy of the United States Drug Wars, 1980–1996.* He examines cultural texts and "investigates the representations of popular culture of the Drug Wars" in the United States since the presidency of Ronald Reagan. Other writers and organizations are interested in representations of drugs, including parent groups for film censorship and the Office of National Drug Control Policy in the United States, which cosponsored the 1999 study "Substance Use in Popular Movies and Music Videos." This study examines both the frequency and nature of representations of drug use (alcohol, tobacco, and illegal drugs) in films produced in 1996 and 1997. Their sample included 200 popular U.S. movie rentals; however, they are not drug films as I have defined them; rather, they include all popular movies produced in 1996 and 1997. Where the Office of National Drug Control Policy is interested in curtailing drug use and counts prodrug representations in film, John Hulme and Michael Wexler, the authors of *Baked Potatoes: A Pot Smoker's Guide to Film and Video*, are interested in providing a user's guide that rates movies according to their quality when viewed under the influence of marijuana. In a similar vein, *Pot TV* provides a series on their Web site, titled "Hollyweed," which offers film clips of cannabis in the movies and representations of users.

They also include segments of animation films and an interview with Tommy Chong, the comember of the stoner-comedy team of Cheech and Chong.
53. Starks (1982) considers educational drug-abuse films similar to Shapiro's (2003) list of U.S. antidrug films shown in schools.

NOTES TO CHAPTER 1

1. Schultes, Hofmann, & Ratsch, 1998.
2. Heron, 2003: 30.
3. Musto, 2002; Warner, 2002.
4. MacAndrew & Edgerton, 1969.
5. Alexander, 1990; Brecher et al., 1972.
6. Booth, 1996: 15–18; Hodgson, 1999: 13.
7. Berridge & Edwards, 1981.
8. Hodgson, 2001: 45.
9. Hodgson, 2001; Berridge & Edwards, 1981.
10. Berridge & Edwards, 1981: 59.
11. Mitchinson, 2002.
12. Gray, 1999: 12.
13. Brecher et al., 1972: 17.
14. Musto, 1987: 73; Weil & Rosen 1998.
15. Carnwath & Smith, 2002: 6, 41.
16. Ibid., 18.
17. Stevenson et al., 1956: 510; Weil & Rosen, 1998: 81–90.
18. Stevenson et al., 1956: 510.
19. Grinspoon & Bakalar, 1997.
20. Ibid.
21. Musto, 2002.
22. Grinspoon & Bakalar 1998; Morgan & Zimmer 1997.
23. Brecher et al., 1972: 42.
24. Ibid., 43.
25. Berridge & Edwards, 1981.
26. Musto, 1987.
27. Berridge & Edwards, 1981.
28. Weber, 1976: 72.
29. Thobani, 2007a: 6, 11.
30. Coomber & South, 2004: 16.
31. Adlaf et al., 2005; Manning, 2007.
32. Coomber & South, 2004: 16.
33. Coomber & South, 2004; Woodiwess, 2001.
34. Berridge & Edwards, 1981.
35. Ibid., 102.
36. South, 1998: 90.
37. Mott & Bean, 1998.
38. Musto, 1984.
39. Ibid.
40. Boyd 1984; Comack, 1986.
41. King 1908: 7, 8.
42. Ibid., 13.
43. Boyd, 1984; Green, 1979; Solomon and Green, 1988.
44. Boyd, 1984, 1991; Comack, 1986.
45. Carstairs, 2006; Murphy, 1973.
46. Mosher, 1998.

47. Carstairs, 2006.
48. Brecher et al., 1971; Musto, 1987; Rose, 1996.
49. Brecher et al., 1971; Musto, 1987.
50. Carnworth & Smith, 2002: 41.
51. Denzin, 1991; Rafter, 2000; Starks, 1982; Stevenson, 2000.
52. Starks, 1982: 54.
53. Gardner, 1987: xi.
54. Ibid.
55. Robertson, 1989.
56. Robertson, 1989: 23–24. The story about how Reid became addicted to morphine is contested; another explanation is that his morphine use was linked to headaches he suffered after being in a train crash (Starks, 1982: 47).
57. Robertson, 1989: 24.
58. Robertson, 1989: 24; Starks, 1982.
59. Robertson, 1989: 25.
60. Starks, 1982: 55.
61. Ibid.
62. Johnson, in Denzin, 1991: 5.
63. Gardner, 1987: 170, 171.
64. Ibid., 171.
65. Ibid.
66. Ibid., 172.
67. Ibid., 170.
68. Starks, 1982.
69. Allemang, 2005.
70. Allemang, 2005: R2.
71. Musto, 2002: 173.
72. Vittala, 2000: 10.
73. EIC et al., 2000: vii.
74. Ibid., viii.
75. EIC et al., 2000: 12.1.
76. Williams, 1979: 190.
77. Ibid.
78. Ibid., 191.
79. Ibid.
80. Robertson, 1989: 25.
81. Starks, 1982: 53.
82. Ibid.
83. Shapiro, 2003: 61.
84. Richards, 1984: 25.
85. Starks, 1982: 42, 53.
86. Home Office papers in Richards, 1984: 26.
87. Richards, 1984.
88. Ibid., 26.
89. Robertson, 1989: 117.
90. Memorandum by Watkins, 1955, in Robertson, 1989: 118.
91. Robertson, 1987: 118.
92. BBFC, Main Issues.
93. Dean, 1981: 3–4.
94. Wise, 2001.
95. R. v. Hicklin (1868) 3 Q.B.D. 360.
96. Boyd, 1984: 13.
97. Dean, 1981: 21.
98. Ibid.

99. Ibid.
100. Ibid., 142.
101. Ibid.
102. Ibid.
103. Boyd, 1984: 47.

NOTES TO CHAPTER 2

1. Foucault, 1979.
2. Razack, 2002: 11.
3. Alexander, 1990: 113.
4. Valverde, 1998: 51.
5. Levine, 1978.
6. Ibid., 165–166.
7. Alexander, 1990: 113; Levine, 1978.
8. Terry & Pellens, 1970; Musto, 2002; Reinarman, 1988: 110.
9. Terry & Pellens, 1970.
10. Breecher et al., 1972.
11. Giffen, Endicott, & Lambert, 1991: 376.
12. Carstairs, 2006: 92; Giffen, Endicott, & Lambert, 1991; Musto, 1987.
13. Whereas Chinese people were the early targets of police profiling following criminalization in Canada, by the 1950s, a primary "White" "addict colony" was identified in the "East End" of Vancouver (Stevenson et al., 1956: 426). These illegal-drug users, referred to as "criminal addicts," were regulated closely by the police. Few escaped long prison sentences (Ibid.; Carstairs, 2006). Because illegal-drug use is what is referred to as a "victimless crime," law enforcement resorted to violence, undercover agents, informants, and broad police powers in order to obtain evidence (Alexander, 1990).
14. Giffen et al., 1991.
15. Carstairs, 2006: 93.
16. Breecher et al., 1972; Giffen, Endicott, & Lambert, 1991; Lart, 1998; Mott & Bean, 1998.
17. Lart, 1998.
18. Morgan & Zimmer, 1997: 132.
19. Berridge & Edwards, 1981; Murray, 1988.
20. Musto, 1987; 2002.
21. Starks, 1982: 37.
22. Nakayama, 2002.
23. Dua, 2003; Thobani, 2007.
24. Berridge & Edwards, 1981: 197.
25. Castro, 2002.
26. Said, 2003.
27. Nakayama, 2002: 94.
28. Ibid.
29. D.W. Griffith also produced the White-supremacist film *Birth of a Nation* in 1915. This film exalts the Ku Klux Klan following the Civil War in the United States. His later films, including *Intolerance* (1916) and *Broken Blossoms* (1919), attempt to problematize racial stereotypes and hatred even though they are unsuccessful.
30. Hannah-Moffat, 2001; Valverde, 1991.
31. Griffen, Endicott, & Lambert, 1991: 62.
32. Morgan & Zimmer, 1997: 132.
33. Carstairs, 2006; Musto, 1987, 2002; Kohn, 1992.

34. Anthony & Solomon 1973.
35. Graham-Mulhall, 1981; Murphy, 1973.
36. Kohn, 1992.
37. Campbell, 2000: 221.
38. Musto, 1987: 133.
39. Ibid., 134.
40. Musto, 2002.
41. Starks, 1982: 49.
42. Alexander, 1990.
43. The films *Kids* (1995) and *Thirteen* (2003) can also be viewed as morality tales that attempt to shock viewers about youth's illegal-drug use.
44. Rafter, 2000.
45. Berridge & Edwards, 1981; Murray, 1988.
46. Brecher et al., 1972; Carstairs, 2006: 54.
47. Brecher et al., 1972.
48. Musto, 1987.
49. Brecher et al., 1972: 69.
50. Ibid., 71.
51. Giffen, Endicott, & Lambert, 1991; Carstairs, 2006.
52. Starks, 1982: 42.
53. Giffen, Endicott, & Lambert, 1991: 16.
54. Musto, 1987.
55. Starks, 1992: 70.
56. See also *Drug Store Cowboys* (1989), *New Jack City* (1991), *Basketball Diaries* (1995), *Trainspotting* (1996), and *Losing Isaiah* (1994).
57. Denzin, 1991: 5.
58. Ibid.
59. Musto, 2002.
60. Valverde, 1998.
61. Reinarman, 2005: 313.
62. Musto, 2002: 164; Reinarman, 2005.
63. Valverde, 1998: 122.
64. The 1962 film adaptation of Eugene O'Neill's play *Long Day's Journey into Night* depicts Katharine Hepburn as a woman addicted to morphine through therapeutic use. She obtains morphine from doctors rather than the illegal market. Her character is represented as unable to face reality and her morphine use is linked to insanity. She is unable to provide a "healthy" home for her son and husband. Her husband is also blamed for her addiction to morphine and family dysfunction because he is depicted as "cheap," always trying to save a dollar; thus, he failed to provide her with proper medical care when she first became sick.
65. Carstairs, 2006: 78; Musto, 1987.
66. Spear, 1984.
67. Reinarman, 2005: 312.
68. Ibid., 308.

NOTES TO CHAPTER 3

1. Musto, 1987: 252.
2. Ibid.
3. Ibid.
4. Brecher et al., 1972; Giffen, Endicott, & Lambert, 1991; Musto, 1987; Young, 1981.

5. The Central Intelligence Agency (CIA) also believed that the drug could be used as a tool of war because it was believed to mimic psychosis; therefore, they thought it could be used to break down people. Today, we know that, throughout the 1950s and 1960s, the CIA approved the administration of massive doses of the drug to prisoners, psychiatric patients, and civilians in the United States and Canada without their consent. For those people whose consciousness was changed without their permission or understanding, the experience was negative and led to lifelong problems (Lee & Shlain, 1992).

6. Wagner, 1997: 14. See Dennis Sullivan's (2007) discussion about altered states of consciousness.

7. Giffen, Endicott, & Lambert, 1991: 7; Musto, 1987; Young, 1981.

8. Healy, 1997, 2003; Lexchin, 1984; Moynihan & Cassels, 2005.

9. NIHCM, 2002; NCPA, 2002.

10. Healy, 2003.

11. Starks, 1982: 141.

12. Ibid., 153.

13. The film *Psych-Out* was produced in 1968 and it capitalizes on what Dick Clark calls, in the DVD notes, the "love children culture" in San Francisco. Jack Nicholson stars in the film and he wrote some of the script. He and many of the other male characters in the film wore absurd long wigs in order to "accurately" portray the youth of the time. The film portrays LSD trips (including a number of LSD and STP freak-out scenes), psychedelic posters, and contemporary bands that are now long forgotten.

14. Malbon, 1998: 277; Manning, 2007: 10

15. Starks, 1982: 122.

16. Martel, 2006.

17. Woodiwiss, 2001: 379.

18. Perry, 2000.

19. Rodriquez, 2007.

20. Fishman, 2002: 181.

21. Agar & Reisinger, 2002.

22. Ibid., 216, 217.

23. Ibid., 224.

24. Lusane, 1991.

25. Robins, Davis, & Goodwin, 1974.

26. Lusane, 1991; Mauer & The Sentencing Project, 1999; McCoy, 1991; Scott & Marshall, 1998; Woodiwess, 2001.

27. Morgan & Zimmer, 1997.

28. Ibid., 134.

29. Reinarman & Levine, 1997: 33, 34.

30. Ibid., 41.

31. Ibid., 22.

32. Reinarman & Levine, 1997; Bourgois, 1995.

33. Weil & Rosen, 1998.

34. Inciardi, Lockwood, & Pottieger, 1993.

35. It is not actually clear in the film what drug the Black man injects into Caroline; however, her relaxation makes it more likely it is heroin rather than the stimulant cocaine.

36. Fishman, 2002.

37. Humphries, 1999; Reinarman & Levine, 1997.

38. Shoatz, 2007.

39. The legality of this action is not explored in the film.

40. See Ross Coomber's 2006 discussion on dealing and ethnicity: 147–148.

41. Mosher and The Sentencing Project, 1999.

42. Reinarman & Levine, 1997: 37
43. Boyd, 1999, 2004; Roberts, 2002.
44. Bufe, 2000: 26.
45. Peele, 1989; Peele & Brodsky, with Arnold, 1999; Rapping, 1996.
46. Alexander, 1990; Weil & Rosen, 1998.
47. Musto, 2002: 173.
48. Ibid., 174–180.
49. EIC, 2000: 12.1.
50. EIC, 2000.
51. Peele & Brodsky, 1991.
52. Reinarman, 2005: 307.
53. Foucault, 1979; Quintero, 2001.
54. Manning, 2007: 26.
55. DeBeck, Wood, Montaner, & Kerr, 2006: 8.
56. Drug Policy Alliance, 2007.

NOTES TO CHAPTER 4

1. Brooks, 2001.
2. Baumohl & Schram, 2000: 213.
3. Bashevkin, 2002; Amnesty International, 1999.
4. Magner, 1996: 4. (Interview with John L'Ecuyer, *The Journal of Addiction and Mental Health*, May–June, 1996, 25(3), 4).
5. See Becker, 1967.
6. Zinberg, 1984.
7. Lart, 1998.
8. Bourgois, 2000; Bunton, 2001; O'Malley, 1999; Valverde, 1998.
9. Brecher et al., 1972.
10. Dole & Nyswander, 1965.
11. Giffen, Endicott, & Lambert, 1991: 401.
12. Spear, 1994.
13. Lart, 1998; Spear, 1994.
14. Lart, 1998: 60.
15. Bourgois, 2000: 167.
16. Ibid.
17. Bourgois, 2000; Boyd, 1999; Alexander, 1990; Alexander et al., 1987; Rosen-baum & Murphy, 1987.
18. Shewan & Dalgarno, 2005: 1.
19. Uchtenhagen, 1999.
20. Drug researchers Andrew Weil and Winifred Rosen also wonder why opium is not offered to illegal-drug users to replace heroin or methadone. They explain that "whole opium, when eaten, is a much safer drug—less concentrated, longer acting, and easier to form stable relationships with. Because it is a gummy solid, it cannot be injected directly into the bloodstream, and though people can certainly become addicted to it—as they did in England and America in the 1800s—the risk is much less" (Weil & Rosen, 1993: 88). We could also ask why coca tablets, coca tea, and elixirs are not made available for cocaine (and crack) users, given that they are less risky than refined cocaine. Representations of these forms of drugs are not shown in illegal-drug films.
21. Walker, 1991.
22. See Peele, 1989; Peele & Brodsky, with Arnold, 1991; Rapping, 1996.

NOTES TO CHAPTER 5

1. See Malbon's (1998) and Feldman's (2001) discussion of space.
2. Razack, 2002: 11.
3. Sarti (as cited in Woolford, 2001: 40).
4. Coomber, 2006.
5. Hodgson, 1999; Starks, 1982.
6. Griffen, Endicott, & Lambert, 1991: 62.
7. Thobani, 2007a: 4.
8. See Sunera Thobani's (2007a) discussion of the nation.
9. From *Human Wreckage* and *Reefer Madness,* respectively.
10. Starks, 1982: 91–2
11. Musto, 1987: 252.
12. See Musto, 1987.
13. Early on, national drug surveys were not available, and many states did not collect data on marijuana use. Marijuana arrest data from California provide some sense of marijuana use and police efforts. In 1954, 1,156 people were arrested for marijuana offences. In 1968, 50,327 people were arrested for marijuana offences (Brecher et al., 1972: 422). In Canada, marijuana arrests were rare, especially on the west coast. Only six people were arrested for marijuana offences from 1946 to 1961 in the province of British Columbia (Carstairs, 2006: 68).
14. Musto, 1987: 252.
15. Castro, 2002; hooks, 1992, 1994, 1996.
16. Musto, 1987: 252.
17. Ibid.
18. Watching the film I was reminded of recent U.S. stereotyping and demonization of people from France following 9/11. U.S. resentment of France obviously runs deep.
19. Mauer and the Sentencing Project, 1999.
20. White, 1991: 115.
21. A multitude of groups and individuals working in the fields of drug policy, health, human rights, social justice, prison abolition, and law enforcement note that drug prohibition causes more harm than criminalized drugs. A legal regulated market is advocated to limit harm to society and individuals.
22. Mosher and the Sentencing Project, 1999.
23. Reinarman & Levine, 1997: 3.
24. Welch & Angula, 2000.
25. CANY/WPP, 2002b.
26. Reinarman & Levine, 1997: 23.
27. Ibid.
28. Reinarman & Levine, 1997: 23.
29. Robb, 2004: 37.
30. Ibid., 38.
31. Ibid.
32. Ibid., 44.
33. Ibid.
34. Ibid., 365.
35. Cowan & Wren, 2001; Muwakkil, 2001.
36. Chomsky, 2000.
37. Office of National Drug Control Policy, 2007.
38. Saunders, 2002.
39. ONDCP, 2007.

40. Boyd, 2004, 2006; Green, 1996; Huling, 1992.
41. See Ekstrand & Blume, 2000; Huling, 1992.
42. Mills, 1975.
43. Boyd, 2006.
44. Boyd, 2004, chapter 6.
45. Feldman, 2001.
46. Ibid., 86.
47. Robb, 2004.
48. Musto, 2002: 173.
49. Saunders, 2000: A2.
50. Wibberley, 2005.
51. Lester, 2001; Robb, 2004.
52. *Spun* (2002) offers a comedic take on young White methamphetamine users who are brought together through their association with a low-level methamphetamine producer and seller, Cook (played by Mickey Rourke). Meth culture is associated with violence, filthy run-down homes and hotel rooms, pornography, and obsession.
53. Foucault, 1977: 210.
54. Internal Centre for Prison Studies, 2007.
55. Dorsey, Zawitz, & Middleton, 2007.
56. Saboi, Minton, & Harrison, 2007: 5.
57. U.S Department of Justice, 2007.

NOTES TO CHAPTER 6

1. Campbell, 2000; O'Malley & Valverde, 2004; Warner, 2002.
2. Murphy, 1973: 162.
3. Ibid., 30.
4. Ibid., 17.
5. Kohn, 1992.
6. Castro, 2002: 84, 85.
7. The father's-rights movement is part of the Western men's movement that emerged in the 1970s. Father's-rights groups challenge family law, custody, and access to their children. They believe that family-court decisions favour mothers. However, empirical evidence does not support their claims. See S. B. Boyd, ed., *Challenging the Public/Private Divide: Feminism, Law, and Public Policy* (1997).
8. Birch, 1994; Chesney-Lind, 1999; Clover, 1999; Faith, 1993; Hart, 1994; Rafter, 2000.
9. Ehrenreich & English, 1973; McLaren, 1990.
10. Oakley, 1984.
11. Chen, 2005.
12. Ibid., 12 .
13. Arnup, 1994.
14. Gusfield, 1972.
15. Berridge & Edwards, 1981.
16. Chunn, 1995.
17. Edwards, 1988.
18. Campbell, 2000: 221.
19. Chen, 2005; Boyd, 1999; Roberts, 2002.
20. Kasinsky, 1994: 121.
21. The penitentiary was still a fairly new concept at this time, having emerged in Western nations in the mid- and late 1800s. Prior to this, offenders were

imprisoned for short periods of time while they awaited punishment or transportation to other countries or colonies. Moral reformers at this time called for the end of corporal punishment. Rather than physical punishment, offenders would be confined long term in penitentiaries, where both the body and soul would be regulated. Early moral reformers, many of them Quakers, saw the penitentiary as a site to do penance. The construction of the early penitentiaries assured total surveillance, enforced solitude, and religious instruction (Foucault, 1979).

22. Heron, 2003.
23. Campbell, 2000: 224, 57.
24. Berridge & Edwards, 1981.
25. Boyd, 1999, 2004; Gupta, 1995; Solinger, 1994; Roberts, 2002.
26. Boyd, 1999, 2004, 2006; Boyd & Marcellus, 2007.
27. Campbell, 2000: 141.
28. Ibid., 142.
29. Boyd, 1999, 2004; Boyd & Marcellus, 2007.
30. Gomez, 1997.
31. Humphries, 1999: 11.
32. Ibid., 19.
33. Reinarman & Levine, 1997.
34. Humphries, 1999: 63–64.
35. Ibid., 64.
36. Frank et al., 2001; Lester, Andreozzi, & Appiah, 2004; Mayes et al., 1992; Morgan & Zimmer, 1997.
37. Arendt et al., 2004.
38. Boyd & Marcellus, 2007; Hepburn, 1993, 2002, 2007; Siney, 1999.
39. Paltrow, 2001; Boyd, 2004.
40. National Advocates for Pregnant Women, 2004.
41. National Advocates for Pregnant Women, 2004; Paltrow, 2001.
42. Boyd, 1999.
43. Roberts, 2002: 9.
44. See Colten, 1980; Dreher et al., 1994; Hepburn, 1993; Jackson & Berry, 1994; Kearny et al., 1994; Klee, Jackson, & Lewis, 2002.
45. Hepburn, 2007: 7.
46. Ibid., 252.
47. Hepburn, 1999.
48. Hepburn, 1993.
49. Boyd & Marcellus, 2007.
50. Weil & Rosen, 1998; Shewan & Dalgarno, 2005.
51. Boyd, 1999; Colton, 1980; Dreher, Nugent, & Hudgins, 1994; Leeders, 1992; Sterk-Elifson, 1996; Sowder & Burt, 1980; Klee, 2002.
52. Fanon, 1967.
53. Monture-Angus, 2000.
54. Alexander, 2001: 19.
55. Alexander, 1998, 2001.
56. Quintero, 2001: 57.
57. See Culhane (2003) and Robertson & Culhane (2005) for a critical perspective about aboriginal and poor women and the DTES.
58. Boyd, 2004, 2006; Carlen, 1998; Green, 1996, 1998; Huling, 1992; Sudbury, 2005; Wedderburn, 2000.
59. CANY/WPP, 2007.
60. Ibid.
61. Chads & Simes, 2002; Correctional Service Canada, 2002–03; Elkins & Olagundoye, 2001; Roberts, 2005.

NOTES TO CHAPTER 7

1. Coomber & South, 2004: 16. See their discussion about drug use beyond the West and Manning's (2006) writing about recreational drug use.
2. Measham, 2004: 211.
3. Ibid., 214.
4. Measham, 2004: 215.
5. Manning, 2007: 9.
6. Ibid.
7. Hogshire, 1999.
8. Ibid., 1.
9. Miltown was the first minor tranquilizer to be produced.
10. *The Constant Gardener* (2005), a drama, also examines the global pharmaceutical industry.
11. Other cable television HBO and Showtime series such as *Six Feet Under*, *The Wire*, and *Weeds* are pushing the boundaries of illegal-drug representations. As well, the BBC series *Absolutely Fabulous* pokes fun at both temperance and AA ideology.
12. ONDCP, 2007.
13. Denzin, 1991.
14. Clement, 2007.
15. Owram, 1996: 160; Clement, 2007; Piven & Cloward, 1979.
16. See The Angel Declaration; The Senlis Council; Transform Drug Policy Foundation; Canadian HIV/AIDs Legal Network; Drug Policy Alliance; DeBeck, Wood, Montaner, & Kerr, 2006; Health Officers Council of British Columbia, 2005; MacPherson et al., 2005.
17. Ibid.
18. Alexander, 1991; Grey, 1999.
19. Alexander, 1991; Brecher et al., 1972; Gray, 1999; Musto, 1987.
20. Ibid.
21. McCoy, 1991.
22. McCoy, 1991: 451.
23. Ibid.
24. Scott & Marshall, 1998: 187.
25. Fazey, 2005; Jelsma, 2005; Meek, 2001.
26. MacGregor, 1998.
27. South, 1998: 90.
28. Stimson, 2000.
29. Coomber, 2006; Woodiwiss, 2001.
30. Correctional Service Canada, 2002–03; Corston, 2007; Elkins & Olagundoye, 2001: 1–4; Saboi, Minton, & Harrison, 2007: 1, 6.
31. National Statistics, 2007: 3.
32. Mwenda, 2005: 4.
33. Ibid., 8.
34. Ibid., 1.
35. International Centre for Prison Studies, 2007.
36. Lloyd et al., 2006: 3.
37. Adlaf, Begin, & Sawka, 2005: 48, 55.
38. Savoie, 2002: 1; Silver, 2006.
39. Silver, 2007.
40. Statistics Canada, 2005.
41. Motiuk & Vuong, 2005: 12.
42. J. Macdonnell, B.C. Corrections Branch, personal communication, July 31, 2007.

43. Debeck, Wood, Montaner, & Kerr, 2006: 7.
44. Department of Finance, 2007.
45. U. S. Department of Justice, 2007.
46. Raphael & Stoll, 2007: 59.
47. International Centre for Prison Studies, 2007; Raphael & Stoll, 2007.
48. Curley, 2007; Raphel & Stoll, 2007: 60.
49. Ibid.
50. Dorsey, Zawitz, & Middleton, 2007.
51. Ibid.
52. Saboi, Minton, & Harrison, 2007: 5.
53. Ibid., 9.
54. Ibid.
55. Corston, 2007: 19.
56. Ferrell, 1997: 146.
57. King, 2003.
58. Coomber & South, 2004: 16.
59. See Sullivan & Tifft (2000) and Sullivan (2007).

References

Adlaf, E., Begin, P., & Sawka, E. (2005). (Eds.). *Canadian addiction survey (CAS): A national survey of Canadians' use of alcohol and other drugs: Prevalence of use and related harms: Detailed report.* Ottawa: Canadian Centre on Substance Abuse.

Agar, M., & Reisinger, H. (2002). A heroin epidemic at the intersection of histories: The 1960s epidemic among African Americans in Baltimore. *Medical Anthropology, 21,* 189–230.

Alexander, A., Beyerstein, B., & MacInnes, T. (1987). Methadone treatment in B.C.: Bad medicine? *Canadian Medical Association Journal, 136,* 25–28.

Alexander, B. (2001). The roots of addiction in free market society. *Canadian Centre for Policy Alternatives,* 1–31. Retrieved September 15, 2002, from http://www.policyalternatives.ca

Alexander, B. (1990). *Peaceful measures: Canada's way out of the "War on Drugs."* Toronto: University of Toronto Press.

Allemang, J. (2005, September 19). *The Globe and Mail,* R1, R2.

Allen, J., Livingstone, S., & Reiner, R. (1998). True lies: Changing images of crime in British postwar cinema. *European Journal of Communication, 13*(1), 53–75.

Altheide, D. L. (2002). *Creating fear: News and the construction of crisis.* New York: Aldine de Gruyter.

Amnesty International. (1999). *"Not part of my sentence": Violations of the human rights of women in custody.* Amnesty International Rights for All: Amnesty International's Campaign in the United States of America.

Anthony, B., & Solomon, R. (1973). Introduction. In E. Murphy, *The black candle.* Toronto: Coles Publishing.

Arendt, R., et al. (2004, February 25). *Top medical doctors and scientists urge major media outlets to stop perpetuating "crack baby" myth.* Retrieved April 20, 2004 from http://www.jointogether.org/sa/files/pdf/sciencenotstigma.pdf

Barak, G. (1994). (Ed.). *Media, process, and the social construction of crime: Studies in newsmaking criminology.* New York: Garland Press.

Barak, G. (1994). Media, society, and criminology. In G. Barak (Ed.), *Media, process, and the social construction of crime: Studies in newsmaking criminology* (pp. 3–45). New York: Garland Publishing.

Bashevkin, S. (2002). *Welfare hot buttons: Women, work, and social policy reform.* Toronto: University of Toronto Press.

Baumohl, J., & Schram, S. (2000). Book review/commentary. *Contemporary Drug Problems, 27*(1), 213–215.

Becker, H. (1967). History, culture, and subjective experience: An exploration of the social bases of drug-induced experiences. *Journal of Health and Social Behavior, 8,* 162–176.

Berridge, V., & Edwards, G. (1981). *Opium and the people: Opiate use in nineteenth century England*. London: Allan Lane.

Best, J. (1995). *Random violence: How we talk about new crimes and new victims*. Berkeley: University of California Press.

Best, J. (1999). (Ed.). *Images of issues: Typifying contemporary social problems*. New York: Aldine de Gruyter.

Birch, H. (1994). If looks could kill: Myra Hindley and the iconography of evil. In H. Birch (Ed.), *Moving targets: Women, murder and representation* (pp. 32–61). Berkeley: University of California Press.

Booth, M. (1996). *Opium: a history*. New York: Saint Martin's Griffin.

Bourgois, P. (1995). *In search of respect: Selling crack in El Barrio*. New York: Cambridge University Press.

Bourgois, P. (2000). Disciplining addictions: The bio-politics of methadone and heroin in the United States. *Culture, Medicine, and Psychiatry, 24*, 165–195.

Boyd, N. (1984). Sexuality and violence, imagery and reality: Censorship and the criminal control of obscenity. *Working papers on pornography and prostitution. Report 16*. Ottawa: Department of Justice.

Boyd, S. (1999). *Mothers and illicit drugs: Transcending the myths*. Toronto: University of Toronto Press.

Boyd, S. (2002). Media constructions of illegal drugs, users, and sellers: A closer look at *Traffic. International Journal of Drug Policy, 13*, 397–407.

Boyd, S. (2004). *From witches to crack moms: Women, drug law, and policy*. Durham, NC: Carolina Academic Press.

Boyd, S. (2006). Representations of women in the drug trade. In G. Balfour & E. Comack (Eds.), *Criminalizing women* (pp. 131–151). Halifax, Nova Scotia: Fernwood Press.

Boyd, S. B. (1997). (Ed.). *Challenging the public/private divide: Feminism, law, and public policy*. Toronto: University of Toronto Press.

Boyd, S., & Marcellus, L. (2007). (Eds.). *With child: Substance use during pregnancy: A woman-centred approach*. Halifax, Nova Scotia: Fernwood Press.

Brady, M. (1998). Specular morality, the war on drugs, and anxieties of visibility. In S. Aiken, A. Brigham, S. Marston, & P. Waterstone (Eds.), *Making worlds: Gender, metaphor, materiality* (pp. 110–127). Tucson: University of Arizona Press.

Brecher, E., & the Editors of *Consumer Reports*. (1972). *Licit & illicit drugs*. Boston: Little, Brown & Company.

British Board of Film Censors (BBFC). Main issues. Retrieved June 28, 2007, from http://www.bbfc.co.uk/policy/policy-mainissues.php

Brooks, X. (2000, February). Requiem for a dream. *Sight and Sound, 11*, 2.

Buchanan, R., & Johnson, R. (2005). The "Unforgiven" sources of international law: Nation-building, violence, and gender in the West(ern). In D. Buss & A. Manji (Eds.), *International law: Modern feminist approaches* (pp. 131–158). Oxford: Hart Publishing.

Bufe, C. (2000). The nature of the problem. In S. Peele, C. Bufe, & A. Brodsky (Eds.), *Resisting 12-step coercion: How to fight forced participation in AA, NA, or 12-step treatment* (pp. 17–43). Tucson, AZ: See Sharp Press.

Bunton, R. (2001). Knowledge, embodiment and neo-liberal drug policy. *Contemporary Drug Problems, 28*, 221–243.

Campbell, N. (2000). *Using women: Gender, drug policy, and social justice*. New York: Routledge.

Canadian HIV/AIDS Legal Network. (2006). Canada's 2003 renewed drug strategy—An evidence-based review. *HIV/AIDS Policy & Law Review, 11*(2/3).

Cape, G. (2003). Addiction, stigma and movies. *Acta Psychiatrica Scandinavica, 107*, 163–169.

Carlen, P. (1998). *Sledgehammer: Women's imprisonment at the Millennium*. London: Macmillan Press.

Carnswath, T., & Smith, I. (2002). *Heroin century*. New York: Routledge.

Carstairs, C. (2006). *Jailed for possession: Illegal drug use, regulation, and power in Canada, 1920–1961*. Toronto: University of Toronto Press.

Castro, D. (2002). "Hot blood and easy virtue": Mass media and the making of racist Latino/a stereotypes. In C. Mann & M. Zatz (Eds.), *Images of color, images of crime* (pp. 82–91). Los Angeles: Roxbury Publishing.

Chads, K., & Simes, J. (2002). *April 2002 monthly prison population brief*. London: Home Office.

Chen, X. (2005). *Tending the gardens of citizenship: Child saving in Toronto, 1880s–1920s*. Toronto: University of Toronto Press.

Chesney-Lind, M. (1999). Media misogyny: Demonizing "violent" girls and women. In J. Ferrell & N. Websdale (Eds.), *Making trouble: Cultural constructions of crime, deviance, and control* (pp. 115–140). New York: Aldine de Gruyter.

Chomsky, N. (2000). *Rogue states: The rule of force in world affairs*. Cambridge, MA: South End Press.

Chunn, D. (2003). Regulating (ab)normal sex: Anti-VD strategies in British Columbia/Canada, 1918–1945. In D. Brock (Ed.), *Making normal: Social regulation in Canada* (pp. 63–86). Scarborough, Ontario: Nelson Thomson.

Churchill, W. (1998). *Fantasies of the master race: Literature, cinema and the colonization of American Indians*. San Francisco: City Lights Books.

Clement, D. (2007, May). *"An Anachronism failing to function properly": How the baby boom generation transformed social movements in Canada*. Paper presented at the Canadian Historical Association annual meeting. Saskatoon: University of Saskatchewan.

Clover, C. J. (1999). Her body, himself: Gender in the slasher film. In S. Thornham (Ed.), *Feminist film theory: A reader*. Edinburgh: Edinburgh University Press.

Cohen, S., & Young, J. (1981). *The manufacture of news: Social problems, deviance and the mass media*. London: Sage.

Colten, M. (1980). A comparison of heroin-addicted and non-addicted mothers: Their attitudes, beliefs, and parenting experiences. In *Heroin-addicted parents and their children: Two reports*. (National Institute on Drug Abuse Services Research Report, pp. 1–18). Washington, DC: U.S. Department of Health and Human Services; Public Health Service; Alcohol, Drug Abuse, and Mental Health Administration.

Coomber, R. (2006). *Pusher myths: Re-situating the drug dealer*. London: Free Association Books.

Coomber, R., Morris, C., & Dunn, L. (2000). How the media do drugs: Quality control and the reporting of drug issues in the UK print media. *International Journal of Drug Policy, 11*, 217–225.

Coomber, R., & South, N. (2004). *Drug use and cultural contexts "Beyond the West": Tradition, change and post-colonialism*. London: Free Association Books.

Correctional Association of New York/Women in Prison Project (CANY/WPP). (2007). The coalition for women prisoners: 2007 proposals for reform. Retrieved July 28, 2007, from http://www.correctionalassociation.org/WIPP_main.html

Correctional Service Canada. (2002–03). *Department performance report (2002–03)*. Retrieved July 26, 2007, from http://www.csc-scc.gc.ca/text/pblct/dpr/2003/section_3_overview_of_changes_e.shtml

Corston, J. (2007). *The Corston report*. London: Home Office.

Cowan, A., & Wren, C. (2001, January 18). Dealing reality: A film's depiction of drugs; "Traffic" captures much of their desperate world, people from the battlefront say. *New York Times*, p. E1.

Culhane, D. (2003). Their spirits live within us: Aboriginal women in Downtown East-side of Vancouver emerging into visibility. *Indian Quarterly, 27*(3/4), 593–606.

Curley, B. (2007). U.S. mayors declare drug war a failure. *Join Together*. Retrieved July 23, 2007, from http://www.jointogether.org/news/features/2007/us-mayors-declare-war.html

Dean, M. (1981). *Censored! only in Canada: The history of film censorship—the scandal off the screen*. Toronto: Virgo Press.

Debeck, K., Wood, E., Montaner, J., & Kerr, T. (2006). Canada's 2003 renewed drug strategy—an evidence-based review. Canadian HIV/AIDS Legal Network, *HIV/AIDS Policy & Law Review, 11*(2/3), 1–12.

Denzin, N. K. (1991). *Hollywood shot by shot: Alcoholism in American cinema*. New York: Aldine de Gruyter.

Department of Finance. (2007, July 23). *A safer Canada: Building a stronger Canada in a modern world*. Retrieved July 23, 2007, from http://www.budget.gc.ca/2007/bp/bpc6e.html

Dole, V., & Nyswander, M. (1965). A medical treatment for diacetylmorphine (heroin) addiction: A clinical trial with methadone hydrochloride. *Journal of the American Medical Association, 193*, 646–650.

Dorsey, T., Zawitz, M., & Middleton, P. (2007). *Drugs and crime facts*. Washington, DC: U.S. Department of Justice.

Dowler, K. (2003). Media consumption and public attitudes toward crime and justice: The relationship between fear of crime, punitive attitudes, and perceived police effectiveness. *Journal of Criminal Justice and Popular Culture 10*(2), 109–126.

Doyle, A. (2003). *Arresting images: Crime and policing in front of the television camera*. Toronto: University of Toronto Press.

Dreher, M., Nugent, J., & Hudgins, R. (1994). Prenatal marijuana exposure and neo-natal outcomes in Jamaica: An ethnographic study. *Pediatrics, 93*(2), 254–260.

Drug Policy Alliance. (2007, April 4). Drug war. Retrieved April 4, 2007, from http://www.drugpolicy.org/drugwar/access/

Druick, Z. (2007). *Projecting Canada: Government policy and documentary film at the National Film Board*. Montreal: McGill–Queen's University Press.

Dua, E. (2003). Towards theorizing the connections between governmentality, impe-rialism, race, and citizenship: Indian migrants and racialization of Canadian citizenship. In D. Brock (Ed.), *Making normal: Social regulation in Canada* (pp. 40–62). Scarborough, Ontario: Nelson Thomson.

Dyer, R. (1999). White. In J. Evans & S. Hall (Eds.), *Visual culture: The reader* (pp. 457–467). London: Sage.

Dyson, M. (1993). Between apocalypse and redemption: John Singleton's *Boys n the Hood*. In J. Collins, H. Radner, & A. Collins (Eds.), *Film theory goes to the movies* (pp. 209–226). New York: Routledge.

Edstrand, L., & Blume, J. (2000). *U.S. Customs Service, better targeting of airline passengers for personal searches could produce better results*. Washington, DC: General Accounting Office.

Ehrenreich, B., & English, D. (1973). *Witches, midwives, and nurses*. New York: Feminist Press.

Eldridge, J. (1993). *News, truth and power*. London: Routledge.

Elkins, M., & Olagundoye, J. (2001). The prison population in 2000: A statistical review. *Findings, 154*, 1–4. London: Home Office, Research, Development and Statistics Directorate.

Entertainment Industries Council (EIC) in partnership with the National Institute on Drug Abuse and the Robert Wood Johnson Foundation. (2000). *Spotlight on depiction of health and social issues: Drug, alcohol, and tobacco use and addic-tion* (3rd ed., Vol. 1). Burbank, CA: Entertainment Industries Council.

Ericson, R., Baranek, R., & Chen, J. (1991). *Representing order: Crime, law and justice in the news media*. Toronto: University of Toronto Press.

Eschholz, S., Bufkin, J., & Long, J. (2002). Symbolic reality bites: Women and racial/ethnic minorities in modern film. *Sociological Spectrum, 22,* 299–334.

Faith, K. (1993). *Unruly women: The politics of confinement and resistance.* Vancouver, BC: Press Gang.

Fanon, F. (1967). *Black skin, white masks.* New York: Grove Press.

Fazey, C. (2005). Where have all the flowers gone? Gone to opium everyone. When will they ever learn, when will they ever learn? *International Journal of Drug policy, 16,* 104–107.

Feldman, A. (2001). Philoctetes revisited: White public space and the political geography of public safety. *Social Text 68, 19*(3), 57–89.

Ferrell, J. (1997). Against the law: Anarchist criminology. In B. MacLean & D. Milovanovic (Eds.), *Thinking critically about crime* (146–154). Vancouver, BC: Collective Press.

Ferrell, J. (2001). *Tearing down the streets: Adventures in urban anarchy.* New York: Palgrave.

Ferrell, J., Hayward, K., Morrison, W., & Presdee, M. (2004). (Eds.). *Cultural criminology unleashed.* London: Glasshouse Press.

Ferrell, J., & Websdale, N. (1999). *Making trouble: Cultural constructions of crime, deviance, and control.* New York: Aldine de Gruyter.

Ferrell, J., & Websdale, N. (1999). Materials for making trouble. In J. Ferrell and N. Websdale (Eds.), *Making trouble: Cultural constructions of crime, deviance, and control* (pp. 3–21). New York: Aldine de Gruyter.

Fishman, L. (2002). The black bogeyman and white self-righteousness. In C. Mann & M. Zatz (Eds.), *Images of color, images of crime* (pp. 177–191). Los Angeles: Roxbury Publishing.

Foucault (1984). *The Foucault reader* (Paul Rabinow, Ed.). New York: Pantheon Books.

Foucault, M. (1979). *Discipline and punishment: The birth of the prison.* New York: Vintage Books.

Fowler, R. (1991). *Language in the news.* London: Routledge.

Frank, D., Augustyn, M., Grant-Knight, W., Pell, T., & Zuckerman, B. (2001). Growth, development, and behavior in early childhood following prenatal cocaine exposure: A systematic review. *Journal of the American Medical Association, 285,*1613–1625.

Gardner, G. (1987). *The Censorship papers: Movie censorship letters from the Hays Office, 1934 to 1968.* New York: Dodd, Mead & Company.

Garofalo, J. (1981). Crime and the mass media: A selective review of research. *Journal of Research in Crime and Delinquency, 18*(2), 319–350.

Gerbner, G. (1990). Stories that hurt: Tobacco, alcohol and other drugs in the mass media. In H. Resnik (Ed.), *Youth and Drugs: Society's mixed messages* (pp. 53–127). OSAP Prevention Monograph-6. Rockville, MD: U.S. Department of Health and Human Services, Office for Substance Abuse Prevention.

Gerbner, G., Gross, L., Signorielli, N., & Morgan, M. (1980). Television violence, victimization, and power. *American Behavioral Scientist, 23*(5), 705–716.

Giffen, P., Endicott, S., & Lambert, S. (1991). *Panic and indifference: The politics of Canada's drug laws.* Ottawa: Canadian Centre on Substance Abuse.

Gitlin, T. (1990). On drugs and mass media in America's consumer society. In H. Resnik (Ed.), *Youth and drugs: Society's mixed messages* (pp. 31–52). OSAP Prevention Monograph-6. Rockville, MD: U.S. Department of Health and Human Services, Office for Substance Abuse Prevention.

Gomez, L. (1997). *Misconceiving mothers: Legislators, prosecutors, and the politics of prenatal drug exposure.* Philadelphia: Temple University Press.

Graham-Mulhall, S. (1981). *Opium the demon flower.* New York: Arno Press.

Gray, M. (1999). Long day's journey into night. *The Drug Policy Letter, 39,* 12–14.

Greaves, L., Varcoe, C., Poole, N., Morrow, M., Johnson, J., et al. (2002). *A motherhood issue: Discourses on mothering under duress.* Ottawa: Status of Women in Canada.

Green, M. (1979). A history of Canadian narcotics legislation. *University of Toronto Faculty of Law Review, 37,* 42–79.

Green, P. (1996). Drug couriers: The construction of a public enemy. In P. Green (Ed.), *Drug couriers: A new perspective* (pp. 3–20). London: Quartet Books.

Green, P. (1998). *Drug trafficking and criminal policy.* Winchester, UK: Waterside Press.

Grinspoon, L., & Bakalar, J. (1997). *Marihuana, the forbidden medicine.* New Haven, CT: Yale University Press.

Guerrero, E. (1993). Spike Lee and the fever in the racial jungle. In J. Collins, H. Radner, & A. Collins (Eds.), *Film theory goes to the movies* (pp. 170–181). New York: Routledge.

Gunasekera, H., Chapman, S., & Campbell, S. (2005). Sex and drugs in popular movies: An analysis of the top 200 films. *Journal of the Royal Society of Medicine, 98,* 464–470.

Hall, S. (1980). Encoding/decoding. In S. Hall (Ed.), *Culture, media, language: Working papers in cultural studies, 1972–79* (pp. 128–138). London: Hutchinson.

Hall, S. (1980). Race, articulation and societies structured in dominance. In *Sociological Theories: Race and Colonialism* (pp. 305–345). Paris: UNESCO.

Hall, S. (1981). The determination of news photographs. In S. Cohen & J. Young (Eds.), *The manufacture of news: Social problems, deviance and the mass media* (Rev. ed., pp. 226–243). London: Constable.

Hall, S. (1983). The problem of ideology—Marxism without guarantees. In B. Mattews (Ed.), *Marx 100 years on* (pp. 57–85). London: Lawrence & Wishart.

Hall, S. (1988). The toad in the garden: Thatcherism among the theorists. In C. Nelson & L. Grossberg (Eds.), *Marxism and the interpretation of culture* (pp. 35–73). Chicago: University of Illinois Press.

Hall, S. (1997). *Representations: Cultural representations and signifying practices.* London: Sage.

Hall, S., Critcher, C., Jefferson, T., & Clarke, J. (1978). (Eds.). *Policing the crisis: Mugging, the state, law and order.* Basingstoke, UK: Macmillan.

Hannah-Moffatt, K. (2001). *Punishment in disguise.* Toronto: University of Toronto Press.

Harrison, P., & Beck, A. (2005). Prisoners in 2004. *Bulletin.* U.S. Department of Justice.

Hart, L. (1994). *Fatal women: Lesbian sexuality and the mark of aggression.* Princeton, NJ: Princeton University Press.

Hayword, K., & Young, J. (2004). Cultural criminology: Some notes on the script. *Theoretical Criminology, 8*(3), 259–273.

Health Officers Council of British Columbia. (2005, October). *A public health approach to drug control in Canada.* Victoria, BC: Authors. Available at: http://www.keepingthedooropen.com/files/hoc_public_health_approach_to_drug_control.pdf

Healy, D. (1997). *The antidepressant era.* Cambridge, MA: Harvard University Press.

Healy, D. (2003). *Let them eat Prozac.* Toronto: James Lorimer & Company.

Heath, L., & Gilbert, K. (1996). Mass media and fear of crime. *American Behavioral Scientist, 39*(4), 379–386.

Hepburn, M. (1993). Drug use in pregnancy. *British Journal of Hospital Medicine, 49*(1), 51–55.

Hepburn, M. (2002). Providing care for pregnant women who use drugs: The Glasgow Women's Reproductive Health Service. In H. Klee, M. Jackson, & S. Lewis (Eds.), *Drug misuse and motherhood* (pp. 250–260). London: Routledge.

Hepburn, M. (2007). Drug use and parenting. In S. Boyd & L. Marcellus (Eds.), *With child: Substance use during pregnancy: A woman-centred approach* (pp. 6–8). Halifax, Nova Scotia: Fernwood Press.

Heron, C. (2003). *Booze: A distilled history*. Toronto: Between the Lines.

Hirshman, E. (1995). The cinematic depiction of drug addiction: A semiotic account. *Semiotica, 104*(1&2), 119–164.

Hodgson, B. (1999). *Opium: A portrait of the heavenly demon*. Vancouver, BC: Graystone Books.

Hodgson, B. (2001). *In the arms of Morpheus*. Buffalo, NY: Firefly Books.

Hogshire, J. (1999). *Pills-a-go-go: Fiendish investigation into pill marketing, art, history, and consumption*. Los Angeles: Feral House.

Holmlund, C. (1994). A decade of deadly dolls. In H. Birch (Ed.), *Moving targets: Women, murder and representation* (pp. 127–151). Berkeley: University of California Press.

hooks, b. (1992). *Black looks: Race and representations*. Boston: South End Press.

hooks, b. (1994). *Outlaw culture: Resisting representations*. New York: Routledge.

hooks, b. (1996). *Reel to real: Race, sex, and class at the movies*. New York: Routledge.

Howitt, D. (1998). *Crime, the media and the law*. West Sussex. UK: John Wiley & Sons.

Huling, T. (1992). *Injustice will be done: Women drug couriers and the Rockefeller Drug Laws*. NY: Correctional Association of New York.

Hulme, J., & Wexler, M. (1996). *Baked potatoes: A pot smoker's guide to film and video*. New York, NY: Doubleday.

Humphries, D. (1999). *Crack mothers: Pregnancy, drugs, and the media*. Columbus: Ohio State University Press.

Inciardi, J., Lockwood, D., & Pottieger, A. (1993). *Women and crack-cocaine*. Toronto: Maxwell Macmillan.

International Centre for Prison Studies. (2007). *World prison brief*. London: King's College, University of London. Retrieved July 27, 2007, from http://www.kcl. as.uk /depsta/rel/icps/home.html

Jackson, M., & Berry, G. (1994). Motherhood and drug-dependency: The attributes of full-time versus part-time responsibility for child care. *International Journal of the Addictions, 29*(12), 1519–1535.

Jelsma, M. (2005). Learning lessons from the Taliban opium ban. *International Journal of Drug policy, 16*, 98–103.

Jewkes, Y. (2004). *Media and crime*. London: Sage.

Johnson, R. (2000). Leaving normal: Constructing the family at the movies and in law. In L. Beaman (Ed.), *New perspectives on deviance: The construction of deviance in everyday life* (pp. 163–179). Scarborough, Ontario: Prentice-Hall.

Jones, J. (1991). The new ghetto aesthetic. *Wide Angle, 13*(3&4), 32–43.

Katovich, M. (1998). Media technologies, images of drugs, and evocative telepresence. *Qualitative Sociology, 21*(3), 277–297.

King, T. (2003). *The truth about stories: A native narrative*. Toronto: House of Anasi Press.

Klee, H. (2002). Women, family and drugs. In H. Klee, M. Jackson, & S. Lewis (Eds.), *Drug misuse and motherhood* (pp. 4–14). London: Routledge.

Klee, H., Jackson, M., & Lewis, S. (2002). *Drug misuse and motherhood*. London: Routledge.

Kohn, M. (1992). *Dope girls: The birth of the British underground*. London: Lawrence & Whishart.

Lalander, P. (2002). Who directs whom? Films and reality for young heroin users in a Swedish town. *Contemporary Drug Problems, 29*(1), 65–90.

Lambertus, S. (2004). *Wartime images, peacetime wounds*. Toronto: University of Toronto Press.

Lart, R. (1998). Medical power/knowledge. The treatment and control of drugs and drug users. In R. Coomber (Ed.), *The control of drugs and drug users: Reason or reaction?* (pp. 49–68). Amsterdam: Harwood Academic Publishers.

Lee, M., & Shlain, L. (1992). *Acid dreams: The complete social history of LSD: The CIA, the sixties, and beyond.* New York: Grove Press.

Leeders, F. (1992). Drug-addicted parents and their children. *International Journal of Drug Policy, 3*(4), 204–210.

Lensing, D. (2002). Pariah among pariahs: Images of the IV drug user in the context of AIDS. *The Journal of American Popular Culture* (1900 to present), *1*(2). Retrieved November 13, 2003, from http://www.americanpopularculture.com/journal/articles/fall_2002/lensing.htm

Lester, B., Andreozzi, L., & Appiah, L. (2004). Substance use during pregnancy: Time for policy to catch up with research. *Harm Reduction Journal, 1*(5). Available at: www.harmeducationjournal.com.

Lester, D. (2001). Army calls up film-makers to provide tactical advice. Retrieved October 10, 2001, from http://news.independent.co.uk/world/ame . . . p?dir=70 &story=98690&host=3&printable=1

Levine, H. (1978). The discovery of addiction: Changing conceptions of habitual drunkenness in America, *Journal of Studies on Alcohol, 39,* 143–174.

Lexchin, J. (1984). *The real pushers: A critical analysis of the Canadian drug industry.* Vancouver, BC: New Star Books.

Lloyd, M., et al. (2006). *Foreign national prisoners: A thematic review.* London: HM Inspectorate for Prisons.

Lusane, C. (1991). *Pipe dream blues: Racism and the war on drugs.* Boston: South End Press.

MacAndrew, C., & Edgerton, R. (1969). *Drunken comportment: A social explanation.* Chicago: Aldine Publishing.

MacGregor, S. (1998). Pragmatism or principle? Continuity and change in the British approach to treatment and control. In R. Coomber (Ed.), *The control of drugs and drug users: Reason or reaction?* (pp. 131–154). Amsterdam: Harwood Academic.

MacPherson, D., Mulla, Z., Richardson, L., & Beer, T. (2005). *Preventing harm from psychoactive substance use.* Retrieved July 13, 2006, from http://www.city.vancouver.bc.ca/fourpillars/pdf/prventingharm.report.pdf

Magner, M. (1996). Interview with John L'Ecuyer. *The Journal of Addiction and Mental Health,* May–June, 1996, *25*(3), 4.

Malbon, B. (1998). "Clubbing": Consumption, identity and the spatial practices of every-night life. In T. Skelton & G. Valentine (Eds.), *Cool places: Geographies of youth cultures* (pp. 266–286). London: Routledge.

Mann, C., & Zatz, M. (2002). *Images of color, images of crime: Readings.* Los Angeles: Roxbury Publishing.

Manning, P. (2007). An introduction to the theoretical approaches and research traditions. In P. Manning (Ed.), *Drugs and popular culture: Drugs, media and identity in contemporary society* (pp. 7–28). Cullomption, Devon, UK: Willan Publishing.

Martel, M. (2006). *Not this time: Canadians, public policy, and the marijuana question 1961–1975.* Toronto: University of Toronto Press.

Mason, P. (2006). (Ed.). *Captured by the media: Prison discourse in popular culture.* Portland, OR: Willan Publishing.

Mauer, M., & The Sentencing Project. (1999). *Race to incarcerate.* New York: The New Press.

Mayes, L., Granger, R., Bornstein, M., & Zuckerman, B. (1992). The problem of prenatal cocaine exposure. *Journal of the American Medical Association, 267*(3), 406–408.

McCarthy, C., Rodriguez, A., Buendia, E., Meacham, S., David, S., et al. (1997). Danger in the safety zone: Notes on race, resentment, and the discourse of crime, violence and suburban security. *Cultural Studies, 11*(2), 274–95.

McCaughey, M., & King, N. (2001). *Reel knockouts: Violent women in the movies*. Austin: University of Texas Press.

McCoy, A. (1991). *The politics of heroin: CIA complicity in the global drug trade*. New York: Lawrence Hill Books.

McLaren, A. (1990). *Our own master race*. Toronto: McClelland & Stewart.

McMullan, J. (2001). Westray and after: Power, truth and news reporting of the Westray mine disaster. In S. Boyd, D. Chunn, & R. Menzies (Eds.), *[Ab]using power: The Canadian experience*. Halifax, Nova Scotia: Fernwood.

McMullan, J. (2005). *News, truth and crime: The Westray disaster and its aftermath*. Halifax, Nova Scotia: Fernwood.

McMullan, J., & McClung, M. (2003, November 5–6, 2003). *Crime out: Press reporting, news truth, and the Westray inquiry*. Paper presented at the Two Days of Canada 2003. Crime in Canada: Law and Dis/Order. St. Catharines, Ontario: Brock University.

Measham, F. (2004). Drug and alcohol research: The case for cultural criminology. In J. Ferrell, K. Hayward, W. Morrison, & M. Presdee (Eds.), Cultural criminology unleashed (pp. 207–218). London: Glass House Press.

Meek, J. (2001). Time is running out in the war on opium. *The Guardian Weekly*, p. 3.

Mills, C. W. . (1975). *The sociological imagination*. New York: Oxford Press.

Mitchinson, W. (2000). *Giving birth in Canada 1900–1950*. Toronto: University of Toronto Press.

Monture-Angus, P. (2000). Aboriginal women and correctional practice. Reflections on the Task Force on Federally Sentenced Women. In K. Hannah-Moffat & M. Shaw (Eds.), *An ideal prison? Critical essays on women's imprisonment in Canada* (pp. 52–60). Halifax, Nova Scotia. Fernwood Press.

Morgan, J., & Zimmer, L. (1997). The social pharmacology of smokeable cocaine: Not all it's cracked up to be. In C. Reinarman and H. Levine (Eds.), *Crack in America: Demon drugs and social justice* (p.p. 131–170). Berkeley: University of California Press.

Mosher, C. (1998). *Discrimination and denial: Systemic racism in Ontario's legal and criminal justice systems, 1892–1961*. Toronto: University of Toronto Press.

Motiuk, L., & Vuong, B. (2005). *Homicide, sex, robbery and drug offenders in federal corrections: An end-of-2004 review*. Ottawa: Correctional Service of Canada.

Mott, J., & Bean, P. (1998). The development of drug control in Britain. In R. Coomber (Ed.), *The control of drugs and drug users: Reason or reaction?* (pp. 31–48). Amsterdam: Harwood Academic Publishers.

Moynihan, R., & Cassels, A. (2005). *Selling sickness*. Toronto: Greystone Books.

Murphy, E. (1973). *The black candle*. Toronto: Coles. (Originally published in 1922)

Murray, G. (1988). The road to regulation: Patent medicines in Canada in historical perspective. In J. Blackwell & P. Erickson (Eds.), *Illicit drugs in Canada* (prepublication ed.; pp. 72–87). Toronto: Methuen Publications.

Musto, D. (1987). *The American disease: Origins of narcotic control* (expanded ed.). New York: Oxford University Press.

Musto, D. (Ed.). (2002). *Drugs in America: A documentary history*. New York: Routledge.

Muwakkil, S. (2001, January 15). Can "Traffic" loosen drug-policy gridlock? *Chicago Tribune*, p. 13.

Mwenda, L. (2005). Drug offenders in England and Wales 2004. *Home Office Statistical Bulletin*. London: Home Office.

Nakayama, T. (2002). Framing Asian Americans. In C. Mann & M. Zatz (Eds.), *Images of color: Images of crime* (2nd ed.; pp. 92–10). Los Angeles: Roxbury Publishing.

National Advocates for Pregnant Women. (2004). *Annual Report.* New York: Authors.

National Centre for Policy Analysis (NCPA). (2002). *Idea house: Pharmaceutical use.* Retrieved May 24, 2002, from http://www.ncpa.org/health/pdh/mar98.html

National Institute for Health Care Management (NIHCM). (2002). *Prescription drug expenditures in 2001: Another year of escalating costs* (rev. ed.). Washington, DC: The National Institute for Health Care Management, Research and Educational Foundation.

National Statistics. (2007). *Statistics on drug misuse: England, 2007.* NHS, Leeds: The Information Centre.

Oakley, A. (1984). *The captured womb.* Oxford: Basil Blackwell.

Office of National Drug Control Policy. (1999). *Substance use in popular movies and music videos.* Office of National Drug Control Policy and Department of Health and Human Services, Substance Abuse and Mental Health Services. Retrieved September 16, 2005, from http://www.health.org/govstudy/media study/new.aspx

O'Malley, P. (1999). Consuming risks: Harm minimization and the government of drug users. In R. Smandych (Ed.), *Governable places: Readings on governmentality and crime control* (pp. 191–214). Aldershot, UK: Ashgate.

O'Malley, P., & Valverde, M. (2004). Pleasure, freedom and drugs: The uses of "pleasure" in liberal governance of drug and alcohol consumption. *Sociology, 38*(1), 25–42.

Owram, D. (1996). *Born at the right time: A history of the baby boom generation.* Toronto: University of Toronto Press.

Paltrow, L. (2001). The war on drugs and the war on abortion: Some initial thoughts on the connections, intersections and the effects. *Southern University Law Review, 28*(3), 201–253.

Parry, R. (2000). Government corruption and complicity in the war on drugs: Analysis of press coverage from the mid-1980s to the present. In *The war on drugs: Addicted to failure* (pp. 52–57). Washington, DC: Drug Policy Project Institute for Policy Studies.

Peele, S. (1989). *Diseasing of America: Addiction treatment out of control.* Toronto: Lexington Books.

Peele, S., & Brodsky, A. (1991). *The truth about addiction and recovery.* New York: Simon & Schuster.

Perry, K. (2000). *Performance.* In J. Stevenson (Ed.), *Addicted: The myth and menace of drugs in film* (pp. 187–197). New York: Creation Books.

Piven, F., & Clowan, R. (1979). *Poor people's movements: How they succeed, how they fail.* New York: Vintage Books.

Postman, N. (1986). *Amusing ourselves to death: Public discourse in the age of show business.* New York: Penguin.

Purvis, T., & Hunt, A. (1993). Discourse, ideology, discourse, ideology, discourse, ideology . . . *Thinking Society, 44*(3), 473–499.

Quintero, G. (2001). Making the Indian: Colonial knowledge, alcohol, and Native Americans. *American Indian Culture, 25*(4), 57–71.

Rafter, N. H. (2000). *Shots in the mirror: Crime films and society.* New York: Oxford.

Raphael, S., & Stoll, M. (2007). Why are so many Americans in prison? *Institute for Research on Poverty Discussion Paper, 1328–07,* 1–94.

Rapping, E. (2003). *Law and justice as seen on TV.* New York: New York University Press.

Razack, S. (2002). When place becomes race. In S. Razack (Ed.), *Race, space, and the law: Unmapping a white settler society* (pp. 1–20). Toronto: Between the Lines.

Reinarman, C. (1988). The social construction of an alcohol problem: The case of Mothers against Drunken Drivers and social control in the 1980s. *Theory and Society, 17*(1), 91–120.

Reinarman, C. (2005). Addiction as accomplishment: The discursive construction of disease. *Addiction Research and Theory, 13*(4), 307–320.

Reinarman, C., & Duskin, C. (1999). Dominant ideology and drugs in the media. In J. Ferrell & N. Websdale (Eds.), *Making trouble: Cultural constructions of crime, deviance, and control* (pp. 73–87). New York: Aldine de Gruyter.

Reinarman, C., & Levine, H. (1997). The crack attack: Politics and media in the crack scare. In C. Reinarman & H. Levine (Eds.), *Crack in America: Demon drugs and social justice* (pp. 18–51). Berkeley: University of California Press.

Reinarman, C., & Levine, H. (2000). Crack in context: Politics and media in the making of a drug scare. In R. Cruthchfield, G. Bridges, J. Weis, & C. Kubrin (Eds.), *Crime readings* (2nd ed.; pp. 47–53). Thousand Oaks, CA: Sage.

Richards, J. (1984). *The age of the dream place: Cinema and society in Britain, 1930–39.* London: Routledge.

Robb, D. (2004). *Operation Hollywood: How the Pentagon shapes and censors the movies.* Amherst, NY: Prometheus Books.

Roberts, D. (2002). *Shattered bonds: The color of child welfare.* New York: Basic Books.

Roberts, M. (2005). *Using women.* London: DrugScope.

Robertson, J. (1989). *The hidden cinema: British film censorship in action, 1913–1972.* London: Routledge.

Robertson, L., & Culhane, D. (2005). *In plain sight: Reflections on life in Downtown Eastside Vancouver.* Vancouver, BC: Talonbooks.

Robins, L., Davis, D., & Goodwin, D. (1974). Drug use in U.S. Army enlisted men in Vietnam: A follow-up on their return home. *American Journal of Epidemiology, 99,* 235–249.

Rodriquez, D. (2006–07). Introduction: American apocalypse. *Journal of Prisoners on Prisons, 15*(2) & *16*(1), 10–50.

Rome, D. (2002). African Americans: Murderers, rapists, and drug addicts. In C. Mann & M. Zatz (Eds.), *Images of color, images of crime* (pp. 71–81). Los Angeles: Roxbury Publishing.

Rose, K. (1996). *American women and the repeal of prohibition.* New York: New York University Press.

Rosenbaum, M., & Murphy, S. (1987). Not the picture of health: Women on methadone. *Journal of Psychoactive Drugs, 19*(2), 217–226.

Saboi, W., Minton, T., & Harrison, P. (2007). Prison and jail inmates at midyear 2006. *Bulletin.* U.S. Department of Justice.

Said, E. (2001). *Orientalism* (25th anniversary ed.). New York: Vintage Books.

Saunders, D. (2000). Editors made deals on antidrug articles. *The Globe and Mail,* April 1, p. A2.

Savoie, J. (2002). Crime statistics in Canada, 2001. *Juristat, 22*(6), 1–22. Ottawa: Canadian Centre for Justice Statistics.

Schultes, R., Hofmann, A., & Ratsch, C. (1998). *Plants of the gods* (rev. ed.). Rochester, VT: Healing Arts Press.

Scott, P., & Marshall, J. (1998). *Cocaine politics: Drugs, armies, and the CIA in Central America.* Berkeley: University of California Press.

Shapiro, H. (2002). From Chaplin to Charlie—cocaine, Hollywood and the movies. *Drugs: Education, Prevention and Policy, 9*(2), 133–141.

Shapiro, H. (2003). *Shooting stars: Drugs, Hollywood, and the movies*. London: Serpent's Tail.

Shewan, D., & Dalgarno, P. (2005). Low levels of negative health and social outcomes among non-treatment heroin users in Glasgow (Scotland): Evidence for controlled heroin use? *British Journal of Health Psychology, 10*, 1–17.

Shoatz, R. (2006–07). Liberation or gangsterism: Freedom or slavery? *Journal of Prisoners on Prisons, 15*(2) & *16*(1), 51–79.

Silver, W. (2007). Crime statistics in Canada, 2006. *Juristat, 27*(5), 1–15.

Silver, W. (2007). Crime statistics in Canada, 2006. *Juristat, 27*(5), 1–15. Ottawa: Canadian Centre for Justice Statistics.

Simeon, R. (Ed.). *Report on the powers of the Ontario Film Review Board*. Toronto: Ontario Law Reform Commission.

Siney, C. (1999). (Ed.). *Pregnancy and drug misuse*. Cheshire, UK: Books for Midwives.

Sklar, R., & Musser, C. (1990). (Eds.). *Resisting images: Essays on cinema and history*. Philadelphia: Temple University.

Smith-Shomade, B. (2003). "Rock-a-bye, Baby!": Black women disrupting gangs and constructing hip-hop gangsta films. *Cinema Journal, 42*(2), 25–40.

Solinger, R. (1994). Race and "value": Black and white illegitimate babies, 1945–1965. In N. Glenn, G. Chang, & L. Forcey (Eds.), *Mothering: Ideology, experience, and agency* (pp. 287–310). New York: Routledge.

Solomon, R., & Green, M. (1988). The first century: The history of nonmedical opiate use and control policies in Canada, 1980–1970. In J. Blackwell & P. Erickson (Eds.), *Illicit drugs in Canada* (pp. 88–116). (Prepublication ed.). Toronto: Methuen Publications.

Sourcebook for teaching science: Television statistics. Retrieved July 27, 2006, from http://www.csun.edu/science/health/docs/tv&health.html

South, N. (1998). Tackling drug control in Britain: From Sir Malcolm Delevingne to the new drugs strategy. In R. Coomber (Ed.), *The control of drugs and drug users: Reason or reaction?* (pp. 87–106). Amsterdam: Harwood Academic.

Sowder, B., &, Burt, M. (1980). *Children of addicts and nonaddicts: A comparative investigation in five urban sites. In heroin-addicted parents and their children: Two reports.* (National Institute on Drug Abuse Services Research Report, pp. 19–35). Washington, DC: U.S. Department of Health and Human Services; Public Health Service: Alcohol, Drug Abuse, and Mental health Administration.

Spear, B. (1994). The early years of the "British System" in practice. In J. Strang & M. Gossop (Eds.), *Heroin addiction and drug policy: The British System* (pp. 3–28). Oxford: Oxford Press.

Starks, M. (1982). *Cocaine fiends and reefer madness: An illustrated history of drugs in the movies*. New York: Cornwall Books.

Statistics Canada. (2005). Adult correctional services. *The Daily*. Retrieved July 27, 2007, from http://www.statcan.ca/Daily/English/o51216/d051216b.htm

Sterk-Elifson, C. (1996). Just for fun? Cocaine use among middle-class women. *Journal of Drug Issues, 26*(1), 63–76.

Stevenson, G., Lingley, L., Trasov, G., & Stansfield, H. (1956). *Drug addiction in British Columbia: A research survey*. Unpublished manuscript. Vancouver: University of British Columbia.

Stevenson, J. (2000). (Ed.). *Addicted: The myth and menace of drugs in film*. New York: Creation Books.

Stimson, G. (2000). "Blair declares war": The unhealthy state of British drug policy. *The International Journal of Drug Policy, 11*, 259–264.

Sudbury, J. (2005). (Ed.). *Global lockdown: Race, gender, and the prison industrial complex*. London: Routledge.

Sullivan, D. (2007). Editor's note. *Contemporary Justic Review, 10*(3), 237–246.

Sullivan, D., & Tifft, L. (2000). *Restorative justice as a transformative process.* Voorheesville, NY: Mutual Aid Press.

Surrette, R. (1992). *Media, crime, and criminal justice: Images and realities.* Pacific Grove, CA: Brooks/Cole.

Terry, C., & Pellens, M. (1970). *The opium problem.* Montclair, NJ: Patterson Smith.

Thobani, S. (2007a). *Exalted subjects: Studies in the making of race and nation in Canada.* Toronto: University of Toronto Press.

Thobani, S. (2007b). Imperial longings, feminist responses: Print media and the imagining of Canadian nationhood after 9/11. In D. Chunn, S. B. Boyd, & H. Lessard (Eds.), *Reaction and resistance: Feminism, law and social change* (chap. 4). Vancouver: University of British Columbia Press.

U.S. Department of Justice. (2007). *Prison statistics.* Bureau of Justice Statistics. Retrieved June 12, 2007, from http://www.ojp.gov/bjs/prisons.htm

Uschtengagen, A. (1999). (Ed.). *Prescription of narcotics for heroin addicts. Main results of the Swiss National Cohort Study (Medical prescription of narcotics).* Zurich: Karger.

Valverde, M. (1991). *The age of light, soap, and water: Moral reform in English Canada 1885–1925.* Toronto: McClelland and Stewart/Oxford.

Valverde, M. (1998). *Diseases of the will: Alcohol and the dilemmas of freedom.* New York: Cambridge University Press.

Valverde, M. (2006). *Law and order: Images, meanings, myths.* New Brunswick, NJ: Rutgers University Press.

Vitalla, K. (2000). The addict as TV entertainment. *The Journal of Addiction and Mental Health, 3*(6), 10.

Wagner, D. (1997). *The new temperance: The American obsession with sin and vice.* Boulder, CO: Westview Press.

Walker, K. (1991). How a medical journalist helped to legalize heroin in Canada. *The Journal of Drug Issues, 21*(1), 141–146.

Ward, C. (1998). *Fantasies of the master race: Literature, cinema and the colonization of American Indians.* San Francisco: City Lights Books.

Warner, J. (2002). *Craze: Gin and debaucher in an age of reason.* New York: Four Walls Eight Windows.

Weber, M. (1976). *The Protestant ethic and the spirit of capitalism.* London: George Allen & Unwin.

Wedderburn, D. (2000). *Justice for women: The need for reform.* London: Prison Reform Trust.

Weil, A, & Rosen, W. (1998). *From chocolate to morphine.* Boston: Houghton Mifflin.

White, J. D. (1997). *Extreme prejudice, excessive force, zero tolerance: Cultural political economy of the U.S. drug wars, 1980–1996.* Unpublished dissertation, George Washington University, Washington, DC.

Williams, B. (Ed.). (1981). *Report of the committee on obscenity and film censorship.* London: Her Majesty's Stationary Office.

Wise, W. (2001). *Take One's essential guide to Canadian film.* Toronto: University of Toronto Press.

Woodiwiss, M. (2001). *Organized crime and American power.* Toronto: University of Toronto Press.

Woolford, A. (2001). Tainted space: Representations of injection drug-use and HIV/AIDS in Vancouver's Downtown Eastside. *BC Studies, 129,* 27–50.

Wykes, M. (2001). *News, crime and culture.* London: Pluto Press.

Young, A. (1996). *Imagining crime: Textual outlaws and criminal conversations.* London: Sage.

Young, J. (1981). The myth of drug takers in the mass media. In S. Cohen & J. Young (Eds.), *The manufacture of news: Social problems, deviance and the mass media* (pp. 326–334). London: Constable.

Zinberg, N. (1984). *Drug, set, and setting: The basis for controlled intoxicant use.* New Haven, CT: Yale University Press.

Index